D0332954

LIBERAL
FAITH
IN A
DIVIDED
CHURCH

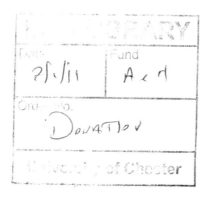
WITHDRAWN

LIBRARY	
Date 2⎰/⎰/11	Fund A e d
Order No. DONATION	
University of Chester	

First published by O Books, 2008
O Books is an imprint of John Hunt Publishing
Ltd., The Bothy, Deershot Lodge, Park Lane,
Ropley, Hants, SO24 0BE, UK
office1@o-books.net
www.o-books.net

Distribution in:

UK and Europe
Orca Book Services
orders@orcabookservices.co.uk
Tel: 01202 665432 Fax: 01202 666219 Int. code
(44)

USA and Canada
NBN
custserv@nbnbooks.com
Tel: 1 800 462 6420 Fax: 1 800 338 4550

Australia and New Zealand
Brumby Books
sales@brumbybooks.com.au
Tel: 61 3 9761 5535 Fax: 61 3 9761 7095

Far East (offices in Singapore, Thailand, Hong
Kong, Taiwan)
Pansing Distribution Pte Ltd
kemal@pansing.com
Tel: 65 6319 9939 Fax: 65 6462 5761

South Africa
Alternative Books
altbook@peterhyde.co.za
Tel: 021 555 4027 Fax: 021 447 1430

Text copyright Jonathan Clatworthy 2008

Design: Stuart Davies

ISBN: 978 1 84694 116 0

All rights reserved. Except for brief quotations in
critical articles or reviews, no part of this book
may be reproduced in any manner without prior
written permission from the publishers.

The rights of Jonathan Clatworthy as author
have been asserted in accordance with the
Copyright, Designs and Patents Act 1988.

A CIP catalogue record for this book is available
from the British Library.

Printed by Chris Fowler International
www.chrisfowlerinternational.com

O Books operates a distinctive and ethical publishing philosophy in
all areas of its business, from its global network of authors to
production and worldwide distribution.
This book is produced on FSC certified stock, within ISO14001
standards. The printer plants sufficient trees each year through
the Woodland Trust to absorb the level of emitted carbon in
its production.

WITHDRAWN

LIBERAL
FAITH
IN A
DIVIDED
CHURCH

Jonathan Clatworthy

WITHDRAWN

BOOKS

Winchester, UK
Washington, USA

This book offers a strong defence of the liberal tradition within Christianity. In particular it highlights the importance that classic Anglicanism has always given to balancing the claims of Scripture, Tradition and Reason and hence to accepting the inevitability of diversity within a single Church. Clatworthy shows very clearly what is at stake in today's debate within the Anglican communion and how tragic it would be if a fundamentalist uniformity were to triumph over a reasoned diversity.

Professor Paul Badham, Department of Theology, University of Wales, Lampeter

For a long time, liberals in the Church of England have been exposed to jibes that they offer a watered-down version of Christianity and have trimmed their sails according to the prevailing winds of secularism. This kind of name-calling leaves many naturally liberal Churchpeople feeling bruised, defensive, and uncertain as to whether they are really representing historic Christian teaching. Now there are signs of a fight-back. Jonathan Clatworthy's book is one manifestation of this. Clearly written, with a firm grounding in the historical and intellectual background of contemporary debates, and plenty of common sense, he argues for the properly theological truth of liberalism. This work will encourage many to move from the defensive to speak out all the more strongly for the rightness as well as the humaneness of a liberal approach.

George Pattison, Lady Margaret Professor of Divinity, University of Oxford

Everything you hoped you'd never need to know about fundamentalism, and were afraid might be true. If you have ever been disturbed by the seemingly invincible advance of literalists and harsh judgementalism within Anglicanism this is the book which will give the confidence to resist.

Clatworthy's arguments and evidence, if anything can, will lead to a resurgence of robust diversity and the intellectual, theological basis upon which it rests. A great deal is at stake. This book is not afraid to takes sides. Are you?

Richard Kirker, Chief Executive, Lesbian and Gay Christian Movement

This is a truly radical book, in that it looks for the roots of a liberal approach to Christianity that is principled, inclusive and undogmatic. Jonathan Clatworthy shows how liberal faith has always striven to temper the wisdom of the past with the promptings of the Spirit in the present. Rather than seeing such an approach as a departure from true orthodoxy, he demonstrates that they lie at the heart of a consistent vision of God's relationship with the world. This book will provide encouragement and sustenance for those who wish for an alternative to absolute certainty, in its secular and religious forms; as Jonathan says, 'Only God is infallible'.

Elaine Graham, Professor of Social and Pastoral Theology,
University of Manchester

What is currently dividing the Anglican Communion is not sexual ethics, but the refusal of a substantial minority to accept diversity and an insistence on getting its own way at all costs. Jonathan Clatworthy's timely book traces the development of the classic Anglican position as inclusive and open to truth wherever it is found, and argues that unless this is rediscovered the result can only be an endless series of rifts, as hardliners find ever more issues on which to hold the church to ransom. It should be read by everyone concerned with our present plight.

Professor John Barton, Oriel College, Oxford

When we find it hard to agree with one another we must re-double our efforts to understand one another. Here Jonathan Clatworthy makes a significant and timely contribution to mutual understanding in a Church where celebrating diversity will do most to heal divisions.

John Saxbee, Bishop of Lincoln

CONTENTS

PREFACE

While writing this book I have often wondered whether the world really needs yet another publication about church leaders and their obsessions with other people's sex lives. News has kept coming in about one report after another threatening disaster unless we get serious about climate change, and church leaders express their concern; but as with most other issues they follow public opinion rather than having a message of their own. Only in the matter of sexual morality do the public faces of Christianity spring to life, determined to forbid acts which do not trouble others. Why not just forget about them?

Because, I believe, our religious traditions still have distinctive insights to offer us. Even though they are often overshadowed by topical issues they are still there, and we will not solve those other problems unless we draw on them.

In writing this book, therefore, my main concern is to understand why liberals and conservatives interpret Christianity in such contrasting ways. The focus of this contrast is, currently, the debate about homosexuality, and I shall draw on it as a way of illustrating the differences; but in so doing I also aim to explore the question of which kinds of religious belief will help us understand ourselves and the way we relate to God and the world around us.

This question has puzzled me since my teenage years in the 1960s. I was brought up in a Church of England vicarage with an Anglo-Catholic ethos; the daily offices were a normal part of life and the weekly Eucharist one of the high points of the week. In my later teens and early twenties I agonized over the widespread view that all religion was unnecessary or even harmful. Religious belief, at the time, seemed to be on the way out. I felt called to defend it.

I still do. If the human race is ever to work out how it can live together in peace and harmony, it needs to be much more critical about which of its visions of the future can, and should, be realized; and this means taking seriously the questions of what is worth doing and what are the possibilities and limits of human behaviour. The conservatives and liberals of western Christianity today offer divergent answers to these questions.

In preparing this text I am indebted to many colleagues and scholars who have given me help and advice in a variety of ways. John Barton, Nigel Yates, Mark Chapman, David Edwards, Pat Starkey, John Saxbee, Richard Kirker and Marilyn McCord Adams have all made suggestions and helped me avoid errors. I am particularly grateful to Paul Badham who has encouraged me throughout the process, offered a great deal of information and suggested directions I should take. No doubt there remain errors, and the responsibility for them is mine; but there would have been many more were it not for the help they have given me.

Finally I would like to thank my colleagues at the Modern Churchpeople's Union. They have provided a community of enquirers with whom I have been able to explore a wide variety of topics and try out ideas. I hope the result will please them, and prove a constructive contribution to the current debates.

INTRODUCTION

Threats to split the church, archbishops refusing to share communion with each other, new bishops being appointed specifically to rival existing bishops. Western Christianity seems to be separating into two increasingly hostile camps of 'liberals' and 'conservatives'.

Talk of a split has been rife in the Anglican Communion for a number of years. Its leaders are struggling to keep it together. In practice this means looking for compromise while giving ground to those who threaten to cause most havoc; so short-term expediency takes priority and the search for good long-term solutions is postponed.

This book is not one more attempt to find a compromise and pour oil on troubled waters. It aims to dig deeper, look for the roots of the disagreements, explain why people understand Christianity in such radically different ways and ask which of these different accounts of Christianity will serve us best. I doubt whether it will help provide a short term fix for the current debate. It is primarily about why Christians believe the things they do; if anything, from the point of view of church politics, it is something of a bull at a gate. My hope is that it will provide resources for a deeper and more long term appreciation of how religious believers can share a church with each other without feeling the need to bully each other.

For some years now the focal issue has been homosexuality. Opponents perceive themselves as the true upholders of the Christian tradition. They accuse its supporters of revisionism, of being influenced by secular society and accepting lower standards of belief and ethics. Supporters of homosexuality in turn accuse their opponents of of making more fuss of this one ethical issue than it merits, of misinterpreting Christianity, of defying publicly available knowledge and of turning their backs on the real world to live in their own fundamentalist bubble.

Homosexuality, the recent story

In the second half of 2002 it became clear that the issue was going to divide the Anglican Communion. An event had taken place which, while normal to many Anglicans, was absolutely unacceptable to others. A campaign of opposition emerged, unexpected by most but very well organized. It soon became clear that the movement behind it had spent many years preparing for a showdown.

The controversial event? The announcement that Rowan Williams, Archbishop of Wales, was to be the next Archbishop of Canterbury. Whatever his strengths or weaknesses it was as though the only thing that mattered about archbishops of Canterbury was their views on homosexuality. Opponents made repeated and heavily publicized demands that he should not be permitted to take up his post. By the time of his enthronement in February 2003 it was clear that the Anglican Communion was in for a rocky ride.

Although an international body with provinces in many countries, Anglicanism has until now understood itself as the international dimension of the Church of England, where it began. The Archbishop of Canterbury remains its titular head but the provinces are self-governing. Recently, though, the province of Nigeria has repudiated the connection with Canterbury as Peter Akinola, its archbishop, believes that stronger disciplinary measures should have been taken against homosexuality.

Within a few months of Archbishop Williams' enthronement at Canterbury a succession of events highlighted the division. Jeffrey John, Canon Theologian of Southwark Cathedral, was named the new Bishop of Reading. He was living with another man in a relationship which, he said, had previously been sexually active, and refused to accept that it had been a sin. In an earlier age an appointment of this type would have generated objections from different quarters, but what happened this time was quite different: a well-organized, high profile campaign which threatened that parishes would refuse to pay their contributions to the common funds. Pressure was put on the new archbishop who in turn persuaded Jeffrey John to withdraw from the post.

In the meantime the Canadian Diocese of New Westminster had authorised a liturgy for blessing homosexual relationships and Gene Robinson, who openly admitted to being in a gay relationship, had been elected Bishop of New Hampshire in the USA. Once Jeffrey John had withdrawn his nomination the focus of the controversy moved to these North American events.

Opponents had two significant threats at their disposal: to split the church and to withhold their financial contributions to the central funds.

In October 2003 the primates - the archbishops of all the Anglican provinces - met to discuss the situation and published a statement which blamed the North Americans for threatening the church's unity. If Robinson's consecration were to take place, they said, 'we have reached a crucial and critical point in the life of the Anglican Communion.' They called on the offending provinces 'to make adequate provision for episcopal oversight of dissenting minorities'. The Archbishop of Canterbury set up a commission chaired by Archbishop Robin Eames to examine the theological and legal implications and make recommendations.

From this time on it has been clear that the majority of the primates, even including the Archbishop of Canterbury, had decided to support the campaigners against homosexuality. The campaigners, while welcoming the support, have repeatedly complained that it does not go far enough. Gene Robinson's consecration as bishop should have been prevented, and once it had happened he should not have been allowed to continue in office. The Anglican church in the USA should be 'disciplined' for allowing it. Anti-homosexual parishes with pro-homosexual bishops should be given the power to seek 'alternative episcopal oversight'. Some preferred to call it 'adequate episcopal oversight', the implication being that a bishop who supported Gene Robinson was, for that reason alone, an inadequate bishop.[1]

They inundated the Eames Commission with submissions. A statement signed by fourteen primates declared that 'The recent action of the Bishop of New Westminster displays a flagrant disregard for the remainder of the Anglican Communion'; the bishop had, apparently, 'placed himself and his diocese in an automatic state of impaired communion with the majority'. The Church of England Evangelical Council complained of 'provocation by a liberal and revisionist elite on an orthodox and unsuspecting Church', a matter of the highest importance because 'homosexual actions leave the actors facing God's judgement without Christ's mediating work... both heaven and hell are genuine alternative destinies'. Anglican Mainstream proposed that the bishops who attended Gene Robinson's consecration should no longer have their ministries recognised, simply because they had attended. There were very few submissions in support of same-sex blessings and the consecration of Gene Robinson. I wrote one on behalf of the Modern Churchpeople's Union, but most liberals felt there was no need to campaign on the matter.[2]

Plans were developed to split the Anglican Communion into two. In January 2004 a confidential letter by the American Anglican Council was leaked to the press. It explained that in public they were asking for 'adequate episcopal oversight' but their real aim, being secretly planned on both sides of the Atlantic, was a major realignment of Anglicanism, a 'replacement jurisdiction' to exclude liberals.[3] Repeated demands for 'adequate episcopal oversight' were kept in the public eye by parish clergy inviting anti-homosexual bishops to conduct confirmations, thereby generating media publicity for snubbing the bishop of the diocese who would normally have performed them.

The Eames Commission published its report, The Windsor Report, in October 2004. Politically it was carefully judged, siding with the conservative position but without supporting their more extreme demands. Since then it has set the framework for the continuing debate; although some of its elements have been abandoned the 'Windsor process' remains at the time of writing the formally accepted process for seeking to resolve the dispute.

In implementing its proposals, the meetings of the Primates have taken a lead. Their first meeting after the publication of the Windsor Report was in February 2005. It was best noted for the refusal of some conservative primates to take Communion with the others. If they cannot even worship together, some asked, had the split already happened? Soon afterwards the Archbishop of Uganda told the North American churches to 'repent and join the flock of God or depart from the Communion'.[4]

The debate has continued to simmer with occasional flashpoints. UK civil partnerships were permitted from December 2005; the Church of England's House of Bishops issued guidelines permitting clergy to register on condition that their relationship was not sexual, advice which impressed neither side.[5] Conservative groups became increasingly bold, holding unconstitutional ordinations and eventually using African bishops to consecrate Americans to serve as bishops in the USA, rivalling the bishops already there.

In June 2006 the Archbishop of Canterbury gave his blessing to the proposal for an 'Anglican Covenant' in which churches would have the option to consult with each other before making innovations, and so 'limit their local freedoms for the sake of a wider witness'. They could not legally be forced to sign a new covenant, but there would be greater unity between the ones who did. Those who did not sign it would still be Anglicans, but the relationship between the two groups 'would not be unlike that between the Church of England and the Methodist Church'. The Primates' Meeting in February 2007 published a draft covenant which gave the primates ultimate authority in matters under dispute.[6]

At the time of writing it seems that *any* public event with a connection to homosexuality can be guaranteed to generate campaigns and demonstrations by religious groups. The rest of the world looks on with bemusement, wondering what kind of Christianity this is.

The nature of the dispute

As controversies go it is most strange. The oddest feature is that it is so one-sided. It is the 'conservatives' who are making the running, not just objecting to homosexuality but insisting that there can be no compromise, no agreeing to disagree. They are well financed and well organized, and are prepared to spend huge amounts of emotional energy on the issue. Every time their view has prevailed there has been no reduction in the threats - and plans - to split the church. It often appears as though they cannot sleep until the church is exactly as it should be. Throughout the process, since 2002, their bishops, archbishops and organizations have described the situation as a 'crisis'. As they see it, supporters of homosexuality are proposing to change the doctrines of the church in order to deny that it is sinful. 'Liberals' see the situation quite differently. They have no concerted programme of change at all. Whether or not they approve of homosexuality, they feel free to disagree with their bishops on any number of issues and see no reason why homosexuality should provoke so much more controversy than anything else. Overwhelmingly they want to avoid a split, but they see no problem with accepting a continuing situation where some bishops are homosexuals and others disapprove of homosexuality. They certainly see no need for a crisis. As a result they tend to leave the campaiging to the organizations catering for gays and lesbians, the people who are most directly affected.

So: why homosexuality? Under the surface it is clear that there lies something else. Despite the decibels and the media coverage there is no real debate about the ethics of gay and lesbian sexual activity. The campaigners operate like stallholders at an open air market, each shouting as loud as they can to be heard and completely ignoring each other.

My own interest in the question stems from my experience of student religion. The 18-21 age group, recently freed from parental supervision and without dependants of their own, are often willing to adopt more extreme views than more mature individuals and more balanced commmunities. I was an undergraduate in Cardiff in the late 1960s. Since my father was an Anglo-Catholic parish priest I knew only too well that being a vicar's son sometimes meant being condemned and despised. What happened at university astonished me. The condemnations continued, but for the opposite reason: because I was *not* a

Christian. On one occasion the Christian Union sent a delegate to my room to spend the evening explaining why I was not. One of their reasons was that I sometimes drank alcohol. Campaigning against alcohol was a major feature of many Christian Unions at that time. Twenty years later I was back in a university, this time as a chaplain at Sheffield. By this time opposition to alcohol was rare; the leaders of student Christian groups knew that many of their predecessors had condemned it, but they now knew that the Bible did not in fact forbid it. Instead they campaigned vigorously against abortion, again on the ground that the Bible forbade it. The Students' Union had a policy of supporting women who wanted abortions. The religious groups would submit motions to repeal it and organize large numbers to attend the debate. They could easily outnumber their opponents and win the vote. Afterwards, not being lovers of Student Union meetings, they would stop attending and it would not be long before their success was quietly reversed.

These campaigns were very common in their time, not just in student religion but in many churches too. Now, though, they have faded into the background as homosexuality takes over. So why alcohol and abortion then, and why homosexuality now? The ethical issue changes but the ethos survives. Is it perhaps the ethos which is the driving force, and is there something about the ethos which likes to focus on one ethical issue at a time?

The evangelical student religious groups I got to know liked sharp distinctions with everything in black and white. They defined who was a Christian. Often they described all non-members of their group as non-Christians. There were no in-betweens. It followed that to become a Christian must be a sudden event; stories of emotional conversion experiences were popular.

The leaders of the group had supreme teaching authority. They were often treated as the ultimate court of appeal on the truths of Christian doctrine; my sermons would be reported to twenty-year-olds who would pronounce judgement on them. Other members were to learn from them, and were warned not to believe anything taught by outsiders like me who might falsely claim to know about Christianity. I often observed student religious leaders making heavy use of that array of thought-policing practices which characterize sectarian religion: telling members exactly what to believe, warning them that doubts and questions are of the devil, giving them strict rules for conversations with non-members. The Christian Union group at one hall of residence discussed in great detail whether it was permissible to sit next to non-Christians over breakfast. The issues were to do with balancing opportunities for evangelism against the danger of being led astray by un-Christian ideas. I promised myself that one day I would study where these ideas came from. The current debate seems an appropriate time to do so.

Student religion is an extreme example, but we should not underrate its influence. Many of today's church leaders were first taught about Christianity in these groups. Most of them have relinquished the simple certainties and black-and-white distinctions of their youth but some have retained them, and a larger number retain some elements - perhaps a tendency to revert to them when in doubt.

This book is not, however, about the psychology of religious belief. I shall concentrate on the theological issues and the philosophies behind them, and on these matters the general ethos of the student religion I have described illustrates the kind of Christianity which the leading opponents of homosexuality are seeking to establish as normative for the Anglican Communion as a whole. To establish it as normative is from their perspective to *defend* the character of the church as they were brought up to understand it; from the perspective of their opponents it is to *impose* one version of it onto the rest of the church.

Just as Christian Union students have often insisted that Anglicans and Roman Catholics are not really Christians at all, leading campaigners against homosexuality are now insisting not only that toleration of homosexuality should have no place in the Anglican Communion but also that the matter is settled and there is no scope for discussing whether it should be reviewed.

Liberals and conservatives

Although the words 'conservative' and 'liberal' have become the usual labels for the two sides they are both misleading, not least because they can mean a great many different things. In this book I am only interested in religious uses of the terms, and it will be helpful to distinguish between three types.

Firstly they are used to describe different views on specific issues. This mirrors non-religious uses of the terms. Institutions find reasons for change, and at their best they allow different points of view to be discussed until a consensus emerges. Within that discussion those who oppose change may be described as conservatives and those who support it as liberals. Similarly in religion those who maintain traditional beliefs in the Virgin Birth or the immorality of homosexuality are often described as conservatives and those prepared to question them as liberals. In this sense it is possible to be a conservative on one issue and a liberal on another without any contradiction.

The second distinction refers to a person's general approach to issues of debate within a subject area. All traditions of enquiry inherit a range of teachings but also have tools to question them and develop new ideas. Within any tradition conservatives tend to give more weight to inherited teachings, liberals to new ideas. There is a spectrum of positions; at the extremes are the very liberal and very conservative, while most people are somewhere in the middle. Some Christians condemn homosexuality but not women priests while others argue the other way round. Some affirm the authority of the first half of Leviticus 20:13 which condemns men who engage in homosexual activity, but not the second half which insists that they should be put to death. In this sense people are more or less liberal, more or less conservative: they value both the inherited tradition and new ideas, and do not believe issues of debate can be answered simply by appealing to one authority or the other. Moderate conservatives of this type may describe themselves as committed to the authority of the Bible, but 'within reason'. They do not, for example, expect to obey every biblical command.

This spectrum - with a few extremists at each end but most people being more or less moderate liberals or moderate conservatives - characterizes many religious traditions as well as non-religious ones. What makes moderate positions possible is that when new ideas conflict with old traditions, neither the new ideas nor the old traditions win the argument every time. There are no all-purpose principles of decision-making which settle every dispute. Each issue has to be judged on its merits, taking into account all the relevant information from whatever source, and applying all the relevant mental processes and decision-making procedures.

The third distinction is a sharper one. It claims that the second, with its spectrum of positions, is itself a liberal process, and conservatives who take part in it are betraying their conservatism. According to this distinction, liberals are those who allow divine revelation to be modified by rational processes, while conservatives insist that the right answers are to be derived from appeal to truths which have been infallibly given by God and can therefore be known with certainty.

This distinction between conservatives and liberals is often found in religious debate but is rarely found elsewhere. It is the one which dominates the current debates, as indicated by the endlessly repeated claims that gays and women *cannot* be legitimate bishops because of what Scripture and tradition decree, and that therefore there is no scope for legitimate discussion about whether they may become acceptable. A church with one gay bishop is a tainted church, even if there is only one and he lives thousands of miles away. Conservatives in this third sense believe that if they ever are persuaded to accept something contrary to what God has revealed they will have deserted the Christian gospel in favour of mere human reason.

This is not to say that all the leaders of the current campaign consistently apply this black-and-white distinction between revelation and reason, or even that they describe themselves in this way. In practice nobody has ever conscientiously lived their life on the basis that every statement in the Bible is true, let alone that they have a moral duty to obey every one of its commands. There are far too many for this to be possible. What happens is that each community which is conservative in this sense, at each stage of its history, concentrates on a small handful of doctrines and commands - perhaps only one - and trumpets its commitment to the Bible's supreme authority by drawing attention to this one while overlooking others. As the church press amply reveals, this provides unlimited opportunities for conservatives to condemn each other as liberals. Group A refuses to have women leading worship and condemns Group B for their women ministers; Group B condemns Group A for permitting divorce and remarriage. Each accuses the other of not being obedient to the whole Bible, and both are right.

This third account of the distinction between liberals and conservatives is therefore the one on which this book will focus. It is important not because it describes real alternative possibilities for holding Christian beliefs and living a Christian life - it does not - but because it dominates the rhetoric of the debate. The *idea* that the Bible condemns homosexuality and that therefore the morality of homosexuality does not need to be discussed any further is a powerful idea. It leads to the conclusion that psychological research into the causes of homosexuality and the effects of permitting or preventing homosexual activity are irrelevant. Revelation has established the matter, and reason has no right to question it.

Within Christianity this idea has a history which I shall describe. Although it is never possible to establish exactly where in history a particular idea begins - they all have forerunners and change from age to age - the medieval 'faith and reason' debate is the stage at which it is first clearly articulated without being denounced as heretical. In Chapter 1 I shall describe how the biblical authors and most early Christians saw matters differently. Chapter 2 describes the medieval debate and the development of dualism, and Chapter 3 its development in Reformation and Counter-Reformation doctrines. Chapter 4 describes how certainty came to be detached from its religious origins and used to establish an alternative secular account of knowledge, known to philosophers as foundationalism. Chapter 5 describes a contrasting tradition, the development of classical Anglican theology by Hooker and his successors who replaced the idea of deriving certainties from a single infallible source with the 'three-legged stool' of Scripture, reason and tradition. In philosophical terms it is coherentist rather than foundationalist.

Around the beginning of the nineteenth century there was increasing anxiety at the prospect of science establishing a reductionist account of reality and disproving all religious belief. Chapters 6, 7 and 8 describe three defensive reactions. The first, adopted by most mainstream denominations, reaffirmed the old dualism between all things religious and the rest of reality and insisted that religious truths were beyond science. The second, generally known as 'fundamentalism', retained the unity of reality together with the Bible as the supreme authority on all things. The third has more recently appealed to postmodernist theories of incommensurability which permit them to retain their religious commitments in defiance of public reason. All three are in their different ways foundationalist defences of religious belief in the face of secularism, and thus express that reactionary stance which gives modern western religion its counter-cultural feel. In Chapter 9 I summarize the nature of religious foundationalism and argue against it.

It is the classical Anglicanism described in Chapter 5 which I wish to defend. In today's reactionary religious environment it counts as a liberal position to hold, and it is sad to see even the leaders of the Church of England apparently so willing to jettison it. In the final chapter I draw out its implications for what we should expect to know in matters of faith and what characteristics we should expect to find in churches which adhere to this kind of liberalism.

There are other versions of Christianity which are often described as liberal but which I do not defend. I have said very little about the 'non-realism' which values Christian worship and the Christian tradition but does not believe in God. If my account of our relationship with God is along the right lines then we should expect that different people engage with religious matters in different ways. Some find acts of worship deeply meaningful but have little or no interest in speculating about the existence and nature of the divine. However the assertion that there is no God does not in itself seem to me to merit the title of religious liberalism, any more than anarchists are political liberals or opponents of capitalism are economic liberals. I do not share the view - common among religious conservatives - that liberals are, so to speak, halfway between conservatives and non-believers. It is indeed true that liberal religious communities tend to be more sympathetic to non-believers than conservative religious communities are; but that is because they are more sympathetic in general to people who do not share their views. The religious beliefs of liberals are at least as strong as those of conservatives, and liberals are no more likely to become unbelievers than conservatives are - except, of course, when liberalism is *defined* to include unbelief. I would prefer to put it the other way round: a liberal faith is a more confident faith, less brittle, less anxious in case its belief structure collapses.

Another tradition which is often described as liberal is the dualist approach which distinguishes sharply between religious and non-religious matters. This is especially popular in the USA where the separation of church and state is still a strongly defended principle. I have more to say about this, largely because it has had an immense influence on western Christianity; but I shall argue that it undermines some of the essential features of religious faith. Many parts of Europe are becoming increasingly anxious about religion; they have traditionally thought of themselves as Christian, but hear a lot from Islamic neighbours who seem to take their religion far more seriously and have a stronger sense of what it is *for*. Many Christians, noticing this, realize that they do not have much idea what they should be expecting their Christian commitment to achieve. I hope to show that it is possible to relate Christian beliefs constructively to all the other things we believe, in such a way that Christianity not only makes sense, but *matters*.

This book, therefore, does not defend everything that can be described as religious liberalism. There are too many liberalisms, and a book which defended them all would contradict itself. Instead I defend a particular type of liberalism, historically associated with classical Anglican theology and philosophically characterized by resisting the temptations of certainty and dogmatism. It is a humbler religion, more tolerant, inclusive and open to change. By insisting that nobody has complete or certain truth it establishes principles for a diverse church in which believers agree to differ without threatening each other. I believe it offers the best method for churches to resolve the disputes which currently divide them.

CHAPTER 1

FAITH AND ITS REASONS IN THE BIBLE AND EARLY CHRISTIANITY

How do people claim to know anything at all about spiritual things? Western Christianity in the twentieth century emphasized a sharp distinction between two processes, *natural theology* and *revealed theology*. Karl Barth, at the beginning of the century, launched an assault on the leading German theologians of his time, accusing them of supporting German imperialism because they allowed themselves to be influenced by natural theology instead of giving supreme authority to the Word of God. His immense influence ensured that most theologians and churches affirmed the authority of the Bible *as opposed to* natural theology.

Natural theology is theology based on nature, but 'nature' means different things. Two are relevant. One refers to 'human nature'. It is natural for dogs to bark and for humans to hear, see and think. In this sense natural theology is theology which uses faculties available to humans in general. In the other sense nature is the physical environment in which we live. In this sense natural theology is theology which bases its ideas about God on extensions of our information about the world of our experience.[1] Most often these two senses are combined, so that natural theology uses universally available mental processes to reflect on what we can see and thence to develop ideas about what we cannot see, as opposed to revealed theology which accepts truths revealed by God and therefore does not need to relate beliefs about the supernatural to the everyday world.

In this book I am concerned with both religious truth claims - doctrines - and ethical norms. The ethical version of natural theology is 'natural law'. Just as scientists, by examining the physical world, find regularities and describe them as laws of nature, so also societies and their moral leaders note that some lifestyles and practices make for a healthy and happy society while others harm it. Religious traditions often justify natural law by arguing that God deliberately creates human minds in such a way that we can reflect on our experience and learn how to live good lives.

Natural law contrasts with positive law. Positive law is laid down by a specific recognized authority and applies where that authority's remit runs. Governments oblige motorists to drive on the right in the USA but on the left in the UK. Similarly religious believers often claim that a particular act is immoral purely because God so decrees and for no other reason.

The concept of natural law is pervasive even when it is not recognized. When people say it is wrong to steal, they may be referring to the law of a state but they also often think of it as a universal rule, morally obligatory regardless of the state's legislation. Similarly, when people claim that a particular law of a state is wrong, or ought (morally) to be changed, they are implicitly appealing to a higher moral authority than the state. Unless they are referring to an international organization like the United Nations, that higher moral authority must be a kind of natural law. This raises the question of where natural laws come from and what authority they have. Sometimes they are justified in terms of 'human rights', but more often they are defended on the ground of being given by God.

Religious believers, then, sometimes base their moral norms on natural law and sometimes on positive law. Characteristically those who believe in natural theology also affirm natural law, and those who deny natural theology base their moral norms on divine command. Problems arise when the two conflict, and homosexuality is a case in point. Divine command theory expects that if an action like homosexual intercourse is forbidden by the Bible, it is immoral *because God says so*. If we ask *why* God so decrees we are asking an illegitimate question, implying that God was constrained by some set of circumstances or had limited freedom.

There is no higher authority than God to explain why God so decrees. Our instructions are to obey, not to understand. The commands, as they stand in the Bible, are supreme authorities and are not to be modified or reinterpreted in the light of other principles or information.

Biblical texts which specifically mention homosexuality – seven at the most, but five is a more realistic figure[2] - invariably condemn it. Scholars believe the ancient Hebrews, like the other rural societies of the ancient near east, had a pro-baby ethic which accepted polygamy, encouraged early marriages and disapproved of homosexuality. Christian defenders of homosexuality sometimes dispute the meanings of the texts.[3] However the main focus of the biblical defence of homosexuality is to accuse conservatives of undue selectivity. So many hundreds of commands are issued in the Bible that nobody makes any serious attempt to obey them all consistently. To select a single command and treat it as the most essential is an arbitrary procedure unless there is good reason for selecting that one.

Many conservatives accept the need to be selective, and use a system of interpretation to justify the selections they make. This brings their position closer to a liberal one; it enables them to discuss what kind of interpretative scheme is appropriate and to compare alternatives. Other conservatives persist in claiming that their opposition to homosexuality is *simply* loyalty to the Bible.

Natural law is also often invoked. It has always had a place in Christian thought; the early Christians often cited Romans 1:20 as a Scriptural example of it and the Roman Catholic tradition has consistently appealed to it. However, since late antiquity they have interpreted it in Platonist terms which expect moral laws to be universal and eternal. From this perspective homosexuality is unnatural for two reasons: it contravenes both the natural function of sexual activity, which is to produce children, and also natural human desire, which is for heterosexual activity. This form of natural law thus establishes a single norm and applies it to everyone. Especially since the nineteenth century, the Roman Catholic hierarchy has increasingly insisted on its own interpretation of natural law as the only legitimate one.

Other defenders of natural law today are more influenced by empirical approaches which value diversity and accept homosexuality as one of many minority variations. The main focus of interest is scientific research on homosexual orientation. If this is an inescapable part of some people's personality it seems that God is responsible for their condition and therefore homosexual activity must be morally acceptable for them. Conservatives argue that homosexual orientation is not sinful but homosexual practice is. On its own this does not solve the problem: it simply raises the question of why God created so many people with such strong yearnings to sin. They therefore attribute homosexual orientation to some misfortune; like alcoholism or megalomania, homosexuality is caused by environmental factors like being brought up by a single parent and the appropriate response is to seek ways to cure it.

In arguments of this type it is often assumed that scientific research should be able to decide the matter. However, no amount of research can settle a question of this type with absolute certainty. It is always possible to challenge the presuppositions, methods or statistics of any study. In practice the best we can do is allow the researchers to continue the debate until a general consensus of specialists emerges, recognizing that even then a minority view may be scientifically defensible.

Such a consensus has, in fact, already been established. It states that homosexual orientation is substantially fixed from the time of birth. There is a greater disposition to it in some families, and among boys with two or more older brothers; but there is no greater disposition among those who have been seduced, or who have attended same sex boarding schools, or have been brought up by single parents.[4] Nevertheless as with other issues like global warming it remains possible to reject the scientific consensus and point to alternative research with different conclusions.

In general, then, two types of argument dominate the Christian debates on homosexuality. Although there is room for variation in both cases, in general biblical commands favour conservatives while rational reflection on scientific evidence favours liberals. This pattern appears in so many ethical disputes today that we may think of it as the characteristic fault line between conservatives and liberals.

Over and above all the detailed arguments about specific issues there persists a general question: what is the relationship between the Bible and reason? If they are both legitimate sources of authority, what happens when they conflict with each other? How should we decide between them? Does the Bible trump reason? Should Christians conclude, for example, that as the Bible forbids homosexuality, no amount of modern scientific study can override Scripture's decree? Or does reason trump the Bible – in which case biblical commands which fly in the face of modern science should be ignored? Or is there a more subtle relationship in which neither is infallible but both contribute to a deeper understanding of truth and goodness?

Natural theology in the Bible

Towards the end of the twentieth century British churches became more sympathetic to the idea that specific actions must be morally wrong simply because the Bible says so. Ethicists, on the other hand, rarely sympathize with divine command theory because it denies that God's commands can be justified in any way except by simply asserting that God decrees them, and so presents them as arbitrary.

Biblical scholars followed Barth's lead for most of the twentieth century and interpreted the Bible as a source of divine commands; but more recently increasing numbers have argued that this account misinterprets what the Bible actually says.[5] The Bible makes different types of authority claims in different places, including a great many appeals to natural law. As this is an important insight I shall offer a number examples drawn from different parts of the Bible to illustrate how natural law is very much at home in the Bible.

The Pentateuch. The first five books of the Bible contain a great many laws; at the time of Jesus every Jew knew that there were 613 of them. The edition which has been handed down to us summarizes them, saying they were all given by God to Moses and by Moses to the people of Israel. Thus the final editors of the Pentateuch present them as positive law in the form of divine commands. On the other hand some of the individual laws within it are accompanied by reasons explaining why they should be obeyed. We often find pragmatic considerations and natural law. This suggests that whereas the final editors of the Pentateuch presented the laws as God's command, their earlier sources had different views of their origins.[6]

Many of these laws seem to us quite barbaric, and others seem pointless. If we can see no intelligible reason for a law, we tend to assume that it must count as divinely-given positive law. This, though, may be because we do not share ancient Hebrew ways of thought. A good illustration is the food laws in Leviticus 11 and Deuteronomy 14 which provide the basis for Jewish dietary rules. Israelites are permitted to eat sparrows but not seagulls, sheep but not camels, cod but not prawns. To us they seem an extreme example of God's inscrutable decree as there cannot be any logical reason for them; but even here, scholars point out, natural law is at work. A reason is given. According to the texts, land animals are 'clean' (permitted as food) if they both have cloven hoofs and also chew the cud, but otherwise not. Such an apparently bizarre explanation leads us, today, to discount it; but Leviticus and Deuteronomy explain the reason as though it made the matter obvious.

One possibility is that the authors of these texts had inherited a list of clean and unclean animals, did not know the reason and hit on cloven hoofs and cud-chewing as a way of rationalizing it. Until recently most scholars took this view. More recently, however, Mary Douglas[7] has argued that the combination of cud-chewing and cloven hoofs was the real reason: people thought there was something wrong with non-ruminant ungulates and non-ungulate ruminants. Douglas drew parallels with other laws, for example the law against wearing a garment made with two different kinds of fabric or sowing a field with two different kinds of seed (Deut

22:9-11, cf. Lev 19:19).[8] It may seem odd to us, but the British objection to eating horse meat seems similarly odd to the French today. Whether or not Douglas' theory is correct, what becomes clear is that something like it is in operation; when we examine the laws closely we find that what had at first sight seemed arbitrary divine commands do in fact have reasons. Our blindness to the reasons is because they would not count as convincing in our society.

There is therefore a tension between the natural law reasons given for specific laws and the divine command justification of the Pentateuch as a whole. Both occur in Deuteronomy. This book explains divine commands in terms of the covenant between God and Israel; Israel must do what God requires without God needing to provide reasons. Nevertheless it is a favourite theme of Deuteronomy that God lays down the laws for Israel's own good.[9] This seems to suggest that human well-being is the reason why God commands them.

The prophets. Old Testament prophecy often combines moral denunciation with a prediction of future events, preceding them with the words 'Thus says the Lord'. Christians have often believed that the prophets were indeed declaring the direct words of God, and that therefore the moral judgements contained in them were divine commands. Scholars have shown that this is an oversimplification. Ancient Hebrew prophecy developed out of earlier practices. The earlier practices are similar to those of pre-modern societies all over the world, and still exist in some places. Prophets or their equivalents would receive messages from their gods in a variety of ways; ecstasy, clairvoyance, observation of omens, examining entrails, necromancy and astrology. They occur in earlier parts of the Old Testament. Later Old Testament texts condemned them.[10]

The literary prophets – those whose prophecies are recorded in Old Testament books – inherited the methods of the earlier prophets but made changes. They continued to practise ecstasy, have visions and give oracles, but did not use clairvoyance, wonder-working, magic, necromancy or astrology. Far from expecting to be paid for their services they made themselves unpopular. They still used the term 'Thus says the Lord', but appealed to a different kind of authority: not to technical expertise in occult skills, but to a combination of the nation's relationship with God and publicly observable events. In other words, the authority to which they appealed was publicly available information rather than occult access to the mind of God. They were taking part in the political and economic debates of the nation.[11]

In the process they often appealed to natural law, though they did not distinguish it from divine law. In Amos 1:3-2:3 the nations surrounding Israel are condemned for enslaving whole populations and torturing conquered enemies. These offences are not forbidden in Old Testament law. The implication is that they should have known that they were morally unacceptable, regardless of which god they worshipped. Other prophets did the same, appealing to moral norms which they expected to be shared by other nations.[12]

An additional factor appears in the growing attractiveness of monotheism. In early Israel Yahweh was one god among others. These gods were closely connected to natural processes; each one worked on nature directly to produce rain, sunshine, the growth of crops and other phenomena. The prophet Hosea described God as more transcendent and therefore more distant from specific natural processes. Koch writes that Hosea 'could no longer conceive of his God as a sexually characterized male giant, who lays himself on the earth, letting his sperm fall on her as rain.' Between the one transcendent God and the people lay something else - God's way of ordering the world - which Europeans would later elaborate as 'laws of nature'.[13]

Thus monotheism encouraged natural law ethics. Direct divine instruction is more at home in polytheism, where gods who are not responsible for natural processes seek to override them. Monotheism, with a single and supreme God, characteristically expects that God has given us whatever mental faculties God intends us to have. Natural law is God's law, and natural reason is the reason God has given us.

Narratives. Natural law judgements are also revealed in biblical stories. Narrators often appear to consider custom, rather than divine decree, a suitable court of appeal. In one text, for example, God declares an intention to destroy an immoral city, Sodom, and Abraham argues that God's action would itself be immoral: 'Shall not the Judge of all the earth do what is just?[14] Many scholars have attemped to reconcile this passage with divine command ethics. Inevitably they fail: the narrative clearly presupposes a standard of justice to which even God should assent.[15]

The wisdom literature. Divine commands are still harder to find in the Bible's wisdom literature. Israel's wisdom writings have close parallels with other ancient near eastern literature, and like them describe moral norms in terms of a more abstract cosmic order. Jews called it 'justice' or 'righteousness'. They understood wisdom as a matter of living in accordance with God's cosmic order and developing appropriate skills, understanding and moral norms. Divine commands, when they do appear, are specific instructions describing how cosmic order should be maintained in particular situations. For much of the twentieth century scholars treated the wisdom literature as marginal to the Bible, partly because they saw it as a foreign influence but also partly because it appeals to natural law rather than positive law.[16]

Jesus. For most Christians Jesus has more authority than the rest of the Bible. He left us no writings of his own and our sources offer contrasting descriptions of him. There is however a strong consensus among scholars that Matthew, Mark and Luke are our most reliable historical sources of what Jesus did and taught. In these gospels Jesus taught primarily through parables. Most of them appeal to well-known features of human society and its environment: a father trying to persuade his sons to do their share of the work, a woman hunting for a lost coin, crops growing while nobody is looking, corrupt servants making money for themselves at their employers' expense. For example, in response to the complaint that Jesus 'welcomes sinners and eats with them' he replies: 'Which one of you, having a hundred sheep and losing one of them, does not leave the ninety-nine in the wilderness and go after the one that is lost until he finds it?'[17] It is characteristic of his parables that he appeals to insights which his hearers can recognize for themselves from ordinary life. There are few occasions when he cites scripture, and even here he is usually responding to scribes who themselves are quoting it. The contrast between Jesus and his Pharisaic and scribal opponents comes across clearly: *they* appeal to scripture, treating it as divine command, while *he* responds with natural theology and natural law ethics.

Acts 15. Christianity's first big internal debate was about non-Jewish converts. The question was whether they should be obliged to obey the laws laid down in the Jewish scriptures. According to Acts 15 a council was held. Peter argued that they should be exempted, appealing to his own authority and the doctrine that God's spirit inspires Jews and Gentiles alike. Paul and Barnabas supported his case by describing the success of their missionary work. The dispute was resolved by an agreement that gentile converts should not be expected to keep the Jewish law, but with four exceptions: they should abstain 'from things polluted by idols and from fornication and from whatever has been strangled and from blood'.[18]

The narrative describes how this decision was reached. James, the undisputed leader of the church at the time, listened to the accounts given by Paul and Barnabas, cited a scriptural text and declared: 'Therefore I have reached the decision what we should not trouble those Gentiles who are turning to God.'[19] They wrote a letter announcing the decision. Instead of writing 'James decided...' they wrote 'It has seemed good to the Holy Spirit and to us...' The decision seems to have been made largely for pragmatic reasons, but was interpreted as divine inspiration. The radical distinction between the two which is so central to religious debate today seems not to have occurred to them.

Paul. Paul's epistles argue for freedom from law and being open to guidance by the Holy Spirit. Much of his teaching aimed to settle disputes within particular churches. In 1 Corinthians, for example, he gave commands about deviant sexual practices, legal disputes, marriage and asceticism, eating food sacrificed to pagan gods, wearing veils, how to celebrate the Lord's Supper, the use of spiritual gifts in worship, the need for women to be silent in church, the resurrection of the dead and a collection of money for other Christians.[20] Behind his instructions lay his theological vision: his conviction, stronger in some epistles than others, that the end of the age is imminent, his emphasis on the death of Christ and his determination to set up communities of the redeemed;[21] but he offered no consistent ethical system. Instead, in some cases he saw an important principle at stake but in others he told them to do what he thought was most pragmatic and explained his reasons. Sometimes he appealed to the teaching of 'The Lord';[22] at other times he specified that the command was his, not the Lord's.[23] When stating that married couples should continue sexual relations he described his instruction as a concession rather than a command.[24] When struggling to justify his command about veils he appealed to custom,[25] and when instructing women to remain silent in church he appealed to Old Testament law.[26] These appeals were there to strengthen his case. Methodologically they are a mixed bag. Some of them are tantamount to divine command ethics – though it is Jesus to whom he is appealing – but most of the time other considerations dominate.

Especially in Paul's epistles, but also scattered throughout the Gospels and Acts, are contrasts between traditional Jews, who believed in keeping all the commandments in the Old Testament, and Christians who were freed from the law and justified by faith. Scholars doubt whether this is a fair account of Judaism, or even of the teaching of Jesus; but this is how many early Christians saw the difference. The old, they said, was bound by outdated laws which were impossible to keep and just made people feel guilty. The new replaces law with guidance by the Holy Spirit.[27]

Eschatology. Many first century Jews had millenarian hopes that God would bring the world order to an end and begin a new age. Most of them thought it would be a continuation of physical life on earth, but with major changes. God would liberate Israel from the Romans. Some believed there would be an end to illness, sin and death. Those more influenced by Greek thought expected the new age to be spiritual rather than physical, and on a different plane.

Not all Christians shared these hopes but many did, and associated Jesus with the new age in one way or another. Three main views can be found in the New Testament. Some authors expected that their own age was about to pass away. This is why Paul, in some epistles, expected his moral teaching to be for a short time only.[28] Others expected that baptized Christians were already in the new age and therefore should live perfect lives. This view was very influential in the church's first few centuries, and led to shocked reactions and harsh penances when the baptized sinned. It is most clearly expressed in Hebrews, though it may also underlie some passages in Matthew.[29] The third group abandoned the expectations of both an imminent end and Christian perfection. Expecting the church to be in for the long haul they offered long-term teaching to regulate church affairs and the lives of Christians. This stance characterizes the pastoral epistles.[30]

Behind these changes we can observe a natural process. At each stage the New Testament authors derived their ethical teaching from what they believed about the new age. If their own age was about to pass, an interim ethic was appropriate and there was no point in having children. If Christians were already living in the new age, perfection was expected. Once they accepted that life was carrying on much the same as before, long-term ethical norms became suitable again and traditional morality was reaffirmed. This is ethics at its best: it is derived from, and makes sense within, the best available theory of the nature of reality. Good ethical norms are derived from good theories of reality.

Development of the canon

Once these writings were accepted as holy scripture they were treated differently. The ancients had an attitude to their scriptures which is very different from ours. Today so many books are available to us that to say a statement is written in a book, even an old one, does not necessarily give it any authority. In the ancient world it did. Jews, Christians and pagans alike had respect for the past and tended to treat as scripture any book which seemed old and venerable. Christians, including New Testament writers, often introduced quotations with the words 'as it is written', without distinguishing between quotations from the Bible and quotations from elsewhere. Odd though it may seem to us today, 'Scripture' was, to them, a loose category.[31]

Gradually this changed. In the heat of debate between alternative Christian traditions church leaders established lists, stating which books were to be read in churches and which were to be rejected as heretical. It was a long time before all the lists agreed, but once there were some lists it became possible to think of the approved Christian scriptures as a unified set. Then some time in the second or third century some Christians combined their authorized Christian scriptures into one volume. This made it possible to think of their scriptures not as 'the books' (*ta biblia,* from which we get our word 'bible') but as 'the book'. From then on it became possible to think of them as a unity, and they began to expect greater consistency between them.[32]

Many biblical texts are difficult to explain as holy scripture. At the time of Christ Jews and pagans were familiar with the problem. In addition Jews needed to defend their scriptures against criticism by pagans. The main issues are still with us.

Irrelevant or harmful texts. Of the many hundreds of commands in the Bible, a large number were simply ignored then and are still ignored today. Thus Leviticus 19:26-28 strings together commands which seem to us not only unimportant, but unrelated to each other:

> You shall not eat anything with its blood. You shall not practise augury or witchcraft. You shall not round off the hair on your temples or mar the edges of your beard. You shall not make any gashes in your flesh for the dead or tattoo any marks upon you

Leviticus 25:3-4 stipulates that all fields and vineyards are to be left untended throughout every seventh year. It is possible to argue that it was God's command to ancient Israelites but not to us; but in that case we need criteria for distinguishing the commands which still apply to us from those which do not.

Laws which have lost their purpose. For example, Leviticus 19:9-10 forbids farmers to reap to the edges of their fields so that they leave some of the harvest for the poor and foreigners. Applying the law in our modern urban society would not achieve this aim. If we insist on the commands as obligatory *because they have been given by God*, and not because we consider them good laws, it seems that we should continue the practice regardless of consequences. On the other hand if we give priority to the intention, and use the biblical text as an argument for modern welfare state provision, we are making greater use of our own judgements and whether they have biblical justification becomes unclear.

Universal norms. Many commands are so common that hardly anyone would disagree with them. Thus one of the Ten Commandments forbids stealing (Exodus 20:15). Jews and Christians may claim that, by obeying them, they are conforming to Scripture. Unbelievers reply that they also obey these commands, but without needing instruction from the Bible. Do Jews and Christians, they sometimes ask, need extra help to be moral?

Immoral commands. Many commands strike modern Christians as immoral. In 1 Samuel 15:9-10, for example, God condemns king Saul for not killing all his defeated enemies. Other examples are the many regulations governing slavery. When Christians find biblical texts morally repulsive, it means that as we read the Bible we bring to it moral values which we hold independently of what the Bible commands, and use them to pass judgement on biblical texts. This raises the question of how we legitimize these external moral values. If they are, ultimately, derived from - or consistent with - biblical values, we need some account of how they relate to these difficult texts.

Development and contradiction. Some biblical texts reveal development in moral thinking, or even contradict each other. The most significant case for Christians is Paul's insistence, noted above, that Christians are freed from the laws laid down elsewhere in

Scripture. If Christians no longer needed to obey them, the question was raised as to why they should read them, either privately or in public worship, and still include them in their scriptures.

Pagans faced the same problems with their own scriptures. By the time of Christ Greeks had long resolved them by interpreting their texts allegorically: their truth, they said, lay not in their surface literal meanings but in their deeper spiritual meanings. Jews and Christians borrowed this pagan solution and allegorized biblical texts. This was especially useful for dealing with obsolete laws which they no longer expected to obey but still regarded as Scripture.[33] An example is Deuteronomy 25:4: 'You shall not muzzle an ox while it is treading out the grain'. Paul responds:

> Is it for oxen that God is concerned? Or does he not speak entirely for our sake? It was indeed written for our sake, for whoever ploughs should plough in hope and whoever threshes should thresh in hope of a share in the crop (1 Corinthians 9:9-10).

Paul's predicament was typical. If he interpreted the text literally it had nothing to say to urban Christians of his own day. If it was to be understood as relevant to his own place and time it needed to be given an alternative meaning. In the fourth century Eusebius even argued that, if we are not to allegorize the trivial details in the Bible, the only alternative would be to fall back on 'incongruous and incoherent fairy-tales'.[34] Later Gregory the Great described biblical texts as having four meanings: the literal or historical, the allegorical or spiritual, the moral and the prophetic.[35]

From the third century onwards biblical commentaries became popular and often attempted to extract a Christian meaning from every phrase. Origen justified this procedure by arguing that the scriptures were written by the inspiration of the Holy Spirit – the real author – and always contained a deeper meaning than what appeared on the surface.[36] Few would attempt to justify this style of interpretation today. Nevertheless it did solve the problem which faced anyone who took the bible at face value. Augustine, for example, was repelled from Christianity by its poor style and obscurity and the unedifying stories of the patriarchs, hardly what anyone would expect from a supreme God, but was converted by Ambrose who explained how to understand them allegorically.[37] After his conversion he could teach that Scripture's obscurities were part of God's plan to discipline the rebellious human mind.[38]

The main problem with allegory is that it allows virtually any meaning to be drawn out of any text; antiquity never established principles for regulating it. The early Christians did not interpret at random, though; in practice they sought to reconcile biblical texts with what they already believed and with each other.[39] They often quoted the Old Testament, drawing out of it references to Christ which could not have been part of the authors' intentions, but they believed that the true author, God, had intended them to refer to Christ. As Barton puts it, 'Since it enshrined the truth, it had to be read as saying what one already believed the truth to be.'[40]

Another change which took place from around the third century was that Christian allegory lost interest in history and instead concentrated on general observations about morality, psychology and philosophy.[41] One result was that the moral teachings which continued to be upheld were treated as universally and eternally binding. What they meant in context was lost.

The combined effect of these changes in biblical interpretation was that Christians sought, and found, meanings which were very different from what their predecessors had found, let alone what the authors had intended. They took it that the true meaning of each text was allegorical rather than literal; that the Old Testament as well as the New was speaking about Christ; that the true meanings of all biblical texts must be consistent with each other and with received Christian doctrine; and that the true meanings related not to historical circumstance but to eternal and universal truths. They justified these beliefs by claiming that the true author of Scripture was the Holy Spirit. As the process developed it became harder to recognize the human wisdom in biblical texts, and Christians were tempted to interpret each one as though they themselves were being directly addressed in it by God.[42]

The text of the bible itself does not justify any of these claims. As we have seen, they were imposed on the Bible because they were the best solutions available to the problems Christianity faced in its first few centuries. Yet despite their artificiality and the lack of biblical support for them the early Christians were convinced that these were the methods for understanding what the Bible was really saying. Today, few Christians are as committed to allegory, or as uncommitted to the Bible's historical statements; but many still believe that the true author is the Holy Spirit, that the Old Testament spoke about Christ, that the Bible is a consistent unity with no disagreements, and that its doctrines and ethical commands are universally and eternally true.

To summarize, then, from the writing of the original biblical texts to their reinterpretation as parts of a larger, consistent and divinely-inspired Bible, there is a pattern of development. Commands are given practical and natural law reasons in earlier texts, but are described as direct divine instruction in later texts. In general it seems that the earlier we probe in the history of any particular command the more likely we are to find reasons for it. Later interpretations, after a bigger time lag, are more likely to treat texts as positive law, given directly by God to be accepted without question.[43] Perhaps the earlier reasons were forgotten, or were no longer relevant or convincing. This type of development, as we shall see, has continued throughout Christian history with subsequent authoritative documents. When the text of a command is accepted as holy scripture, and therefore becomes part of a body of literature which is read in worship, even if it no longer seems appropriate or relevant it cannot be quietly forgotten. It is therefore reinterpreted; a deeper meaning needs to be found.

The nearest we get, in the Bible, to an opposition between divine command and natural law is in the teachings of Jesus and Paul. In the debates between Jesus and the scribes, Jesus appeals to natural law while the scribes appeal to scripture. However, the gospels do not describe these disagreements as an opposition between divine law and natural law. In Paul's epistles the doctrine of freedom from law is combined with openness to new guidance from the Holy Spirit. Scripture's commands are no longer binding. The rhetoric of these claims still echoes around countless churches, largely as a result of Luther's influence. Today's debate about homosexuality makes it sound odd. Has Christianity swapped sides? Has it become just as much of a fossilized, law-bound relic as the early Christians said first century Judaism was? Is it equally due for replacement by a newer and better faith? Or can it find within itself the resources to renew itself?

Opposition to natural theology

So far then it seems that the biblical authors and early Christians appealed to both direct divine instruction and natural theology, but did not see them as opposed to each other. Characteristically, they did not reject reason. Some affirmed it. John's Gospel begins: 'In the beginning was the *logos*, and the *logos* was with God, and the *logos* was God'. Although *logos* is usually translated 'word', it could equally well be translated 'reason'. The early apologist Justin thus identified Jesus the Logos with God's reason.[44] Some early Christians did claim to reject reason; best known is Tertullian's 'What has Jerusalem to do with Athens?' However as Ayers shows he offered no reason-denying account of Christianity; on the contrary he used all the rational tools at his disposal.[45]

Others, however, did develop theories of religious knowledge which distinguished sharply between divine information and human reason. From its beginning Christianity was a diverse movement, including not only the versions which came to be established as normative but also a wide range of Gnostic traditions. It was only very slowly that church leaders suppressed them in the interests of a more unified Christianity. For a long time the beliefs of the Gnostics were only known through the writings of their opponents, but since the discovery of the Nag Hammadi texts in the middle of the twentieth century it has been possible to read their own writings. Scholars still debate some of Gnosticism's features and vary in their evaluations of it. Some find it inspiring and regret the fact that church leaders suppressed it;[46] others are more critical and lament the fact that its ideas are so prevalent in Christianity today.[47]

What is of interest here is not disputed: the bulk of the literature expresses a distinctive account of the nature of reality and human existence, in which a number of themes reinforce each other. It is a very negative evaluation of the physical world, including human bodies. It is evil, and to be despised. The literature describes in detail why this is so, chiefly through elaborate myths.[48]

Why was the world created evil? This question is answered by an immense variety of polytheistic literature. The common theme is to affirm the existence of a supreme good God, who is distant from this earth and powerless to intervene. The world has been created, and is governed, by evil or ignorant gods.

If the world is so evil, why do most humans accept it as it is? This question is answered in similar vein; human minds have been created in such a way as to deceive us about our true predicament. Many texts dismiss ordinary reason as complete ignorance. Sometimes they express extreme disgust at it; one describes it as 'the fabric of ignorance, the base of evil, the bond of corruption, the dark wall, the living death, the perceptible corpse, the grave you carry around with you, the robber within you, who hates through what he loves and envies through what he hates'.[49]

How, then, can we be saved from this situation? Gnosticism offers knowledge of how to escape. Our spirits are trapped in physical bodies, but when we die they may be able to escape the earth and find their way to the supreme God. Salvation is interpreted in terms of the fate of the spirit after death, and offers a particular type of knowledge, *gnosis,* as the means to a desirable afterlife. Detailed instructions are given about how the individual's spirit is to travel from earth, through the many different heavens - each controlled by a different god - and finally reach its true home in a far distant heaven.

According to these texts nothing in the world can possibly enlighten us as to the true state of reality. The unenlightened are often described as being asleep and the enlightened as those who have woken up.[50] However, if the mental processes which all humans share are deceptive, and to be despised, who is the 'I' who despises them and is not deceived by them? For this account of humanity to be coherent, the inner self, the 'real me', must be completely separate from, and qualitatively different from, our ordinary minds.

Many Gnostic texts therefore divide humans into three parts: body, soul and spirit. The soul is the mind created by the inferior gods and is designed to deceive; the spirit is the 'divine spark', the element which hears the message of salvation, welcomes it and learns to despise the physical world. Myths describe each human spirit as a 'spark' of an original divine being which longs to be reunited. Some accounts describe the creation of human bodies as a deliberate act by evil gods to trap these sparks on earth. Once people are enlightened they understand their physical bodies as prisons and long to escape from them.

This raises another conceptual question. If we are all so deceived how can anybody find out the truth? The only possible source of enlightenment, in these accounts, is divine intervention to bring a message to selected people and warn them about their true nature and calling. Myths describe how the supreme and distant God has sent a messenger to earth to inform those willing to hear. The messenger undergoes many dangers in order to deceive the evil gods as he passes through their heavens in disguise. Characteristically Jesus is the messenger. He is often described as a divine figure disguised as a human in order to deceive the evil gods. Those who accept the message learn about the divine spark within them, whose true home is in a far distant heaven, and long to return there.[51]

The content of the message did not of course tally with the historical reminiscences of Jesus handed down from the apostles, but the apostles themselves had shown a way round this problem. They had claimed to see Jesus risen from the dead. The non-canonical gospels include many teachings which Jesus is purported to have given to selected disciples after his resurrection. Anybody, of course, could claim to have seen and heard the risen

Jesus and it was possible for some to interpret their dreams and imagination in this way. As time went on it became increasingly difficult to distinguish the historical teachings of the pre-crucifixion Jesus from the teachings derived from these claims. Fortunately for us, the 'early catholic' movement set out to establish what could be reliably affirmed from the reminiscences of the apostles. Perhaps Luke, realizing that his gospel did not do enough on the matter, designed the first chapter of Acts to acknowledge a period of time in which resurrection appearances took place, while insisting that they had come to an end.

In this Gnostic literature we have an account of divine revelation which claims to be the only possible source of truth. All natural theology, in this view, is misleading; *only* direct divine revelation, accepted by those who have learned its source, can provide true information about the human condition. The contrast was clear enough at the time. The theory of these Gnostics required at least two gods, a good one and an evil one. It was not compatible with the monotheism which Christianity had inherited from Judaism. Church leaders responded by closing the canon of the New Testament to stop their writings being read in churches. From then on it was only minority sects which did read them. The idea of a polytheistic Christianity, with Jesus as a divine messenger, was thus suppressed. Nevertheless one Gnostic doctrine - that human reason is altogether deceived about the nature of reality – survived, and remains popular today in many Christian circles.

Despite the contrast, however, there is one feature which all the ancient theologies described in this chapter share which sets them apart from most of modern western Christianity. Religion, for us, is a distinct part of our culture. It is science which explains the way the world works, and it does so without referring to divine beings. Before the development of modern secularism this distinction was not recognized. All over the world, beliefs about the divine contributed to a unified account of who we are, who made us, and how the world works. For the ancients, to attempt to describe how the world works without mentioning any gods would be as absurd as attempting to describe the way the world appears to us without mentioning colour. The authors of the Bible, their pagan contemporaries and the Gnostics all shared that unified approach to the search for truth. They expected their beliefs about the gods to *explain* the way things are.

An example is illness. In ancient Assyria and Babylon, all ill health was attributed to demons. Over the years priests developed long tables listing the different illnesses, which demon was responsible for each one and which incantations, prayers and rituals would drive the demons out.[52] By keeping careful records of symptoms and remedies they developed their theories on the basis of trial and error. To the modern ear nothing could be less scientific, but this is because we do not accept their initial presupposition about the cause of illness. It is now recognized that all science makes some presuppositions; their presuppositions were very different from modern ones, but the manner in which they developed their theories about demons and exorcisms was as scientific as it could have been.

The Old Testament offered a contrasting theory, that illness was due to divine punishment for sin. This theory often seemed inconsistent with people's experiences; after all, many people might think they knew which of their neighbours were in good health and which of them were the biggest sinners. The book of Job examined the problem at great length.

Here, then were two contrasting theories about the causes of illness. Both attempted to account for it in ways which did justice to the experiences of ill people but were also consistent with the nation's other beliefs about reality. Both needed to be consistent with the empirical evidence. Whether we agree with either of them, or reject them both, they witness to a unified view of reality. Pagans, Jews and Christians alike combined their observations of human life and the physical world with their theories about the gods, in order to produce accounts of reality which *explained* the way things are: who made us, for what purpose, and how therefore we ought to live. In the next chapter I shall describe how later theories laid the foundations for a very different kind of religion.

CHAPTER 2

FAITH AND REASON IN THE
MIDDLE AGES

Every society claims to know things, and has disagreements about what it knows. Most claims to knowledge are based on two processes. One is the empirical appeal to evidence produced by the five senses: we can justify a statement like 'an aeroplane has just gone overhead' by adding 'I saw it myself'. The other is the rational appeal to logic and mathematics, where we reach conclusions by deducing them from other things we know.

Many knowledge claims are indirect. We may claim to know something because we read it in a book, in which case we depend on the evidence of someone else's senses. Whether it counts as good evidence then partly depends on how reliable the book is. Modern research is based on the principle that the process of gathering data, and the content of the data gathered, are publicly described so that the resulting knowledge claims or hypotheses can be assessed by critics. Modern science would have been quite impossible without the gradual process of gathering evidence, forming hypotheses, criticizing and refining which needs to be done in the public domain. It may not always work out like this – researchers may sometimes cut corners and get away with unjustified claims – but in principle all knowledge, in all subject areas, derives from publicly describable sense experiences and calculations by one or more people, which can then be checked by others. This is true of research in all subjects.

With one exception: religion. Many believe that all these processes are inappropriate for religious matters. Instead they urge us to put aside the evidence of our senses and the rational questioning in our minds. Other forms of justification, which would be considered quite inadequate anywhere else – an autocratic tradition which refuses to reveal the reasons for its judgements, or voices in the head - are, in religious discourse alone, considered higher authorities. This of course is why religious authorities are treated with so much disdain today; their truth-claims seem to be nothing but unjustified dogma.

To many believers it may seem obvious that religious information must be different in these ways from other information. It has not always seemed obvious; the idea has a history.

As far as we know, human societies have always enquired about the nature of God, or the gods, how we relate to them, what kind of world they have made and what they expect us to do in it. In the last chapter I described how in ancient times these questions were treated together without separating religious elements from others. The early Christians spent much of their time debating questions like the incarnation and the Trinity which seem to us to be disconnected from any public evidence. Most churches today treat them as authoritative doctrines, hallowed with age, making statements which rarely seem relevant to people's lives. To question them and try to improve on them is usually discouraged. The early Christians on the other hand spent centuries in intense and bitter debate doing just this. They did so because the questions at issue were important to them. From their Jewish roots they had inherited the belief that there is only one God, but they were also making increasingly bold claims for the divine status of Jesus. In order to hold together these two doctrines they made extensive use of Greek theories about the nature of reality. In this way early doctrines, which later Christian tradition was to describe as reason-free divine revelation, were in fact hammered out over centuries using all the reasoning tools available.

There were limits. Just as mainstream Christianity refused to reject reason, it also refused to treat reason as the *only* source of truth. A remark of Augustine has often been quoted; although not entirely consistent on the point, he did write 'Do not seek to understand in order that you may believe, but believe in order that you may understand'. Centuries later Anselm echoed the sentiment.[1] It was a significant point. It is not just that neither Christian doctrine nor the existence of God can be deduced with certainty from rational processes, so we need to make an act of trust: in addition, *all* our reasoning processes depend on presupposing that the things we see around us really exist, and that our basic calculations in arithmetic and logic produce true results. If we do not make these presuppositions we cannot make any sense at all of our lives. Yet we cannot prove them: and even if we could logically prove that logic is reliable, it would be a circular argument. What differentiates Augustine and Anselm from the Gnostics described in the last chapter is their belief that our minds have been designed by a good God to understand those aspects of reality which we need to understand. It was an act of *faith*. To say the same thing in scientific language, it was a *hypothesis*; and as it was the best hypothesis available to them they took it to be true.

Reason and its opponents

From the fifth century onwards educational standards in western Europe declined. In this situation it became natural to think that greater wisdom could be found in the writings of the ancients than in the new ideas of contemporaries. The church did more than any other institution to maintain educational standards and came to be respected for its learning. This was true not just of theological matters but of all learning, and continued to be true after the revival of educational standards from the eleventh century onwards.

Modern western histories have often described the seventeenth and eighteenth centuries as 'the Age of Reason' and contrasted it with the medieval 'Age of Faith'. In fact the medieval schools and universities invested heavily in developing their understanding of reason. They did so in unprecedented detail, analyzing its scope and the rules for its use. They also promoted 'natural philosophy', the precursor of modern science, which engaged in empirical studies.[2]

In their researches they would search the ancient documents available to them for answers to questions on any subject. Chief among those documents was the Bible. Over time, however, scholars began to reach conclusions which contradicted traditional views. This meant disagreeing with church leaders and even sometimes biblical texts. Some church leaders perceived the new learning as a threat and defended traditional beliefs against it. In the process they came to perceive the church less as a truth-seeking community with a dynamic process of reflection on old and new ideas, more as the defender of a fixed set of truths which needed to be accepted as they were. They opposed both rational analysis and empirical research.

The study of logic was central to the medieval schools and universities. In the eleventh and twelfth centuries they applied it to matters of faith, like the doctrines of the Eucharist and the Trinity, just as rigorously as to all else. At the beginning of the thirteenth century the Dominican order was founded specifically for the purpose opposing heretics with rational arguments.[3] However there were opponents who argued that to analyze the church's doctrines in these ways was an act of heresy. True piety, they believed, meant accepting its teachings without question. Direct knowledge of God and contemplation were the proper tools of meditation on Christian truth. The eleventh century Peter Damian rejected reason so far as to argue that God could reverse the effects of a past injustice or even cause it not to have happened in the first place. Although this would produce a contradiction and therefore undermine logic, he claimed that this indicated the superiority of faith over logic.[4] Later Bernard of Clairvaux, condemning Abelard in a letter to a cardinal, wrote:

He has defiled the Church; he has infected with his own blight the minds of simple people. He tries to explore with his reason what the devout mind grasps at once with a vigorous faith. Faith believes, it does not dispute. But this man, apparently holding God suspect, will not believe anything until he has first examined it with his reason.[5]

Genesis 1:7 states that God placed waters above the sky. Empirical researchers had their doubts about them, but had nowhere near as much influence as church leaders. Their researches could be severely hampered by ecclesiastical hostility to any findings which contradicted tradition. To minimize conflict, they defended the authority of reason *only* over the regular processes of nature, while allowing the authority of tradition over all else. They made use of a distinction between God's *regular* power, expressed in normal processes of cause and effect, and God's *absolute* power to do anything logically possible. So Adelard of Bath argued in the 1120s:

> I take nothing away from God, for whatever exists is from Him and because of Him. But the natural order does not exist confusedly and without natural arrangement, and human reason should be listened to concerning those things it treats of. But when it completely fails, then the matter should be referred to God.[6]

One more step was to argue that the processes of nature, which we understand through reason, are the work of nature *as opposed to* God. According to William of Conches,

> It must be recognized that every work is the work of the Creator or of Nature, or the work of a human artisan imitating nature. The work of the Creator is the first creation without pre-existing material, for example the creation of the elements or of spirits, or it is the things we see happen contrary to the accustomed course of nature, as the virgin birth and the like. The work of nature is to bring forth like things from like through seeds or offshoots, for nature is an energy inherent in things and making like from like.

On this basis he argued that the authority of the bible and the early Christian theologians should be limited to matters of religious faith and morals. When dealing with the works of nature, on the other hand, it should be permissible to disagree with a biblical statement.[7]

Previously Christians and pagans alike had believed that the non-human natural order was entirely the work of the gods they believed in. To assert that nature operates independently of God, with the exceptions of the initial creation and occasional miracles, is to separate God from the reality which humans normally experience, and to set a barrier between them, namely 'nature'. God, instead of being responsible for regularities and irregularities alike, could be thought of as only responsible for the irregularities, while the regularities were explained by the 'laws of nature'. For the first time in Christian history it was being proposed that God was irrelevant to most of human experience. Behind this move lay the influence of Aristotle, who had taught that once God had created the world he allowed it to operate according to its own regularities and took no further interest in it.

The motivation is clear enough: research into the natural world could not make progress as long as theologians had the power to prescribe the results. It was at first very much a minority view, but it was to continue for many centuries; the best known debates are later ones focusing on Galileo and Darwin. In the case of Darwin there still are religious traditions committed to denying his scientific theory. Since the end of the nineteenth century many opponents of religious belief have argued that religion and science are incompatible; the view is often described as the 'warfare' model of the relationship between the two. Opponents of religion can find many texts, not only of medieval church leaders repressing empirical studies, but also of their successors through the ages doing the same. Defenders of religion can also find many texts illustrating church leaders supporting these researches. The temptation is for the proponents of each position to emphasize one side of the picture at the expense of the other. Both happened. My argument will be that bad religion does indeed conflict with science but good religion supports it.

The solution proposed by the twelfth century natural philosophers aimed only to free empirical research to reach its own conclusions. They had no intention to oppose Christian doctrine as a whole; all that concerned them was that when the words of the Bible conflicted with the conclusions of natural reasoning, something had to give. We can agree with the need for a solution without agreeing that theirs was the right one. It would have been better to accept that the biblical authors and the inherited Christian tradition were sometimes wrong; but the commitment to the authority of the past was still too strong. The dualistic solution suited the purposes of the empirical researchers well enough.

At the time their main opponents were theologians anxious to defend God's freedom. Empirical studies of the physical world were closely linked to the Neoplatonist tradition, which described physical reality as an emanation from God. The idea of emanation had two implications. One was the regularity of nature, which is an essential presupposition of science. The other was determinism: Neoplatonism's God, unlike the Christian God, had no option but to produce the world. Many Augustinians were therefore determined to insist on God's freedom. In order to do so they denied that nature was predictable. Some denied that there are any laws of nature, arguing that each natural process takes place as a direct result of God's decree. From this it followed that scientific investigation cannot yield useful results.

Of those who tried to reconcile these two schools the best known is Thomas Aquinas. Aquinas set out to give due place to both reason and revelation within a single account of how we know things. He pictured the sciences in a hierarchy in which each one presupposes truths which it cannot itself establish, but which are established by another. Philosophers of science still accept this hierarchy of the sciences. Aquinas added to it by placing theology at the top. He believed that human endeavour, rightly directed, aspires towards God, and theology is the science which directly treats God as its subject. In this way, he argued, theology functions like other sciences; it uses information provided by other sciences, but also provides truths which the others cannot discover.[8] Within this account Aquinas believed there was a place for both reason and divine revelation. Natural theology uses reason: by reflecting on the finite and natural world we come to learn about the infinite and the supernatural. Revealed theology begins with God, and provides information much of which we would not have been able to discover through reason. Human rationality can take us so far; what God has revealed through his grace takes us further; but the human quest for knowledge will not be finally achieved until we come to know God in heaven.[9]

One of Aquinas' reasons why special revelation is needed was that if natural reasoning were the only means to the knowledge of God, only a few people would achieve it. It seemed to him that the ability to reason without error was not widely available. The doctrines of the church, however, were. In the seventeenth century natural theologians, in very different circumstances, would argue the exact opposite.[10]

Although Aquinas' theory was eventually rehabilitated, at the time it pleased neither side. Many of the Bishop of Paris' condemnations in 1277 were aimed at his teachings, and the reactions against him deepened the divisions.[11] Augustinians complained that to attribute to God a constant mode of operation took away God's freedom. Instead they argued that God is free to act in ways which transcend all human analysis.

Of course it is possible to believe that a free, powerful and good God chooses to do many things regularly in order to provide humans with the regularities needed for a good life. This was the point of the distinction between God's regular and absolute power. What made a resolution on this basis impossible was the determination of many theologians to defend specific traditional teachings about the physical world, like the waters above the sky. Faced with mounting evidence against them, they did what countless people have done before and after them when they were on the losing side: they denied the value of reason.

If the principle of God's freedom is applied to all natural processes, science of course becomes impossible. The resolution of the conflict which was eventually accepted by both sides was a revived dualism. If a biblical text contradicted the findings of scientists about the natural world, reason was to be followed; but reason was not applicable to religious matters, where revelation reigned supreme.[12] Because this dualism is a central theme of this book, in order to avoid confusion I shall restrict my use of the term 'dualism' to this tradition – though there are many other dualisms equally deserving of the term.[13]

A central figure in the development of dualism was William of Ockham. Ockham emphasized God's absolute power to the extent that God can, in principle, even overturn the categories of good and evil or cause and effect, or award salvation on the basis of no ordered system. However, he also believed that God had decreed that the laws of creation should be constant. This made science possible, though he retained strict limits to its scope; all our knowledge, he argued, comes from our senses which give us awareness of individual things but nothing else. It follows that we cannot even know the existence of causation, since whatever God does by means of a cause God can also do immediately without needing the cause.[14] On theological matters, on the other hand, he believed all certainty rested on the doctrines of faith. Since our senses do not provide knowledge of God's existence, reason cannot tell us anything about God. Doctrines such as the Trinity and the soul's immortality are beyond rational examination as our senses cannot perceive them. We simply believe them by faith.

Recently scholars have argued that Ockham was not a true dualist. At times he denied that there was an absolute distinction between the two spheres - so that, for example, the statement 'God is wise' can be derived from both theology and natural reason. Nevertheless he increased the restrictions on natural theology and some argue that when his followers embraced a thoroughgoing dualism they were revealing the inevitable result of his logic.[15] The same applies in ethics. Part of Ockham's legacy was that all morality is based simply on the arbitrary decree of God. Some of his followers, Robert Holcot and Adam of Woodham, took the argument further and claimed that God can even lie and sin.[16]

For present purposes it does not matter exactly where we locate the development of dualism; what is significant is that it became sufficiently well established to be a major influence in the Reformation debates. To accept dualism was to liberate empirical studies from theological censure and pave the way for modern science to develop. There was a price to pay in the need to distinguish between the spiritual and the natural, and this was done by counting observables as natural and unobservables as spiritual. Today scientists propose many unobservables as hypotheses to explain the behaviour of observables, but the tradition of denying their existence is still influential.

Dualism's effects on theology were more wide-ranging. It denied that there is any way human reason can understand traditional doctrines: we have to just accept them as divine revelation. This of course flies in the face of the way they were in fact developed. The late medievals had available to them no shortage of information to recognize that the church's doctrines had been hammered out through centuries of debate among the early Christians, using all the rational processes available to them. Nevertheless, the dominant solution to the debates of the time demanded that these doctrines should be reason-free revelations given directly by God, and so they were decreed to be.

Effects of medieval dualism

That great watershed of European history, the end of the Middle Ages and the beginning of the modern era, is marked by the production of alternatives to holistic accounts of God, the world and humanity. Dualism provided two contrasting ways of knowing things, revelation and reason. At the time, theological discourse was far more influential than scientific research. That was to change. Empirical research, freed from theological censure and encouraged to make full use of reason, went from strength to strength. Nobody at the time could have foreseen how the new paradigm would lead to the marginalization of religious belief; but it did because theology was given a much poorer set of tools. Before adding later ideas into the mix, let us reflect on the implications of this dualism as they have been worked out over the subsequent centuries.

Theology's scope was restricted. It was to apply only to the unobservable and non-physical. Previously this had not been the case. Throughout the Middle Ages popular European society was full of beliefs about invisible beings intervening to affect observable physical events. The most Christianity could do was to reinterpret these beings as angels, evil spirits or saints. The new theory restricted religious belief to the non-physical, which it equated with the unobservable. As a matter of principle religion was to be nothing to do with the way the physical world works.

Although this is widely taken for granted now by both supporters and opponents of religious belief, at the time it was a radical innovation and would have seemed counter-intuitive outside the universities. However, because of the tensions within them, it was a necessary price to pay for empirical research to develop. The one part of religious belief which was useful to science was retained, for a few more centuries, as an exception to the rule: the doctrine that the world has been intentionally created by God in an ordered manner. Otherwise, religion was to keep its nose out of worldly matters.

Theology became backward-looking. With divine revelation the only source of information, there was no source of new ideas. It is of course possible to believe in new revelations from God: enthusiasts of the Reformation era claimed to receive them, and some charismatics today do. In practice, however, new ideas rarely arise in this way, and even when they do they present their churches with the dilemma of whether to accept them. Churches which have not renounced reason are able to evaluate new ideas on their merits. Those which have renounced it have no means to justify change. It is inevitable that all the influential revelation claims of dualist churches appeal to the past, whether church tradition or the Bible.

Thus the historical circumstance of the centuries immediately after the collapse of the Roman empire, when the best insights were the insights of the distant past, was elevated into an eternal truth about all religious matters. Although theologians have often been far more creative than dualism allows, ever since the fourteenth century it has been possible for the opponents of new ideas to cite religious authority against the very possibility of new ideas being acceptable. Truth comes from revelation, and revelation comes from the past.

Christianity became exclusive. Dualism denies that there is any role at all for natural theology; *only* Christianity's divine revelations can offer knowledge of God. It is true that the Catholic church already had, and still has, a tradition of appealing to natural theology. However it had limits. It argued that although its doctrines could be deduced from the Bible, appeals to reason made them accessible to anyone who reflects on them, not just to those who already accept the Bible's authority. Reason could therefore be used to present Catholic teaching to non-Catholics. However the same did not apply the other way round. Catholic natural theology emphasized universal truths deduced with certainty from other universal truths, with comparatively little interest in empirical observations. For example, Roman Catholic moral rules with respect to abortion, euthanasia and killing in war are based on the universal rule that it is always gravely sinful directly to kill an innocent person on one's own authority. Contextual empirical information is used to establish how to apply the rule in particular situations, but is not given the authority to challenge the rule itself. In this way the Catholic church could present the doctrines and moral norms derived from its own natural theology as divinely revealed certainties and therefore beyond challenge by reason.

Thus divine revelation, by dualism's logic, is restricted in two ways: not only to the past but also to Christians. Catholics had long believed there was no salvation outside the church, but dualism distinguished Christians from non-Christians more sharply than before. Non-Christians, according to the theory, must be in complete ignorance of God and all religious truths. If this is true it must follow that a non-Christian who describes God using the same words as Christians use cannot possibly mean the same thing as a Christian would mean, or at least cannot understand it in the same way. To dualists this bizarre conclusion needs to be held as a principle of faith regardless of evidence to the contrary. Many conservative evangelicals today, for example, claim that Islam's Allah is a different god from the Christian God – despite the facts that both faiths teach that there is only one God, and that 'Allah' is the Arabic translation for the English word 'God'.

Religious truth was accepted as absolutely certain. Since divinely revealed statements were supposed to transcend reason it followed that they were true even if they contradicted all reason. From the human perspective there was no way they could possibly be false. The idea of certainty therefore took on an absoluteness which it had not previously had; the certainty of Christian doctrines gave them a different quality from all other types of information. In the current Anglican debate, for example, many conservatives argue that because the Bible condemns homosexuality no amount of human reason can legitimately question its verdict: homosexuality is wrong with a certainty which transcends anything that new research into homosexual orientation may produce.

Moral rules are not rationally justified. Morality, like religious truth, is based on divine revelation and owes nothing to human experience and reason. For God to have a reason for decreeing an act right or wrong would imply that God's freedom is limited. Ockham argued that, because God's will is completely sovereign, everything that is good or bad is good or bad simply because God says so and for no other reason.[17] Critics have noted that the social results of this doctrine have been disastrous. To believe one has a duty to do right and avoid wrong, when one has no understanding of *why* some things are right and others wrong, is to create insoluble dilemmas in situations where the rules are unclear. When, for example, homosexuality is condemned simply because the Bible forbids it, homosexuals point to the fact that they, like heterosexuals, engage in a wide variety of acts. In some cases it is not clear whether the act should be described as sexual. To observe the rule against homosexuality they would need to ask questions of the type 'Is *this* a homosexual act? If it is, is *that* also a homosexual act?' If the moral rules transcend all reason and all we have to work from are the biblical texts, questions of this type cannot be answered. On this account of morality, therefore, however hard we try to do good and avoid evil we are only making guesses in the dark.

Reason is narrowed. The Platonist tradition offered a wide account of reason; the highest forms of reality, it taught, were eternal and spiritual essences, and reason enabled humans to know about them. Reason, therefore, was able not only to know about non-physical realities, but to reflect on them and understand them. Aquinas, while rejecting much of the Platonist tradition, still interpreted reason widely, to refer to a variety of processes for seeking truth other than divine revelation. Opponents of this view argued that knowledge of the way things are implies regularity, and regularity limits God's freedom. For early opponents like Peter Damian, *any* attempt to understand the way things work, whether in spiritual or physical matters, presupposes regularity and therefore denies God's freedom. If Peter's voice had been heeded, the sciences would not have been able to develop. Ockham's account, while allowing a role for reason, restricted it tightly in order to defend God's freedom: physical, observable things, he said, operated according to regularities and human reason apprehends individual things through the five senses. It cannot apprehend anything non-physical, or indeed do anything at all except apprehend physical things and make logical deductions. This contrast between wider and narrower accounts of reason informs later debates; characteristically, those committed to the search for certainty prefer narrower accounts of reason while others prefer wider accounts.

There is an increased authoritarianism. A change took place in the nature of authority. In every field of study a lively, confident tradition usually feels able to reject even central features of its belief system without feeling threatened. Thus Einstein could challenge Newton's theory without being accused of undermining physics as a whole. Before late medieval dualism the same was true of religion: biblical authors felt able to affirm some parts of their tradition while changing others.[18] The objective was truth. However, when a tradition loses its self-confidence and becomes defensive it turns its old ideas into certainties above question. By exalting Christian doctrine to a position above rational questioning, dualists in effect gave church leaders the right of veto over all theological ideas. Intending to preserve the tradition, they made it more authoritarian.

This dualistic account of knowledge was established as a popular theory in the later Middle Ages and from then onwards has had immense influence on religious thought. In the last chapter I described how biblical doctrines and commands could be initially justified by natural theology but later asserted as divine revelation. Dualism encourages this process. A theory, or law, is first defended for reasons of natural theology or practicality. Practices often last longer than the reasons for them. However intensely these reasons are initially debated, as time passes they are forgotten or lose significance. Meanwhile the very fact that they have been inherited from a past age gives them an aura of venerability. Eventually it becomes easier to defend them in the name of tradition and present them as God's law imposed simply because God says so.

The Nicene Creed, for example, was established as orthodoxy at the Councils of Nicaea and Chalcedon in the Church's debates of the fourth and fifth centuries. The reasons for establishing it as official doctrine were to do with the conflicts of the time: if there had been no rational debate before the councils were held, there would have been no need to hold them. This means that the councils produced a change in the authority of their doctrines. Before they pronounced on the issues under debate, a variety of views were in circulation and were publicly debated. After they had pronounced their verdict, the majority view became the only acceptable one. Christians were expected to hold it for a new reason: *because the church had so decreed.*

The same has happened many times: the Westminster Confession, the Thirty-Nine Articles and the Council of Trent all had the same effect. More recently, in the Church of England's debate over homosexuality, *Issues in Human Sexuality*[19] was published in 1991 as a discussion document, specifically denying that it was the last word on the matter. At publication it was heavily criticized from all directions. Eleven years later, when

Rowan Williams' appointment as Archbishop of Canterbury was announced, and in the following year in the debates about the appointments of Jeffrey John and Gene Robinson, it was widely cited by the opponents of homosexuality *as the church's teaching*.[20]

It is a characteristic trend. Genuine debate leads to an official resolution which imposes the successful view as the only legitimate one. Unsuccessful views, previously legitimate though contested, become forbidden. The successful view, previously defended for publicly debated reasons, no longer needs to be rationally justified. The original reasons for it fade from view and are eventually forgotten. It then becomes all the more important, for its defenders, that it should be accepted by all simply because it is the church's doctrine.

At every stage in Christianity's history believers have inherited doctrines from a variety of different debates but have also engaged in contemporary debates carving out new doctrines. We know about the reasons for and against the different positions in the debates of our own day. We are more inclined to accept earlier decisions without question; many of them, after all, have no practical significance today so we find them boring. They lurk in the archives, waiting to be revived when some new movement finds them useful. The long-term result is an ever-increasing pile of doctrines which, in theory, one has to believe in order to count as a true Christian, or a true member of a particular denomination. Churches with long histories are now far too top-heavy with accumulated formally approved doctrines. They need – but have not yet established – a system for regular doctrinal spring cleaning.

Dualism denies that this happens at all. It has no method for recognizing innovation because it claims that all the truths of religion are given by revelation. It enables Christians and atheists alike to argue that all religious beliefs are dogmas without rational support - the former in order to justify their version of it, the latter in order to dismiss all religion as mere superstition.

When doctrines and moral norms are reinterpreted in dualistic terms, therefore, they lose touch with the reasons why they were introduced in the first place. Moral norms are no longer defended in terms of their positive value and instead become arbitrary decrees by a God whom we cannot understand. Doctrines, similarly, cease to explain why reality and human life are the way they are and instead simply transfer snippets of spiritual information from God to believers. It is hardly surprising that, in a culture where religious belief is understood in this way, the vast majority of the population simply do not care whether or not the doctrines of Christianity are true. They no longer matter. In order to matter they would have to explain something and in order to explain something they would have to *make sense*.

CHAPTER 3

SCRIPTURE AND CERTAINTY IN THE

REFORMATION DEBATES

If religious truth is revealed to us by God without being mediated by human reason, as the dualism described in the last chapter argued, how do we find it out? Who tells us what it is? As long as the Catholic church was dominant in western Europe, there was one obvious answer. Come the Reformation, competing churches claimed to teach the true faith. How could the faithful know which of them was right?

Because the Reformation produced new religious institutions which are still popular today, many scholars and church leaders are motivated to either attack or defend its doctrines. To a lesser extent the same is true of Roman Catholicism; it did not begin at this stage but the Council of Trent clarified many doctrines, hardened opposition to Protestantism and reduced the options for Catholic belief. This chapter therefore deals with many people's deeply held commitments, and no account of them will please everyone.

My aim in this chapter is to show how the Reformers and Counter-Reformers set the terms for much of subsequent western Christianity, and so note the price we pay for accepting them. Some of their ideas have remained authoritative in their respective denominations from that day to this. Others were popular for a while, died out and were revived later. Others again died out and have not been revived; but such is the reverence for the Reformers among Protestants and for conciliar decrees among Roman Catholics that it remains possible for polemicists to revive long-forgotten statements and attribute authority to them. When they do, the original context is often ignored; Luther and Calvin can easily be proof-texted just like the Bible, ignoring the fact that sixteenth century Protestants and Catholics alike were engaged in lively and developing debate and could change their minds.

It was a fertile period for new ideas and new analyses of old ones. Nevertheless there were some dominant theories and some characteristic changes. Most significant for present purposes is the dualism, inherited from the later Middle Ages, which dominated both Protestant and Catholic thought. Both sides effectively rejected the use of reason, except for the purpose of deducing truths from revelation. During the sixteenth century the clearest voice in defence of reason came from the Socinians, a small group condemned by both sides. Among the Reformers, Melanchthon defended the scholastic concept of a balance between reason and revelation; otherwise, Catholics and Protestants alike argued that the only things we can know about matters of faith are what God has revealed.[1] Some explained reason's limitations by appealing to the Fall. Luther taught that ever since Adam's sin natural human reason would be better described as unnatural.[2] Calvin taught that nature still offers us some awareness of God, but humanity is so conditioned by sin that we can no longer read the book of nature rightly.[3]

Overwhelmingly the Reformers and Counter-Reformers accepted from late medieval dualism the principles that theological truth is only to be found in the Bible, which is God's revelation; that Christian truth is therefore restricted to doctrines already established; that the truths known through revelation are known with certainty; and that moral commands are laid down purely because God so decrees. In their changed circumstances, however, they developed these convictions in new ways.

The authority of the Bible

Whereas the authority of the Bible was unchallenged, how to interpret it was a matter of great debate.

Sufficiency. Catholics believed that Scripture is a necessary rule of faith but accepted that many passages were difficult to understand or contradicted each other. There must be another authority, namely the church, to interpret it. From the twelfth century onwards Waldensians, Albigensians and Lollards had responded to preachers sent to convert them by quoting the Bible back at them. The Catholic response was that it was the church's responsibility to determine how to interpret Scripture; after all it was the church which had decided which books counted as Scripture.[4]

Many of the Reformation's leaders were influenced by Renaissance humanism. The humanist slogan *ad fontes*, 'back to the sources', meant treating ancient texts as authoritative in their own right and reading them without the use of medieval commentaries. In the same way the Reformers rejected the church's authority as interpreter of the Bible. The Bible alone was authoritative; nothing was required for salvation unless it was contained in it or deducible from it. This was their principle of *sola scriptura*: going far beyond anything the early church had proposed, they insisted that the *only* authority to which appeal should be made was the Bible. They accused the Catholic church of producing new doctrines not found in Scripture.[5]

Counter-Reformation theologians agreed that it was wrong to produce new doctrines, but replied that the church's definitions merely explained the true sense of Scripture or drew out its implications. Suarez, for example, denied that the Church of his day knew more than the apostles had learned from Jesus; instead he insisted that the apostles had explicitly known every doctrine which the Church had subsequently declared.[6]

Ethical authority. Nearly all the Reformers rejected natural law ethics. Moral norms, they believed, are based on God's decree as expressed in the Bible and apply to all times and places regardless of their effect on human well-being. Bucer and Cartwright believed the Bible provides ethical instructions for all spheres of human life, and Cartwright went so far as to claim that we should refrain from doing anything not commanded in it. In practice, of course, nobody systematically attempted to apply all the Bible's ethical commands to their own lives, let alone refrain from actions not mentioned in it. Like their successors today they ignored most of them but focused on a few which related to the issues of their own day. The Anabaptists came closest to a systematic application with their attempts to carry out consistently the demands of the New Testament, especially the Sermon on the Mount. The task was made easier by the fact that they did not accept the ethical authority of the Old Testament.[7]

The Bible records a great many immoral acts, like the polygamy of the patriarchs and the suicide of Samson, without any hint of disapproval and sometimes with approval. The medieval church had usually treated the stories allegorically, and it was also possible to argue that there must have been extenuating circumstances. The Reformers rejected both these explanations; instead they argued that the biblical characters must have received a special command from God. This was consistent with their belief that God's will is necessarily right however immoral it may seem to us. However it raised the possibility that God might command people in their own day to commit acts which were otherwise immoral. The Anabaptists at Münster believed this of themselves - they had been given a special revelation from God to fight against unrighteousness - but most Reformers believed that God now spoke only through Scripture.[8]

By interpreting the Bible this way Protestants rediscovered the ethical problems which the early church had faced; but they added to the difficulties by expecting Scripture to be a complete guide to life. Many spent much time, and some still do, seeking ways to interpret the Bible as a realistic and comprehensive guide to life. If, as they believed, what God demands of us is quite independent of our bodily or mental well-being, we are bound to experience a persistent tension between what we want and what God commands. This tension has had a major influence on modern ethical theory, secular as well as Christian. It easily leads to a strong sense of alienation: puritans, like the earlier Gnostics and Manicheans, often thought of themselves as a saved soul trapped in an evil body in an evil world. E C E Bourne has argued that an anticosmic attitude inherited from them lay behind puritan views.[9]

Scientific information. In the sixteenth century science did not have the status it has today. Many still considered the Bible's teaching on scientific matters more reliable than the theories of scientists. Luther cited the text in Joshua where the sun stood still as a refutation of Copernicus' theory.[10] Calvin took a more dualistic view, arguing that the Bible is primarily concerned with the knowledge of Jesus Christ and should not be treated as a textbook on astronomy, geography or biology. He was not, though, prepared to accept that the Bible might be in error. He therefore developed the theory of 'accommodation': just as good orators adjust their language to their audiences, so God's revelations are accommodated to their recipients.[11]

Thus the Reformers expressed two contrasting ways to interpret the Bible's supreme authority. One declares it authoritative on scientific matters; the six-day creation and Noah's flood are to be believed because the Bible's reliability is greater than that of science. According to the other, Scripture's sufficiency relates to matters of faith but no more.

Unity. Luther sometimes accepted that the Bible consisted of distinct literary works, and denied that they had the same value. His criterion for evaluating them was the extent to which they witness to Christ. He believed that John, 1 John, Romans, Galatians, Ephesians and 1 Peter were of supreme value. Romans is 'really the chief part of the New Testament and the very purest Gospel', whereas James has nothing of the nature of the Gospel about it and is dismissed as 'straw'.[12] More often the Reformers thought of the Bible as a single, unified body of literature. The Neoplatonist tradition had contributed: in the fourteenth century, for example, Wyclif had viewed the Bible as an eternal form, the primal image of all eternal truth, containing all universal concepts and moral laws.[13] Among the Reformers Zwingli accepted the complete Bible as a disclosure of God's will, equally authoritative throughout. Luther, despite the distinctions noted above, could also say of it that 'God is in every syllable' and 'no iota is in vain'; everything in it is to be believed because the book constitutes a whole, 'and he who does not believe one statement cannot believe anything'. Similarly Calvin saw the Bible as the Word of God to humanity, written down and preserved in order to build up the

Church.[14]

Perspicuity. When the Reformers rejected the Catholic church's claim to be the authoritative interpreter of Scripture, they did not have an alternative tradition of interpretation with which to replace it. They claimed that the Bible did not need to be interpreted. This meant that it could, and should, be understood and obeyed *as it is*. This was the doctrine of perspicuity. Scripture, they said, is clear and persuasive, so that anybody at all should be able to understand it. Luther seems to have believed that anybody could make perfect sense of what it said.[15] To Zwingli 'The Word of God, as soon as it shines upon an individual's understanding, illuminates it in such a way that he understands it.'[16] To Calvin, Scripture reveals the evidence of its own truth every bit as clearly as black and white things do of their colour, or sweet and bitter things do of their taste. For a while it was a common view.[17]

Perspicuity would have been easier to defend if Protestants had not disagreed about the meanings of texts. It was not long before Luther and Zwingli disagreed over the words of Christ on which eucharistic doctrine depended: 'This is my body'. Some reformers showed much ingenuity in harmonizing conflicting texts: Andreas Osiander, in his *Harmonia Evangelica* (1545), argued that each event must have occurred in as many forms and on as many occasions as was necessary to validate all the versions. Christ must have been crowned with thorns and clothed in purple twice, and Peter must have warmed himself at the fire four times. Calvin emphasized that the biblical writers were 'the mouthpieces of God' and their utterances were infallible, but also believed they could be mistaken about factual details, as in the conflicting accounts of the burial-places of the patriarchs.[18]

Another matter of debate was the accuracy of the Latin Vulgate translation of the Bible. Medieval scholars had accepted it without question, but humanists checked it against Greek and Hebrew texts and found discrepancies. Which version was inspired by God? Despite their earlier commitment to perspicuity, Zwingli and Luther came to believe that to understand Scripture one needed knowledge of Hebrew and Greek. This, of course, implied that most people did after all need a human authority to interpret Scripture for them. The Anabaptists retained their commitment to perspicuity, and with it the Vulgate.[19]

Perspicuity was bound to fail the test of time. The English Interregnum was a test case. When the puritans were in government, they sought to reform the church on Scriptural principles, expecting that every individual could read for themselves what those Scriptural principles were. The two proved incompatible: puritans could not agree with each other about what the Bible commanded.[20] Despite its weaknesses, however, the idea has proved attractive to later generations. Today the idea of 'the clear teaching of Scripture' remains a popular slogan for many evangelicals.[21]

Timelessness. The Reformers inherited a static view of history. Many comparatively static societies conceive of history in discrete stages. They believe that their own pattern of human settlements and lifestyles with its traditions of worship and moral rules were established in a very different age, and that their own age simply maintains them unchanged through the generations. Medieval Christianity fitted its theological story into this pattern. The creation, Fall and redemption were in the past and the second coming was in the future; between the two was the present age in which life carried on basically unchanged.[22] This implied that there is a fixed set of truths in matters of faith, all of which have already been authoritatively revealed, and that there cannot be any possibility of discovering new ones until the second coming.

Another common idea of the time was that history is characterized by alternations between golden ages and dark ages. The idea of a 'renaissance' was often linked with the theory that a thousand-year golden age had ended with the collapse of the western Roman empire, and the subsequent thousand-year dark age was just then giving way to a new golden age. Protestants could borrow the theme by associating medieval Catholicism with the dark age and the new golden age with a return to the Bible.

Protestants and Catholics alike thought in these unhistorical terms until well into the eighteenth century; it was not until the nineteenth that theories of doctrinal development were propounded. Thus Nowell's *Catechism* of 1570 declared that 'it were a point of untolerable ungodliness and madness to think, either that God had left an imperfect doctrine, or that men were able to make that perfect, which God left imperfect'.[23] Bucer's recommendations for ordering the church consisted almost entirely of quotations from the New Testament because 'we do not want to introduce anything anywhere which is not manifest and certain teaching and the clear and undoubted command of our Lord Jesus Christ'.[24] Their failure to acknowledge changing circumstances was expressed in their claim that the Bible was written 'for us' - that is, for the people of their own day. Even the Old Testament histories, they believed, must have something significant to say about their own time and place.[25]

Catholics argued from apostolic tradition. The church had received its doctrines from the apostles and the apostles from Christ. Since they are necessary for salvation, God would not have permitted them to be altered. Agreeing with Protestants that change is error, they argued that only the Catholic church has remained unchanged. When it defined doctrines and made new articles of faith it was merely using logical words to clarify the content of the original revelation.[26]

There was of course much evidence of gradual historical change, and sometimes it was recognized. Protestants and Catholics accused each other of innovating. Nevertheless the ahistorical view of time produced a general sense that truth, and the way things are, have been given to the age between the New Testament and the second coming as a complete and unchanging package. There cannot be any new truths so there is no point in looking for them.

Inspiration. These claims for the sufficiency, unity, perspicuity and timelessness of the Bible needed defending. Here lay a difficult question: what authority did they have for asserting the supreme authority of the Bible? Logically there are two possible types of answer. One is to look for evidence within the contents of the Bible. Luther used this argument.[27] Its strength depends on the judgements of readers; those who read the Bible without becoming convinced of its supreme authority have no reason to be persuaded. The other is to establish the Bible's authority by appeal to something external to it. If no church suffices, it must be God. So Zwingli emphasized that the whole Bible had been inspired by the Holy Spirit.[28] Calvin agreed: God is the true author of every biblical text, and it has nothing merely human mixed with it. Opinions differ as to whether he believed in verbal inspiration (that God selected the exact words) though most think he did.[29]

The question of the Holy Spirit's role was therefore critical. To Catholics the pope was guided by the Spirit. If the Spirit were not concentrated in one person there would be many different interpretations of Christian doctrine.[30] Protestants needed to explain why they did indeed differ from each other. The most common theory was that those with erroneous interpretations had not sufficiently allowed the Spirit to guide them. To Luther, 'They most sadly err who presume to interpret the Holy Scriptures and the law of God by taking hold of them by their own understanding and study'; instead, each person must attend to Scripture themselves under the Spirit's guidance.[31] Calvin taught that it is through the witness of the Spirit that the Scriptures impress themselves on the human heart as divine and life-giving wisdom. This testimony of the Spirit is, he believed, unique: it applies to the Bible and nothing else. Once we have received this assurance from the Spirit, then the other reasons for submitting to Scripture's rule acquire added force.[32]

These ideas helped Protestants establish the only possible solution to their conundrum. Despite their theories they could not agree with each other about the plain, uninterpreted meanings of biblical texts. Scripture did not function at all well as a supreme authority. Another authority was needed, and if no human one was acceptable a divine one was the only alternative. Nevertheless it opened a Pandora's box. If the individual Protestant was to learn true doctrine by reading Scripture, but also needed to learn the meaning of Scripture by the Spirit's inward guidance, it seemed that the Spirit was doing the work; perhaps Scripture was superfluous. Protestants held a range of opinions on the matter. Those who emphasized the Spirit's role came to be known as the 'enthusiasts'.

The enthusiasts accepted the traditional distinction between 'sanctifying grace', which makes people fit for salvation, and 'edifying grace' which enables them to teach others, speak in tongues, work miracles, discern spirits, heal and prophesy. Most Protestants believed that edifying grace had been restricted to the biblical prophets and apostles. The enthusiasts believed it was available in their own day. Many of them claimed to possess it, and thereby claimed for themselves the authority to teach things not in the Bible.[33]

Attitudes to opponents change with theories. As long as the interpreting authority is the church, anyone who disagrees with it is rejecting the Church's authority and is therefore a heretic. When authority shifts to the perspicuity of every biblical text, I read it and understand it, so those who disagree with me are refusing to accept the clear teaching of Scripture. Why they so refuse is a puzzle; perhaps they are not reading it carefully enough, or perhaps the devil's influence is at work. When the authority shifts again, to the inner guidance of the Holy Spirit, the nature of the disagreement changes once more. I know that I have the Spirit's guidance because I have the required feelings inside me. My opponent also claims to have the required feelings and therefore the Spirit's guidance. If I am guided by the Spirit, my opponent must be guided by something else capable of entering people's hearts in opposition to the Spirit. It can only be the devil. My opponent is not just in error but is speaking the devil's words. To disagree is not enough; his or her words need to be denounced, driven out, exorcized. Many of course did not go that far, but some did. Such discourse did, and still does, generate that over-confidence which refuses to tolerate those who disagree, and which in any other context would be condemned as pure bigotry.

The afterlife
Today many people wonder why on earth sixteenth century

Christians felt so passionate about their religious beliefs. To them, uncertainty about the afterlife was a pressing issue. There is a tension in human hopes. We would like a favourable afterlife for ourselves and those we love, but there are other people of whom we disapprove so strongly that we hope they will be punished severely in the next life. One biblical text, Revelation 14:10, has been taken to imply that one of the greatest joys of the blessed in heaven will be to watch the damned being tortured in hell. It was explicitly taught by the early Christian theologian Tertullian, and endorsed by the medieval scholars Peter Lombard and Thomas Aquinas.[34]

To the early Christians, those to be given a blessed afterlife[35] were either the whole human race or the righteous or Christians. Augustine taught that 'outside the Church there is no salvation' - that is, baptized Christians are destined for heaven and others for hell.[36] Towards the end of his career, however, in his debates against Pelagius, he came to believe in predestination: God chooses who is to be saved even before they are born. Pelagius believed living a good life can secure salvation, and his view was condemned as heresy. The victorious view was that none of us deserves salvation, and thereafter it became common to believe that we are all so sinful as to deserve eternal damnation.[37]

Since then three doctrines have lived in uneasy tension: our eternal fate depends on whether we live good lives, or on whether we believe the true faith, or on God's decision made before we were born. Predestination dominated official Catholic teaching in the later Middle Ages, but local teaching varied. Many taught that God would reward those 'who did what lay within them'. The combination of helpless anxiety with this one straw still available to be clutched led to an outpouring of religious tension in a variety of 'good works', among them repetitive prayers, emotional displays of repentance, buying indulgences and praying for the dead.[38]

If anything can be described as the starting-point of the Reformation, it is Luther's appeal to justification by faith in reaction against the sale of indulgences. His experience of Catholic priests was that they played on the fear of hell and offered sacraments and other practices as ways to heaven after a limited time in purgatory:

> When I was a monk, I made a great effort to live according to the requirements of the monastic rule. I made a practice of confessing and reciting all my sins, but always with prior contrition; I went to confession frequently, and I performed the assigned penances faithfully. Nevertheless, my conscience could never achieve certainty but was always in doubt and said: 'You have not done this correctly. You were not contrite enough. You have omitted this in your confession.'[39]

He intended his doctrine of justification by faith to be a more positive, liberating alternative. He continued to believe that all human nature since the Fall is so corrupt as to deserve eternal punishment in hell, but argued that those who put their confidence in what God has done through Christ are justified by faith and can rest secure that God pronounces them justified.[40] His successors still interpret the doctrine in different ways. Some take it to mean that God is not punitive at all, so those who suffer anxieties about damnation are simply wrong about God's intentions. Others interpret it to mean that only those who have faith in God will be justified. Luther himself later modified his doctrine because the Anabaptists also professed a true faith, and he could not accept that they too were saved. He therefore added that faith needs to be tested by Scripture, or to be based on the illumination of the Spirit.[41]

Calvin emphasized predestination, at least in his later writings: God is free to save or damn anybody regardless of merits. To ask *why* God decrees like this is to ask for a justifying reason, and there cannot be one because God is the highest authority:

> The will of God is the supreme rule of righteousness, so that everything which he wills must be held to be righteous by the mere fact of his willing it. Therefore, when it is asked, why the

Lord did so, we must answer, Because he pleased.[42]

Modern defenders of Calvin argue that predestination was peripheral to his thinking, and that double predestination is a later development by his followers.[43] For present purposes this debate is not important; whether we put the emphasis on Calvin himself or others, a doctrine which had been inherited from the Middle Ages was re-emphasized in different circumstances. Pessimistic though it may seem to us, to the Reformers it seemed better than the alternative. In their view to extend reason to the heavenly realm would be to assume that God is bound by regular laws. Calvin's doctrine of total depravity taught that if God had been bound by moral law we would all, without exception, have been condemned to hell; it is only because God is *not* bound by laws of moral justice that we can retain hope in God's reason-defying mercy. The corollary is that we cannot know about our eternal fate through reason.[44] To the extent that predestination was promoted in order to allay anxieties, it failed. By re-emphasizing it and denying purgatory the Reformers removed shades of grey and emphasized the stark alternatives of eternal heaven and hell.

Modern society does not reflect on the next life so anxiously. Either we doubt whether there is one or we feel confident that nothing dreadful is in store for us. Their anxieties, though, were quite rational: the possibilities of eternal bliss or torment logically outweigh all the short-term considerations regarding this life. The puzzle needing to be explained is not why sixteenth century Christians who believed in eternal hell spent their lives panicking about it, but why Christians who believe in it today do not.

Pastorally, a more destructive doctrine has never been devised by the human imagination. Believers were faced with the prospect of either eternal bliss in heaven or eternal suffering in hell, and no way of knowing which of the two it was to be. Even if they did know, there would be nothing they could do about it. It was comparatively easy for Christians before the Reformation to believe that Jews and heretics were destined for eternal damnation, especially if one did not personally know any. It was quite another to believe it of the next door neighbours, one's own children or even oneself. Calvin tried to ease the anxieties of believers with his doctrine of assurance. There were, he said, inner *signs* of election: a feeling of illumination and inspiration accompanying the individual's faith, and a holy life. Those other criteria of salvation, a holy life and true doctrine, therefore survived within Protestantism as contributors to the question of who was saved. Puritans debated the question at length. William Perkins, recognizing that hypocrites knew God's word and assented to it, sought to distinguish between true believer and hypocrite within the same sect. He offered many criteria of true faith: it is completely persuasive, it is characterized by zeal, repentance, love for the brethren and obedience to the Commandments. In the end though he had to admit that his criteria could also be met by reprobates.[45]

We can see why they struggled. Their theories generated the sharpest possible distinction between the afterlives of the saved and the damned, together with complete ignorance of who was to face which fate. The combination could not fail to produce intense anxiety. Believing that they and their followers were among the elect, they looked for criteria to reassure themselves that they were saved while the majority were damned. Real life does not provide any.

Three results have often been observed. One was a driving need to prove themselves; there has been much discussion of the role this played in generating modern capitalism. The second was that, for those who could feel assured that they were among the saved, the reduction of anxiety was accompanied by awareness of belonging to a superior elite, very different from ordinary unsaved humans. Quite literally, they saw themselves as God's favourites. Thirdly, as long as they retained anxiety about their own salvation the thought that the vast majority of the world's population were to be damned for eternity did not trouble them so much. The more anxious we are about our own future the less mental energy we have to desire the best for others.

Beiser argues that the roots of modern atheism are to be found here. The rise of atheism is often attributed to Hobbes' materialism. However in the early seventeenth century, even before Hobbes' challenge, large quantities of Puritan literature warned believers of the dangers of unbelief. Satan, according to these writings, was constantly leading the worried to despair of salvation, telling them that they could not meet the demands of true faith and that they might be damned in any case, and tormenting them with visions of the terrors of hell. Burdened with all this the worried believer would succumb to temptation and deny God, thus giving Satan another soul.[46] The fact that there is so much of this literature strongly suggests not only that there must have been unbelievers, but that they must have abandoned belief because of their anxieties about salvation. Not everybody could convince themselves that their lives showed the signs of true faith and holy living. Some, faced with the threat of damnation by such a cruel and arbitrary deity, appear to have made pacts with the devil, who after all would appear the only hope.[47] For others, the best hope was that God did not exist.

Certainty

Certainty, therefore, was no longer simply a matter of recognizing the supremacy of revelation; instead, it became both essential and impossible. Medieval Catholicism had not expected every believer to be educated in matters of doctrine; it was enough to accept and trust the teachings of the church. The Reformers, by rejecting the church's authority and replacing it with the Bible, put the onus on the direct relationship between each individual and God. At the same time, in addition to the Catholic church there was a range of Protestant churches each claiming to be the only way to salvation. Believers had to decide between them. Eternity was at stake. The anxious naturally felt dissatisfied with probabilities; they wanted to be *certain* that they were saved.

This made Protestantism intensely individualistic. If each person's eternal fate depended on what that person believed, and authorities disagreed with each other, it did not make sense to trust anybody else's judgement; the onus was on each individual to work out their own salvation. Puritanism's victory in the English Civil War revealed the tension which the situation produced. On the one hand they intended to reform the state according to Scripture. On the other, each individual was to be responsible for their own spiritual life and biblical interpretation, without interference by ecclesiastical authority. Differences in scriptural interpretation made it impossible to do both at once. The result was an increasing demand for freedom of conscience and toleration of diversity.[48]

If the eternal destiny of each person depends on what is going on in their mind, the nature of true faith is crucial. To Luther, faith was more of an experience than an intellectual position: God's work within people, and the soul's openness to God.[49] Nevertheless he expected a sense of certainty: against Erasmus, who argued that we could not know the answers to many theological questions, he insisted that the Holy Spirit has written 'no doubts or opinions' but 'assertions, more certain and more firm than all human experience... Not to delight in assertions is not the mark of a Christian heart'.[50]

Calvin stressed the cognitive element of faith rather than feeling: faith is 'a firm and certain knowledge of God's goodwill towards us, founded upon the truth of the freely given promise in Christ, both revealed to our minds and sealed upon our hearts through the Holy Spirit'. It was not enough implicitly to believe without understanding or investigating. On the other hand he also believed assent should be of the heart rather than the brain. It is the testimony of the Spirit which brings certainty; rational proof is unnecessary and impossible.[51]

In these ways certainty changed. As something that every individual needed for salvation its meaning was loosened. It retained the idea of *intellectual* certainty - knowing that a belief cannot possibly be false - but it also came to mean a *psychological feeling* of being certain. Public debate had shown that intellectual certainty was not, in fact, available. Psychological certainty was offered to Catholics through the authority of the church and to Protestants through inner feelings. This inner sense was destined to have a major impact on subsequent evangelicalism; it opened the door to an emotional type of religion which emphasizes the individual's *feeling* of closeness to the Spirit.

It was not really satisfactory. To be relieved of anxiety about the hereafter, they needed not just to feel certain but to be certain. It therefore became common to interpret the inner feeling of certainty as God's way of giving intellectual certainty. Thus according to Calvin's doctrine of assurance God gives true believers an inward sense that they are saved. Since then it has been the practice of some Christian traditions to encourage their members first to develop an inner feeling of psychological certainty, and then to interpret the feeling as God's assurance that they are indeed saved.

Not long after Calvin's time assurance proved harder to defend than he had anticipated. Some assured believers deserted the faith. Since God's decrees cannot change, the deserters must have been predestined from the start for damnation. While they were believers, then, they must have been mistaken about their election. This implied that other people, currently assured of election, might also be mistaken. Perkins and other puritans concluded that no believer could be sure of election. They should therefore scrutinize themselves for signs of grace with intense self-examination. Assurance, they concluded, only comes with a mature faith; the struggle with doubt and sin characterizes the Christian life. Good works, though they did not merit salvation, became for puritans a sign of election. This inward-looking piety, though later swamped by evangelical enthusiasm, still survives in some places such as the highlands of western Scotland.[52]

Catholics too faced new problems with certainty. The very fact that Protestants were openly disagreeing with their doctrines made it harder to insist that they were beyond question. Nevertheless Counter-Reformation Catholicism, far from modifying its claims, accentuated them. Faith, they said, is an absolute God-given certainty, an assent leaving no room even for high probabilities, let alone doubt. Owen Chadwick illustrates their approach with the Spanish theologians' debates about the validity of baptism. By putting together the statements 'The church tells me that valid baptisms regenerate' and 'I know that I fulfilled the conditions for validity when I baptized that baby', one reaches the conclusion 'That baby is regenerate'. However, whereas the first premise is absolutely certain as it derives from the church's teaching, the second is less certain as it derives from human experience. We today would have expected our own memory of what we have just done to be more certain than inherited doctrines, but they insisted that it was the other way round.[53] Similarly Ignatius Loyola urged 'That we may be altogether of the same mind and in conformity with the Church herself; if she shall have defined anything to be black which to our eyes appears to be white, we ought in like manner to pronounce it to be black'.[54]

To justify the church's authority, Catholics argued for papal infallibility. There was apostolic tradition: Christ instructed the apostles to form a church and the pope is the successor to St Peter. God would never permit the beliefs necessary to salvation to be mutilated through transmission. To have a united church, a sovereign authority is essential. In a legal sense, therefore, the pope's decisions were above correction - though the claim that his decrees are always true was yet to be developed.[55] Thus the Council of Trent delivered what leading Catholics felt they needed: a defence of their tradition against Protestant attacks and the reaffirmation of revelation, as handed down by the church, over mere human reasoning. Counter-Reformation Catholicism became less creative, more defensive and more anxious to defend tradition.[56] Stephen Toulmin summarizes:

> In the High Middle Ages, Christian theology... was more relaxed and adventurous than it became after the late 16th century. Medieval theologians were spared the Vatican monitoring and censorship to which a Hans Küng and a Charles Curran are subjected today. Nicolas Cusanus taught doctrines for which Bruno was to be burned at the stake; Copernicus gave free rein to his imagination in ways no longer permitted to Galileo; Aquinas took up and reanalyzed the

positions of Augustine and his other predecessors, and reconciled them not just with each other, but with the texts of such non-Christians as Aristotle and Cicero. In short, the Church operated with an academic freedom that ceased to exist, once the Protestant and Counter-Reformation theologians were joined in confrontation. After the Council of Trent, ecclesiastical censors in Rome started to monitor the work of theologians in the Provincial Churches in a new way; the Holy Office, rooting out "heretics" in ways that are all too familiar, became more widespread and vigorous; and for the first time Catholic teaching hardened into theses (or "dogmas") that were no longer open to critical discussion, even by sympathetic believers, and whose immutable truth it was politically indispensable to assert, for fear of yielding to the heresies of the Protestants. Instead of free-wheeling *Summas*, the 17th century was fed a diet of centrally authorized *Manuals*; and the Roman authorities began to intervene formally in moral theology by laying down general rulings about moral issues, or *responsa*, with the full force of authority.[57]

Conclusion

In these ways Protestants and Catholics, through the Reformation debates, developed the ideas they had inherited. The tradition had already affirmed the Bible's unity, timelessness and divine inspiration. Protestants, determined to reject the church's authority to interpret it, added that it was sufficient on its own and therefore perspicuous. In the course of the debates the threat of eternal damnation became a more pressing issue and the search for certainty more intense. This in turn led to individualism and appeals to inner feelings and spiritual guidance.

These ideas are certainly not the main themes of the Bible. Every one was defended with biblical texts; but the texts were their justifications, not the real reasons why they believed them. Herein lies a tension between doctrine and practice. Reformers and Counter-Reformers alike claimed loyalty to the authority of Scripture and denied any role for reason in matters of faith. In fact they used all the reasoning powers at their disposal to attack their opponents and defend their own beliefs, appealing to biblical texts as and when it suited them. These hotly debated sixteenth and seventeenth century doctrines had explanatory value; they were rational attempts to explain the way people relate to God. At the same time they insisted that Scripture is to be accepted as it is and reason has no place in matters of faith. This gave Catholics and Protestants alike ample scope to accuse each other of using reason instead of accepting Scripture.

What they meant by Scripture was Scripture as interpreted in a particular way. Over the centuries Catholics had developed ways of interpreting difficult texts to reconcile them with the church's teaching. The Reformers, by insisting that it is not only a unity but also self-sufficient and perspicuous, established expectations regarding what it *ought* to contain. Deducing that there cannot be two biblical texts disagreeing with each other, for example, they read the Bible determined not to find any.

The Reformation debates are a major source of the doctrines to which conservatives appeal today. When they claim that their doctrines are revealed through Scripture and therefore transcend human reason, they are giving western Christianity the backward-looking and exclusive mood it has today, unable to reflect on its weaknesses, respond to changing circumstances, develop new ideas or reach out to other faiths. When every issue which arises can only be examined through the lens of the Bible or the church's decrees, far too much weight is put on these authorities. When drunkenness is the issue of the day, the Bible has to be read as condemning the consumption of alcohol, even though it does not. When abortion is the issue of the day, biblical verses are made to condemn it, even though not one mentions the practice. These inventions would have been unnecessary if the Bible had not been forced to carry a heavier burden than it can bear.

There is an irony in the authority given to these doctrines. It is because they failed to satisfy that they produced conflict, culminating in a succession of religious wars. It is because of the conflicts that new denominations were founded, and it is because new denominations were founded that their leaders authorized these doctrines and imposed them upon the faithful. The Council of Trent, the Thirty-Nine Articles and the Westminster Confession, for all the wisdom in them, would have been better if they had been hammered out without the heat of controversy and without the intention of condemning opponents. That never happens. Wiser ages, with fewer failures and less conflict, are not driven by determination to impose statements of faith on each other and suppress alternatives. The doctrines of Luther, Calvin and the Council of Trent have become standards for their respective denominations not because there was any consensus about the wisdom of their teachings, but precisely because there was no consensus. If the views of the Reformers had been more widely accepted there would have been no schism. Luther and Calvin would have been contributors to the church's teachings, and no new denominations would have been founded in their names determined to uphold their doctrines. In exactly the same way the 2005 *Windsor Report* declares that the Anglican Communion, at the 1998 Lambeth Conference, 'has made its collective position clear' on the immorality of homosexuality,[58] while knowing full well that if there had been a collective position the Conference would not have seen any need to debate the matter.

The Reformation era, like the era of the creeds, was a time of bitter conflict between Christians. We have inherited from it statements of what we must believe, statements full of hostility to opponents whom we no longer oppose and may have long forgotten. Other ages have produced more thoughtful and positive expressions of Christian believing without obliging us to accept them. However, we should not blame the leaders of the Reformation debates for our situation. They did what they believed right at the time. If we grant more authority to those who tell us what to believe than to those who allow us to think for ourselves, that is our folly, not theirs.

CHAPTER 4

FAITH AND CERTAINTY IN
ENLIGHTENMENT REASON

Modern western society has a strong self-awareness. We know we are very different from all other societies the world has known. We locate the main differences in our science and technology, and we are proud of them. Usually we think our society, and our way of life, is better. A common refrain is that other societies failed to develop a truly scientific understanding because their beliefs about the world were influenced by religious and superstitious theories.

How western Europe came to adopt its distinctive attitude to the physical universe, with its determination to understand it in ever-increasing detail but without any reference either to God or to any religious concepts, has been much discussed in recent years especially in the light of the many complaints that it is largely responsible for environmental destruction.[1] One of the driving forces behind the change was the seventeenth century reaction against religious authority. Throughout the sixteenth century the Christian metanarrative was still the controlling one. Judaism and Islam shared much of it. The world has been created by God, flawed but originally intended to be a good place to live in. The whole human race is created, and given its purpose, by God. God provides moral rules by which we are to live and notices every time we obey or disobey them. When we die God will remind us of our obediences and disobediences, and whatever rewards and punishments are due to us will commence. The practical issues of life - the laws about money, status, sex, land, crime and war - were designed to cohere with this metanarrative by expressing God's purposes for us and the world.

This account of reality broke down under pressure from two

developments. The first was the dualism described in Chapter 2. For the metanarrative to work it needs to be sanctioned by tradition, but it also needs to be adaptable - so that each generation can use it in appropriate ways to judge what should be done about the issues they face. Once the inherited doctrines of Christianity had been redescribed as divinely revealed certainties which transcended all human reason, sealed in formaldehyde tanks where they could never change, they could no longer serve this purpose. Subsequent challenges, which would otherwise have initiated new adaptations, could only be treated as threats to the whole system. The idea is well expressed today by the opponents of women priests who see the ordination of women as an attack on the whole church.

The other development was an inevitable result of the first. It became harder to contain disagreements and the church split. Europe was faced with competing accounts of what divine revelation was. As a result the old metanarrative could no longer work. It broke down into competing alternatives, each claiming to offer the one true account of divine revelation. People had to decide which one to believe. All the attempts to distinguish true from false revelation - the unchanging nature of the Catholic church, perspicuous Scripture, the Holy Spirit's guidance of the individual - failed to resolve the conflicts.

A major practical effect was the question of government. When Europeans disagreed about God they also disagreed about who should govern, and how. Worse still, since authority provided certainty but reason did not, there was no way to resolve the disagreements. There followed a succession of wars. The commonly heard criticism that religion causes wars is an echo of the European wars of the sixteenth and seventeenth centuries, when it did. It was a tragic era with much blood spilt. Scholars today disagree about how to describe it. Opponents of religious belief emphasize the dogmatism and bigotry of powerful church leaders who could not agree to differ peacefully. Others prefer a more favourable account of church authorities and emphasize non-religious causes of the conflicts. My aim is to offer something in between: to recognize the harm done by religious dogmatism determined to establish religious truth, but attribute it to bad religion rather than religion in general.

To resolve the conflicts sooner or later reason would have to be reaffirmed. In some ways Protestantism encouraged it. Although Luther and Calvin made a self-evident, reason-transcending Scripture the rule of faith and warned their followers not to judge its authority, they also taught that faith was an act of individual commitment and believers should know the grounds of their faith. Inevitably the two conflicted: Scripture needed some argument on its behalf and this meant giving reason some authority. Perkins, struggling to find a criterion which would enable believers to know whether they were saved, appealed to the concept of the conscience and described it literally as the individual's 'knowing together' with God about one's own spiritual state, 'a little God sitting in the middle of mens hearts, arraigning them in this life as they shal be arraigned for their offences at the Tribunal seat of the everliving God in the day of judgement'. It is the voice, he concluded, not just of the heart but of reason, since reason is 'the more principall part serving to rule and order the whole man', placed within us as 'the wagginer in the waggin'. Thus puritanism was driven by the logic of its doctrines to reaffirm reason and reduce the gap between the unknowable God and the human mind.[2]

Religious conservatives today often complain that the Age of Reason, by promoting reason at the expense of faith, led to secular society with its atheistic assumptions. The accusation presupposes that faith *ought* to repudiate reason; but ancient and medieval religion, Christian and pagan alike, failed to produce significant numbers of atheists despite their extensive uses of it. The Age of Reason would be more accurately described as a reaction against a particular kind of religion, religion which suppresses reason. Secularism appeared attractive because Reformation and Counter-Reformation religion were so unattractive.

In this chapter I shall examine one element of what postmodernists call 'Enlightenment reason', the commitment to the power of natural human reason to produce knowledge with certainty. In the next I shall describe an alternative reaffirmation of reason which does not expect certainty.

The medieval scholastics followed Aristotle in distinguishing between opinion and *scientia*, which can be translated 'knowledge' or 'science'. Knowledge, to Aristotle, was the result of demonstration, characterized by logical syllogisms or geometrical equations, and produced certainty. Opinions, on the other hand, were not demonstrable and were only more or less probable. This distinction began to break down towards the end of the Middle Ages. The certainty of knowledge was undermined by those who argued that since God might at any time do anything which was not self-contradictory, humans could not know with certainty anything much at all. There was speculation about different levels of certainty; a common category, for example, was 'moral certainty', used to describe statements which were not quite certain but were certain enough to be a basis for action.[3] In effect the concept was being expanded to incorporate what we today would describe as varying degrees of probability.

Probability also changed. Today we often think of it in terms of percentages: we might say, for example, that something is thirty per cent probable. This idea first developed in the 1660s. Before then it was judged in terms of approval by authority; an opinion became more probable if it was supported by better authorities. As the numbers of discordant authorities increased, especially after the Reformation, it became increasingly difficult to judge how much authority a disputed opinion could command.[4] In the later decades of the seventeenth century, therefore, the idea of levels of certainty was incorporated into the new concept of probability and the medieval distinction between knowledge and opinion was abandoned.

These changes applied across many disciplines. In science, for example, at the beginning of the seventeenth century Francis Bacon believed certainty was its aim and rejected the use of hypotheses because they could not produce it. By the end of the century his successors had learned that hypotheses were an essential part of scientific development and had restricted certainty to mathematics, logic and perhaps some metaphysical principles.[5] More recently it has been recognized that even the process of developing hypotheses does not follow an ordered pattern. Poincaré has shown that in practice science proceeds not only by gathering data but also by leaps of the imagination and creative use of intellectual models, and Popper has shown that although hypotheses can be disproved they can never be proved to be true. Even our scientific knowledge, far from being certain, consists of the best available hypotheses.[6]

Foundationalist knowledge

René Descartes and John Locke, the two most influential figures of early Enlightenment philosophy, both still sought absolute certainty. Their reasons were those already noted: neither Europe's political conflicts nor the individual's anxieties about the afterlife would be resolved until all doubts could be assuaged.[7]

Descartes' method was to begin by doubting everything that was not absolutely certain. This process, he found, left him with the certainty 'I think, therefore I am'. Even if his mind was being deceived by an evil demon, he noted, he must still exist. From this point he proceeeded to deduce, as also certain, the existence of God and thereafter the existence of the world external to his mind. His arguments for the existence of God were adaptations of the ontological and cosmological arguments previously developed by Anselm and Aquinas respectively. He turned them into absolute logical proofs: the existence of God, he said, was as certain as any geometrical proof could be.[8] His argument for the existence of the physical world was that a good God would not deceive: 'The desire to deceive bears evidence without doubt of weakness or malice'. God has given him a power of judgement, 'and, as he would not wish to deceive me, it is certain that he has not given to me a power such that I can ever be in error, if I use it properly'.[9]

Philosophers now call his system 'foundationalism'. It has two parts. The first is to establish a first principle which can be known with certainty. The second is to deduce other certainties from it, using logical procedures which cannot err. Foundationalism has had immense influence ever since Descartes' time, and some philosophers still defend it.

The idea of seeking truth by beginning with known certainties and logically deducing other truths from them was a standard procedure of the medieval scholastics. Descartes' innovation lies in the starting-point. For the scholastics the starting-points were to be found in Scripture and the church's teachings. There were many of them and their truth could in theory be taken as certain, but in practice they led to many conflicting points of view. Descartes replaced Scripture and the church with a starting-point which could be known to be certain, by any individual, purely by the process of introspection, without needing to trust the authority of anyone else; and being single it offered the hope of a unified system which would not produce contradictions.[10]

Philosophers have found weaknesses in his method, among them a circular argument regarding the role of God. Descartes' system is founded on the self-evident intuition 'I think, therefore I am'. On the other hand it is the reliability of God, who would not engage in wholesale deception, which guarantees other truths. He therefore justified the existence of God by means of his intuition, but also justified the reliability of his intuition by appealing to God's goodness.[11] Critics pointed out that if God does deceive, Descartes' intuition, and the process of logical deduction, may lead to error.

He inherited the dualism of spirit and matter described in Chapter 2 and accentuated it. His theory describes not just different ways of knowing different aspects of reality, but two distinct realms. The physical one is open to observation by scientists and consists of atoms pushing each other according to the laws of nature. It includes not only animals but also human bodies. The spiritual realm is where the human soul relates to God.[12] This separation of the spiritual from the material realms has had two long term effects in subsequent thought. Firstly it distanced God from the world. There was no place for God to be present in the strictly deterministic system of matter moving according to laws of nature. Secondly it presented the human being as primarily a soul; our bodies are secondary. Because of the radical distinction between the two realms he had difficulty explaining how soul and body relate; his suggestion that the soul influences the body through the pineal gland was never satisfactory. His account of how humans relate to the physical world is often described as that of the 'detached observer', looking at what goes on in the world but not part of it.[13]

Whereas the rationalists stressed the active role of the mind in getting information from the world, the empiricists emphasized the role of the senses. The most influential of them was John Locke. Locke pictured the mind as in its own 'box', separated from the material world, with the capacity to reason. To explain how it can know about the world he described how the senses penetrate into it with information. The mind then uses reason to make sense of the information and build up a picture of reality.

Medieval scholars had explored the question of whether the mind has innate notions, ideas given by God to all humans. Locke denied them. He believed that the minds of new-born babies are blank like a sheet of white paper. Then the paper is marked by the natural impact of ideas which the senses let in. The mind, he believed, has just three faculties: it has awareness of its own inner states and operations, it receives information through the five senses, and it has 'reason' by which he meant logical deduction. Because there are no innate notions the only sources of ideas in the mind are information from the senses and logical analysis of them. The grounds for assenting to propositions, even religious ones, are entirely natural human ones.

Critics asked how we can know that the images in our minds do in fact represent the world outside it. I look outside my window and get a mental image of a tree; but how do I know that the tree really exists, and has the same colour and shape as the image in my mind? Locke offered two arguments. One was that the senses support each other in building up our ideas. The other was - as for Descartes - that a good God would not give us senses which systematically deceive.[14]

Reason, he believed, could defend both the Christian faith and the existence of God better than dogma could. One of his examples is the flood described in Genesis. Christians, he noted, felt certain that it happened because it is recorded in Scripture; but they were not as certain as Noah was, because Noah *saw* it.[15] By recognizing that Noah must have been more certain than we are, we acknowledge that our senses provide information with greater certainty. He did not deny revelation, but relativized it: 'Whatever God hath revealed is certainly true; no doubt can be made of it. This is the proper object of faith: but whether it be a divine revelation or no, reason must judge'.[16] Therefore 'Reason must be our last judge and guide in everything'.[17]

By denying the existence of innate notions and accounting for all human knowledge in terms of processes which anybody could recognize in their own minds, he offered the prospect of knowledge with certainty. At last, Cragg observed, contemporaries could feel that Locke had explained the workings of the mind in such a way that reason stood on firm foundations, its authority above question.[18]

Two implications of Locke's theory became central features of early Enlightenment thought. One is the devaluation of tradition. We have seen why the modern search for knowledge needed to be liberated from traditional dogmas. Locke's accounts of reason and the mind opened up the prospect that the search for knowledge could abandon tradition, begin from scratch and build up a body of knowledge with more certain foundations. There appeared to be no need for historical development.

The other was individualism. Locke's account implied that every individual should in principle be able to gain knowledge by using their own reason and the evidence of their senses. This was necessary in matters of religion. He thought it unrealistic that people should be expected to give unquestioning assent to the views held by their religious authorities. This, of course, is what most people have done throughout human history. The reason why it seemed to him so unreasonable was the situation prevalent in his day, with its rivalries between Christian groups each threatening their opponents with eternal hell. To put one's trust in one religious authority and thereby reject another was to gamble with one's eternal destiny. In the circumstances to offer people a way to work out for themselves the way of salvation was to relieve them of an irresolvable dilemma.

If it was unwise to entrust one's eternal destiny to church authorities who might be wrong, many people felt it also unwise to put all their trust in their own individual judgement. However Locke replied that *whatever* decision each person made - even the decision to renounce all responsibility and just trust another authority - it was the individual believer who was making it. We decide for ourselves, as individuals, what to believe and whom to trust, and we make our decisions for *reasons*.

We today accept a wide range of hierarchical professions. Doctors, accountants, computer manufacturers and car mechanics all have expertise which other people do not have. They sometimes disagree with each other and no one person is completely reliable; but despite these limitations we value and use their skills. What Locke and his contemporaries have bequeathed to us is a refusal to accept professional expertise in two areas, government and religion. By so refusing we continue a tradition established by Enlightenment philosophers to resolve the conflicts of the Reformation debates.

Locke's theory owed a great deal to Ockham, but his conclusions were very different. The medieval nominalists had argued that reason, being limited to sense perceptions, had no authority in matters of faith. Locke set out to show that even such a limited reason could still establish the truth of the Christian faith. He was expressing a more confident mood, a widespread optimism that reason should be able to establish complete and certain knowledge.

A significant change had taken place. For Augustine and his successors, it was faith in God which legitimated reason. For Descartes and Locke, it was reason which legitimated faith in God. Throughout the seventeenth century there were sceptics arguing that we have no guarantee that either our reasoning processes or our sense impressions are accurate. In rejecting scepticism Descartes and Locke, like many of their contemporaries, appealed to the argument that a good God would not design our faculties in such a way as to systematically deceive us. They did not seriously question the existence of a good divine creator who designed our minds to understand the world around us. Nevertheless they had made reason, not faith, the supreme court of appeal.

Rational defences of Christianity

How, then, can reason prove the truths of faith? Locke argued that by using reason we can know the existence of God with a certainty equal to mathematical certainty.[19] He and many of his contemporaries developed arguments to establish the truth of religious belief in general and Christianity in particular. I shall describe the Christian ones first.

The most popular argument appealed to the biblical miracles. When we judge the truth of a reported event, Locke argued, we generally take two factors into account, the strength of the evidence and its intrinsic likelihood. In the case of a very unlikely event we are unlikely to believe even the best of witnesses.[20] Normally we would not believe the miracle stories. However the general rule only applies to natural events. If we have a well-grounded rational belief that there is a God willing and able to intervene, and if we consider the sorts of purposes God may have in so intervening, we may judge an event of the right sort to be probable even though it would be most improbable otherwise. In the case of the biblical miracles God's purpose was to reveal Christianity as the true religion. The rational religious believer, searching history for signs of a religion coming from God, can find them in the biblical miracle stories. These stories reveal that God was at work not just in the miracles but in the whole Bible. In this way Locke argued that Christianity is both uniquely true and universally available.[21]

Previous ages had understood miracles differently. To Augustine nothing could be contrary to nature because God is the cause both of the nature of things and of what happens; the miraculous is contrary only to what we know of nature.[22] Aquinas agreed: a peasant will find an eclipse miraculous but an astronomer will not. It is best to restrict the word 'miracle' to events whose cause is 'hidden absolutely and from everyone', but miracles are no more or less caused by God than regular events.[23]

Locke was applying a later idea. When medieval natural philosophers, seeking to defend their researches from church censorship, emphasized the distinction between regular events and God's interventions, they bequeathed to early modern scientists the idea that the 'laws of nature' were not descriptions of what God does regularly but intermediate forces, halfway between a more distant God and mundane events. Many people today still think of them in this way.[24] This led to accusations of atheism as they seemed to be explaining the ways of the world without reference to God. There were two ways to reply to the accusation. One was to draw attention to the new discoveries about the world and the solar system and argue that they give greater cause for admiration of their divine creator, as natural theologians did. The other was to reassure sceptics by pointing to events which could not be explained by laws of nature and therefore must be attributed to divine intervention. This is how Locke argued: the biblical miracles break the laws of nature and therefore only God could have performed them. They were God's way of indicating the truth of Christianity.

A similar argument appealed to the biblical prophecies. Thus Samuel Clarke's Boyle Lecture of 1705 argued that 'The Proof of the Divine Authority of the Christian Revelation, is confirmed and ascertained, by the Exact Completion both of all those Prophecies that went before concerning our Lord, and of those that he Himself delivered concerning things that were to happen after.'[25]

However strange this line of reasoning may seem to us it filled a gap in early Enlightenment philosophy. Claims to divine revelation and inspiration had been thoroughly discredited. This left a conceptual vacuum which had to be filled: if Christianity was true it had to be rationally *proved*. The argument made it possible to present biblical statements as certainties proved by reason.[26]

The appeal to miracles and prophecies, still popular today in some circles, was heavily attacked by both believers and unbelievers. Believers objected that it only enabled a minority of the world's population to receive revelation, that many biblical miracles like the exorcism of devils into the Gadarene swine were not worthy of a divine power, that the healings should have been performed more widely,[27] and that miracles would mean we were living in an orderless, chaotic world.[28] Stories of miracles performed by the saints were popular among Catholics but Protestants had long treated them as signs of superstition. Should the biblical miracles be treated with the same suspicion? The obvious conclusion could not be avoided for ever, and in 1749 Conyers Middleton made it: the presence of miracle stories in a text is a sign that, far from being divinely inspired, it should not be trusted.[29]

David Hume's arguments against miracles proved more attractive to non-believers. One was theoretical. Defining miracles as transgressions of laws of nature, he argued that by definition the laws of nature cannot be broken.[30] For Hume, unlike Locke, the unbreakability of these laws had become supreme. As critics have observed it is a weak argument. The laws of nature are derived from generalizations about what we observe, and therefore cannot prove that singular, unrepeated events cannot possibly have been observed.[31]

His other arguments are more practical. Firstly, the witnesses to a miracle need to be of sufficient number and of good sense and education, beyond suspicion of any desire to deceive. This cannot be said of the biblical witnesses. Secondly, when judging the truth of a report we usually consider more usual events to be more probable. In the case of miracles, the most unusual and improbable, we are attracted by the elements of surprise and wonder and mistakenly allow our judgements to be influenced by them.[32] Thirdly, miracles are only observed 'among ignorant and barbarous nations... *It is strange*, a judicious reader is apt to say, upon the perusal of these wonderful historians, *that such prodigious events never happen in our days.*'[33] Fourthly, if the biblical miracles prove the truth of Christianity then similar miracles in the scriptures of other religions must prove their truth too; but since the different religions contradict each other they cannot all be true.[34]

The use of miracles to prove the truth of Christianity seemed convincing for a while. The laws of nature are eternal and unbreakable. Only God can break them. The bible records occasions when they were broken. Therefore they must have been broken by God. Eighteenth century atheists, following Hume, stood the argument on its head. The laws of nature are eternal and unbreakable. The bible records occasions when they were broken. Therefore the bible cannot be trusted.

Rational defences of God's existence

With reason once again permitted in matters of faith, natural theology flourished. One aspect of its thought - the one philosophers today most commonly associate with it, though at the time it was only one of many - was the attempt to use reason to prove the existence of God. Descartes defended the ontological argument. More popular was the cosmological argument. Aquinas had argued that everything has a cause, and there must either be an infinite regression of causes or a first cause capable of accounting for the existence of everything else. Locke agreed.[35] Most popular of all were the interventionist and design arguments.

The interventionist argument appealed not only to the biblical miracles but also to natural events not explained by science. In one of his letters Isaac Newton claimed to have written his *Principia* with 'an eye upon such principles as might work with considering men, for the belief of a Deity', by showing that the orbits of the planets could not be explained mechanically and therefore God must intervene from time to time to correct them.[36] Recently this has been called the 'God of the gaps' argument. From the outset it was poor. Leibniz rejected it on theological grounds, as flaws in the system indicate an imperfect creation.[37] A more common criticism is that generation after generation of Christians have pinned their faith on some aspect of the physical universe which they thought could not be explained by science, only to find science explaining it. Today it has been thoroughly discredited for this reason, though its echoes can still be heard; insurance policies describe a sudden and unexpected storm, but not a calm sunny day, as an 'act of God'.

The immensely popular design argument sought to show that by examining the natural world one could observe signs of intentional design and infer a divine creator. The first substantial defence of it was John Ray's *Wisdom of God* (1692); the most popular, William Paley's *Natural Theology* (1802), widely read well into the twentieth century.

Hume's criticisms of the argument are still influential today. Firstly he argued that order is not proof of design. We see order in many situations but only in a minority do we know it is caused by an agent. Secondly we consider one thing the cause of another when we have observed that the effect follows the cause with regularity, but since there is only one universe we cannot appeal to any regularities. Here Hume, like Locke, misdescribed how scientists operate. Far from restricting themselves to establishing certainties by generalizing about regularities, they often develop theories about singularities. However he was right to observe that the inference to a designer does not amount to proof.

His third argument is that when we deduce a cause from an effect, all we know about the cause is what the effect indicates. If the universe has indeed been created by God, this shows that God possesses the amount of power, intelligence and benevolence revealed in the universe but no more. He criticized religious philosophers for tacitly assuming that they knew more about God than the design argument could establish if it were valid; perhaps the universe was made by a committee of designers, or was a poor experiment in universe-making, perhaps by an inferior deity, or was created by a god who has lost interest in it and allows it to continue regardless of its condition until it breaks up with age.[38]

This argument is worthy of note because it reveals the extent to which Hume and his contemporaries had, by the middle of the eighteenth century, lost touch with traditional forms of religious speculation. Among the ancients Aristotle and Epicurus had taught that the divine creator had indeed lost interest in the world, and Gnostics and Manicheans had believed that the world was indeed the product of inferior deities. They had taught these things, and Jews, Christians and Platonists had disagreed with them, because each tradition believed that its own doctrines provided the best explanation for the way humans experienced the world to be. Ancient and medieval religion, in other words, had painted on a wide canvas. These richer speculations had become inaccessible to Hume and his contemporaries because religious doctrines had been disconnected from continuing attempts to explore the nature of reality. Once Descartes' dualism had transferred all value, purpose and morality to the spiritual sphere of human souls and spiritual beings, while leaving the physical universe as an agglomeration of atoms with only instrumental value,[39] empiricists could allow the spiritual realm to fade from sight while they concentrated on the physical realm where God was only relevant as its original creator. Once this point was reached the original creation of the world became the only reason for believing God exists. It was at this point, and only then, that Hume's argument became convincing.

Hume also presented more general arguments against belief in God. All our thoughts depend on our sense impressions; philosophical and theological terms which do not so depend are meaningless. If we describe God as loving and merciful but believe that God permits great suffering and threatens everlasting hell for transient offences, the words 'loving' and 'merciful', when applied to God, cannot mean anything remotely comparable to what they mean when applied to humans. Unless we can explain exactly what they do mean they do not tell us anything about God. He also argued that some subjects simply lie beyond human understanding.[40]

Before the seventeenth century the project of using reason to prove God's existence with absolute certainty would not have seemed appropriate. In any case there was no need for such proofs as there were very few doubters. However, once the project had been established, and these arguments for the existence of God had been incorporated into it, Hume and his successors could show that they failed to serve their new purpose.

Secularization

As the influence of religious leaders declined the fractured Christian metanarrative was replaced by a secular one. According to the old account religious doctrines provided an overall description of the nature and purpose of the world and human life, and thereby established how governments should govern and subjects should obey. The Reformation produced conflicting religious authorities and conflicting accounts of government. The most destructive of the religious wars, the Thirty Years' War, ended with agreement that the ruler of each state should determine its religion. This brought peace, but without conviction. Protestants denied that Christians should leave doctrinal questions to others; it was up to the individual to hold the correct beliefs, and eternity was at stake. To accept the judgement of one's ruler on matters of faith would mean, as Locke put it, that 'Men would owe their eternal Happiness or Misery to the places of their Nativity'.

The problem was how to resolve the twin crises of religious wars and the threat of eternal damnation. There were increasing calls for religious toleration. In order to achieve it, Locke argued, there would have to be a clear line of demarcation between state and church. The state is fundamentally a society of individuals constituted for the 'procuring, preserving and advancing of their own civil interests' – life, liberty, health and possessions. A church is also a society of individuals, but a voluntary one composed of those who wish to worship God together in whatever manner they choose: 'True and saving Religion consists in the inward perswasion of the Mind; without which nothing can be acceptable to God. And such is the nature of the Understanding, that it cannot be compell'd to the belief of any thing by outward Force'. With the exception of atheists and Roman Catholics, who he believed could not be trusted to be loyal subjects, the church poses no threat to the state so the state has no need to interfere in the church's affairs.

Religion was therefore to be a private matter with no relevance to political issues. Here we have the Protestant ecclesiology which still characterizes western society today: each church should be free to regulate itself by its own laws without government interference, on the understanding that its activities are restricted to public worship and the acquisition of eternal life:

> All Discipline ought therefore to tend to that End, and all Ecclesiastical Laws to be thereunto confined. Nothing ought, nor can be transacted in this Society, relating to the Possession of Civil and Worldly Goods.[41]

This is the source of the modern claims that religious leaders should not interfere in politics and that freedom of religious belief is a basic human right which governments do not have the right to withdraw. Nothing could be further removed from medieval Catholicism with its social teaching about just wages and prices and the moral obligation to give to beggars; or from the Christianity of the ancient Roman empire, when allegiance to Christ as an alternative 'lord' or 'king' was a way of rejecting the political establishment.

Similar processes took place in other disciplines. In legal theory Grotius and others developed a system of natural law which could be internationally recognized independently of beliefs about God. Whereas Descartes' dualistic metaphysics preserved a 'spiritual' realm where the human soul could think and relate to God, later materialists explained the human mind as a result of brain processes, concluding that human thought was just as determined by the laws of cause and effect as the rest of the universe. This paved the way for early sociologists and economists to explain human society in deterministic terms unconnected to religious accounts of humanity. At the end of the eighteenth century Kant could claim that not even our moral norms are based on religious beliefs.

Thus secularization developed. Today it is widely proclaimed as a major achievement, an essential step on the way to becoming a modern civilized society, and western governments welcome opportunities to impose it on other nations. A central element of the westernization of non-western countries is the repeal of legislation enshrining religious norms in the constitution, on the principle that individuals should be free to adopt the religion of their choice. What makes other societies reluctant to accept the principle is that they do not share our presupposition that people's religious beliefs do not tell them how the state should be governed. Secularization was not the result of a universally valid insight. It resulted from a specific problem in a particular place and time: oppressive religion. Is it a good thing anyway? Now that religion no longer performs the role it used to, are we missing anything?

We replaced one metanarrative with another. The Christian one gave an organic account of how the various fields of study related to each other and to God's purposes. Law, government, logic, the natural sciences, ethics, medicine, mathematics and theology all had their place; they related to the bigger picture in ways which established the positive role they were to play, and thus gave them their purpose.

When this metanarrative broke down the Enlightenment produced an alternative one based on reason. It is harder for us today to understand the newer one because it still dominates western society - especially the USA, where it was from the start one of the nation's founding principles - and therefore seems to most of us to be no more than common sense. Compared with the older one, the fundamental change was that reason and God had changed places. In the old one Christianity held the ring, within which different accounts of reason, knowledge and government could be debated. In the new one reason holds the ring, within which different accounts of religion can be debated just like other issues. It was not an equal exchange. Religion, as holder of the ring, had given each discipline its purpose in the divine scheme of things and therefore its role, its value. Reason, unable to do this, only provides a classification of subject-matter; it allows greater autonomy to the practitioners of each discipline but expects them not to trespass on others. Just as secularism understands government as concentrated in the state, economics in capitalism and intimacy in the family, it also understands religion as concentrated in the church.[42]

Modern religion is in this sense an invention of the new metanarrative: one social phenomenon among others, with its own spheres of competence - prayer, worship and the afterlife. It has come to seem increasingly credible that beliefs about God are irrelevant to anything outside these 'religious' matters. This difference between the traditional and modern roles for religion remains a matter of tension today; much of the conflict between Islamic and western social attitudes reflects the fact that Islam has largely retained the older view. Similarly the recent revival of interest in spirituality in western Europe responds to the awareness of the divine which continues to characterize human life but finds modern Christianity disconnected from it.

Secularism separated religion from all understanding of the physical world, systematically and as a matter of principle, insisting that all attempts to understand the universe count as science and therefore must exclude any reference to God, so that theories about God no longer explain anything. Inevitably, any religion which accepts this disengaged role must become exactly the kind of religion which many of the first Christians accused Judaism of being - so wrapped up in outdated doctrines and ethical commands which had no practical relevance that they lost contact with the real issues which concerned most people.

In the secular metanarrative reason is treated as self-authenticating. It can neither prove the truth of religious beliefs nor find a use for them. Locke's attempt to do so was based on a narrow theory of reason which had been developed in the Middle Ages specifically with the purpose of *excluding* spiritual matters from its remit. It could not have succeeded even if the expectations of the age had not required all knowledge to display the stamp of certainty. Enlightenment natural theology began with high hopes but gradually got thinner as the number of rationally defensible religious concepts declined. Despite his ambitions to the contrary Locke's narrow reason could only produce an empty religion.

Positivism

For those who recognized its shortcomings there were two possible responses. One was to return to a richer account of reason, which I shall describe in the next chapter. The other was to persist in the hope that narrow reason would provide a complete and certain account of reality, and therefore deny the existence of whatever it could not prove.

This is positivism. It was at its most popular in the nineteenth century. Mandelbaum classifies it into two phases. In the first it made ambitious claims for science; by gathering data through empirical observations it would be possible to establish the laws of nature, understand how the world works and make predictions. On this basis Comte and others hoped to establish a general account of knowledge which would integrate the laws of all the sciences into a single account of reality.[43] This tradition had immense influence throughout the nineteenth and twentieth centuries and remains common today. Positivists characteristically see themselves as defenders of scientific method, affirming that we can know, as facts, what is established by empirical observation, while denying that alternative procedures can produce knowledge. Its most common refrain is that the existence of God has been disproved. A present day example is the work of Richard Dawkins.[44]

Reflection on this first phase led to the second. If all knowledge is based on human experience, everything which lies beyond our experience cannot be known. The laws of nature are nothing but generalizations from observed regularities; to speculate about deeper explanations like true causes is beyond the scope of science.[45] To establish science on a properly positivistic basis scientists must dispense with all their metaphysical ideas; but what will be left? Mach argued that, according to positivist theory, the physical objects we see are just bundles of sensory experiences to which we give names, and scientific concepts are likewise just bundles of experience. Concepts like 'force' and 'atoms' therefore have no proper place within science.

This was to undermine the optimistic hope of a complete and

certain account of reality. Other late nineteenth century developments raised similar questions. One was human determinism. If nature is deterministic and humans are part of nature, our science just orders our experience in ways which suit our needs and interests. Darwinian theory, the best known example, would imply that all scientific research is to be explained in terms of how it helps us struggle for survival. Instead of being a model for establishing certain knowledge, it becomes instead merely a determined effect of our physical characteristics.[46] As Patricia Churchland has put it more recently,

> Boiled down to essentials, a nervous system enables the organism to succeed in the four F's: feeding, fleeing, fighting and reproducing. The principal chore of nervous systems is to get the body parts where they should be in order that the organism may survive... Improvements in sensorimotor control confer an evolutionary advantage: a fancier style of representing is advantageous *so long as it is geared to the organism's way of life and enhances the organism's chances of survival* [Churchland's emphasis]. Truth, whatever that is, definitely takes the hindmost.[47]

Another development was research into the relation of the mind to the brain. Descartes had described the human as primarily a mind who possesses a body. Empirical research, on the other hand, indicated that the mind depends on the brain; if the brain is damaged, so is the mind. Positivism led to the view that there is nothing to the mind except processes within the brain.[48] Yet all knowledge, including scientific theories, depends on the assumption that mental thoughts are caused by other mental thoughts. If you think it is Thursday today, your thought is justified by thoughts like remembering that it was Wednesday yesterday. However, if all our mental thoughts are caused by chemical processes in the brain, we have no basis for expecting the contents of our minds to bear any particular relationship to the world outside our heads. For knowledge to be possible at all the mind must be more than just physical brain processes. Although philosophers continue to debate the issue, scientists almost invariably accept the reality of the mind as more than just by-products of brain activity. This means accepting that there is more to reality than can be empirically observed.[49]

Positivism's most extreme form was logical positivism, which flourished from the 1920s to the 1950s. Here the emphasis was on linguistics, and the central claim was that statements which could not be verified either rationally or empirically were not merely untrue but meaningless. In the case of religious belief this meant not merely that God did not exist, but that the very notion of God had no meaning.

Once stripped of presuppositions it could not justify, it became clear that positivism denied too much. If God's existence could not be proved by rational and empirical methods, neither could many other things we take for granted. The list is worth noting.

Mathematical formulae, the rules of logic and scientific axioms. These all depend on basic principles which cannot be independently proved true. To deny them would be to reject these practices in their entirety.

Statements about the past. It is theoretically possible that the world came into existence two minutes ago, complete with our history books and our misleading memories of past events. It is not a helpful hypothesis because if we are so radically deceived we shall have no idea what to do, but it cannot be disproved.

Other people's minds and feelings. It is possible, dear reader, that you are the only real human being. The rest of us are robots without minds or feelings. Or maybe we are conspirators with the creator of the universe, deliberately playing the role of human beings as part of an experiment to see how you will behave. Again it cannot be disproved, but life would be impossible on this basis.[50]

The search for certainty through rationalism and empiricism alone has ended in failure. Nevertheless positivism remains influential. The idea of a sharp distinction between 'facts' which have been proved with certainty by scientific methods, and 'beliefs' or 'opinions' which have not, remains popular. So also does the idea that the existence of God has been disproved. It was unfortunate that logical positivism was still popular when religious liberalism was revived in the 1960s; because many people believed that reason had disproved the existence of God, what resulted were accounts of religion which had no place for the divine.[51]

The coherentist alternative

We seem to have come full circle. In the ancient world there were many contrasting theories of reality, based on how the gods have made us and what faculties they have given us. Among the questions asked were the two on which science depends: is the universe in principle intelligible, and if so is the human mind capable of understanding it? Medieval monotheism, Jewish, Christian and Islamic alike, answered yes to both questions and justified their answers by describing the divine creator and designer as omnipotent, good and purposive. The complete truth about reality is a consistent unity known by the mind of God. God gives humanity not complete knowledge but knowledge of what we need to know. The faithful can come closer to a 'God's eye view' through prayer, godly living and accepting revelation.

Early Enlightenment philosophy transferred complete and certain knowledge to natural human reason, as given by a good God who would not systematically deceive. After Hume appeals to God's goodness lost credibility. What remained was reason, interpreted as self-authenticating and expected to produce certainty through science. Eventually it became clear that reason is not self-authenticating; we cannot stand outside our own reason and adopt a detached observer's standpoint from which to check whether the universe is intelligible or the human mind can understand it. To reject the appeal to God, therefore, was to squeeze the search for certainty at both ends. At one end, complete and certain knowledge could no longer be located in the mind of God; if it was possible at all it would have to be located in the human mind. At the other, there was no longer good reason for confidence that the human mind can understand reality.

What kept the search for certainty going was that jewel in

modernism's crown, the countless successes of science. In fact, though, science does not work simply with certainties. Induction and hypothesis-formation are essential tools of scientific research; all its successes were established *despite the absence* of certainty. While science made progress without certainty, others pointed to science as proof of what certainty could achieve. The search for it was based on foundationalism, the idea that truths could be deduced from self-evident first principles. Although there are still some foundationalist philosophers today the theory has lost popularity. The alternative is described as 'coherentism'. In our searching for knowledge we do not begin with self-evident first principles; we begin with a variety of things we think we know, some more probable than others. If we think of foundationalism as a building with everything secured to the foundations, coherentism is more like a web with a network of links between one piece of knowledge and another. What holds the web together is that the various parts of it cohere. When one part turns out to contradict another, an adjustment needs to be made. As we learn new things we keep adjusting the web and adding new threads. To use another analogy, our view of the world is more like a junior clerk than a managing director; we do not have a balanced overall view of the whole enterprise, but we know a fair bit about the part we are in and this enables us to make informed guesses about some of the other parts. The more our web of beliefs survives pressure the more confidence we develop in it, but we never reach absolute certainty.

Philosophers' definitions of knowledge are now much humbler. They are generally variations on the theme of 'justified true belief'.[52] Knowledge is described no longer as a public accumulation of certainties but as more subjective, varied and relative. It varies not only in degree of certainty but in the degree of certainty required for any given purpose. Hospers, for example, lists the sources of knowledge as not only empirical sensations and rational deduction but also introspection, memory, faith, intuition and testimony. They sometimes lead us into error but we need them all and we no longer expect error-free knowledge.[53]

The *idea* of certainty remains popular. In general discourse it is still useful as many beliefs are true enough for most purposes. To insist on foundationalist certainty has, however, become less common in western society. It is most commonly found in two discourses: religions which appeal to the traditions described in Chapters 2 and 3, and atheistic attacks on religion. Both these discourses often give the impression of being outdated, speaking the language of a past age. The claim to absolute certainty, with that all-too-familiar intolerance of those who are considered certainly wrong, no longer rings true to the way most people think today.

What, then, would a certainty-free modern religion be like? This is what I shall describe in the next chapter.

CHAPTER 5

REASON WITHOUT CERTAINTY IN ANGLICAN THEOLOGY

In the last three chapters I described some theories of knowledge which grant supreme authority to a single source of information: tradition, the Bible and reason respectively. In each case it was claimed that all knowledge can be derived with certainty from that one source.

I shall describe religious theories of this type as 'foundationalist' religion. In the last chapter I described the foundationalist philosophy of knowledge developed by Descartes and his successors, who claimed that knowledge begins from a self-evident starting-point which cannot be false and that other truths can be deduced from it with certainty. Descartes' starting-point, his 'I think, therefore I am', was his own; but the idea of beginning with certainties which cannot be questioned and deducing further certainties from them had already been common practice among the medieval scholastics and was continued by those who appealed to revealed certainties, Protestants and Catholics alike. Their starting-point was divine revelation rather than introspection but otherwise their approach to establishing knowledge was a forerunner of Descartes' philosophy.

The type of religion which appeals to reason-transcending divine revelation is often described as 'dogmatic' or 'fundamentalist'. These terms however also have more specific meanings. Instead I think it is appropriate to call it 'foundationalist' religion, despite the unfamiliarity of the term outside philosophical circles, because it is accurate; it draws attention to the type of knowledge claims being made by those who believe not only that they know the answers to questions of doctrine and moral norms but that those answers are so well established that there is no scope for discussing whether they are true. For example, in the current debate in the Anglican Communion opponents of homosexuality are arguing not just that homosexuality is immoral but that those who believe otherwise should not be permitted leadership positions in the church. What makes this view a foundationalist one is the claim that the immorality of homosexuality is not open to reassessment by human reason. It is a *given*, a certainty, and therefore not to be debated.

This chapter describes the alternative, religion without foundationalism. It affirms the value of reason but does not expect certainty. In philosophical terms it is coherentist. In the last chapter I described how early Enlightenment philosophers who sought certainty defined reason narrowly, confining it to rational deduction and empirical observation. Those who did not expect certainty could affirm wider accounts of reason. They could appeal not only to Aquinas but also to the Renaissance humanists, especially Erasmus, who believed that God has endowed all human minds with other forms of knowledge over and above logical deduction and empirical observation.

Hooker used the word 'reason' widely, to refer to universally available mental faculties and distinguish them from special revelation. Herbert of Cherbury agreed that there are many universally available mental faculties but gave them other names and retained the narrow sense of the word 'reason'. While they used the word differently they both believed that God has provided enough mental faculties for a variety of purposes, both spiritual and material, and has designed them to represent reality well enough for human purposes.

In this chapter I shall focus on the Anglican tradition beginning with the writings of Richard Hooker who was writing towards the end of the sixteenth century. The continental European churches, under greater pressure to distinguish themselves from their rivals, tended to define themselves through doctrines; the English church, being the national church of a clearly defined nation, was not under the same pressure. Nevertheless the Elizabethan theologians did need to defend Anglicanism, in the heat of controversy, against both Catholics and puritans. They did not intend to make doctrinal changes; in keeping with the mood of the age they aimed to preserve the truth they believed had been once and for all delivered to the saints. Everything needing to be believed for salvation, they claimed, was to be found in Scripture, which revealed it clearly without need of interpretation. However there were also some doctrines relating, for example, to Christology and the Trinity, which were not clear in Scripture without assistance; on these matters Anglicans appealed to the consent of antiquity and the general councils of the early church.

Hooker

This was the background to Hooker's work. Since the nineteenth century many scholars have credited him with defending the church of his day by articulating the Anglican 'middle way' between Calvinism and Catholicism. More recent scholarship has shown that this is an anachronism. When he was writing there was no middle way; most senior clerics in the Church of England were of a decidedly Calvinist outlook. This leaves an uncertainty which is still debated today. His position is unclear partly because his earlier writings were more Calvinistic than his later ones, and partly because he wrote in an oblique style and is often difficult to understand. There are two possibilities: either he did indeed defend the church of his day - in which case he was more of a Calvinist that he was previously taken to be - or his views were more original despite his claims that he was defending the tradition.

The best known defender of the latter view is Peter Lake, who argues that 'Hooker's whole project had represented a sort of sleight of hand whereby what amounted to a full-scale attack on Calvinist piety was passed off as a simple exercise in anti-puritanism'.[1] His case has recently been well defended by Nigel Voak. If Hooker agreed with the Calvinism of his day it is difficult to explain the texts which diverge from it; if on the other hand his real views were different his apparent conformity was necessary for the circumstances in which he was writing. Although he openly opposed puritans and presbyterians he could not afford to attack Calvinism as a whole; as an Anglican clergyman he needed to avoid opening himself to the charge that he disagreed with any of the Thirty-Nine Articles.[2]

He is perhaps best known for his 'three-legged stool', his proposal that authority in matters of faith requires the use of Scripture, reason and tradition. 'What scripture doth plainly deliver, to that the first place both of credit and obedience is due; the next whereunto is whatsoever any man can necessarily conclude by force of reason'. Thirdly, he adds, 'After these the voice of the church succeedeth'.[3] He had much to say on all three.

Reason. Hooker's puritan opponents had two main theological arguments for limiting the power of reason. One is that we can only understand reality if it is ordered, and to claim that the world is ordered is to restrict God's freedom of action. Against this view Hooker appealed to the medieval distinction between God's absolute power to do anything logically consistent and the regular power which expresses God's goodness: 'The very being of God is a kind of law to his working: for that perfection which God is, giveth perfection to that which God doth'.[4]

The other puritan doctrine was total depravity. Because of the Fall, they claimed, the practices of true religion and moral virtue are not only contrary to human nature but cannot even be understood by it. Hooker's view was closer to that of Aquinas: reason is a faculty implanted by God, enabling us to understand the truths which God reveals in both nature and scripture, and can therefore gain knowledge about reality.

Reason was not simply a matter of adding together the knowledge gained from scripture and empirical science. Because Hooker, like Aquinas, had a richer understanding of reason he could extend its reach further: God has made us for self-transcendence, so it is in our nature to seek what is beyond our nature.[5] On the other hand he did not believe that reason has the all-encompassing powers which secular philosophers would later give it; it does not enable us to know everything or to have certainty.

Scripture. Like the Reformers Hooker accepted that Scripture teaches us all things necessary to salvation with a perspicuity that makes their message available even to the simple. However the puritans believed that Scripture should be the supreme authority in every aspect of life and looked for biblical justification for every action they took, however small. Against them Hooker argued that we have been given other means to know God's will; Scripture does not tell us how to build houses, solve mathematical problems or rake up straw. We learn some things from Scripture but others from nature, reason, experience and practice.[6]

The puritans accepted Calvin's principle that the Bible is self-authenticating. Hooker saw that it cannot be. Self-authentication can mean two things: either that the Bible has authority because the Bible says so, or that its authority is self-evident. The first is a circular argument and the second is a proper subject for rational examination.[7]

Tradition. During the sixteenth century Catholics and Protestants alike tried to show that their churches agreed with the teaching of the primitive church. Catholics believed they were being true to the original tradition, Protestants that they were reforming the church rather than creating a new one. Both sides believed that the theologians of the first few centuries had accepted the ultimate authority of Scripture. Many Anglicans attributed authority to them only to the extent that their interpretations of difficult biblical texts could provide guidance to their successors. Thus the authority of 'tradition' primarily meant the teachings of the early church.[8] Inheriting this account, Hooker - unlike later Enlightenment rationalists - believed part of the role of reason was to take into account the insights of tradition and historical development.[9] At the same time, because he rejected the puritan idea that all behaviour should be guided by Scripture, he was able to argue that in many matters the church of his own day was free to make changes, guided by natural reason. The church 'has authority to establish that for an order at one time, which at another it may abolish, and in both do well'.[10]

In matters of doctrine he argued that in most cases - for

example the doctrine of Mary's perpetual virginity - certainty is not available. Decisions must therefore be made according to probability. He referred to these as *adiaphora*, indifferent matters. In such cases, he argued, we may 'lawfully doubt and suspend our judgement, inclyning neyther to one side nor other'.[11] This argument was a significant development. By denying that all of scripture is clear and thereby establishing a category of doctrines which were unclear, he concluded that they could not be essential to salvation. It was a stark contrast with the puritanism of his day which still thought of Christian doctrine as authoritative in every aspect of life. By limiting essential doctrines Hooker opened up an arena for freedom of belief without fear of damnation, and therefore provided a basis for legitimate freedom of enquiry.

In matters of ethics, again following Aquinas, Hooker argued that God has created the world to operate according to regular laws and has given the human mind the capacity to perceive them. These laws include both what we now call the 'laws of nature' and moral norms. Both have been established by God and designed for the greatest good. The moral norms, as 'natural law', are to be distinguished both from the revealed laws of Scripture and from the positive laws imposed by states.[12] This view is the origin of the secular notion of 'human rights'; the 1948 Universal Declaration of Human Rights, for example, stands in this tradition.

Great Tew

Among those who developed Hooker's ideas were the Great Tew circle, the Cambridge Platonists and the Latitudinarians. The Great Tew circle were a group of friends who met at Lord Falkland's Oxfordshire estate in the 1630s. Their leading theologian was William Chillingworth.

They were concerned to preserve unity in the church. The traditional view was that there should be one church in the land and that its liturgy, doctrine and government should accord with Scripture. Roman Catholics, Arminians, Lutherans and many puritans disagreed about which church that was, but they all agreed that the true church had the right to impose uniformity and punish dissidents. The main alternative view was that God's will was revealed through the spiritually inspired individual. The enthusiasts had their own accounts of the divine inspiration they had received, and often demanded the right to leave the church on the ground that its constitution and practices were unscriptural.[13]

The Great Tew theologians accepted the aim of a united church but opposed the intolerance and dogmatism of the competing factions. As Hales noted, 'Men are very apt to call, their own private conceit, the Spirit'.[14] They therefore sought to maintain unity while at the same time defending the rights of individual consciences. Their proposal was fundamentally the same as Hooker's: the unity of the church should be founded on doctrines with which all Christians agreed. On other matters freedom of conscience should be permitted. They expressed this theologically by saying that the necessary features of the true church were very few; most of the questions under dispute were on inessentials, *adiaphora*, and could be settled according to reason rather than scripture. In this way they revived the vision of a doctrinally 'broad church'.[15]

They therefore emphasized the role of reason. Reason, they believed, included not only analytical processes but also 'common notions' or innate principles which are shared by all, among them universal moral principles upon which individuals could act and states could govern. Understood in this way reason provides a basis upon which people can listen to each other, reflect on the differences between their own views and those of others, and thereby come to agree about the fundamental nature of the church, true faith and the moral life. They hoped reason could thus provide order based on consent, a middle way between the twin dangers of papal infallibility and the anarchy of separatism. In any case, they argued, it was already being used in this way. Catholics gave supreme authority to the pope and enthusiasts to inspiration because they believed they had good reasons for doing so; even if they did not acknowledge it, therefore, they were giving greater authority to reason than to pope or inspiration.[16]

They continued to claim that Scripture is the rule of faith while in practice emphasizing the authority of reason. Chillingworth's chief work, *The Religion of Protestants*, declares: 'The Bible, I say, the Bible only, is the religion of Protestants!' Commentators have noted that he really meant the Bible as interpreted by reason.[17] Accepting that reason cannot provide certainty they argued that God does not expect of us more belief than the evidence warrants. This of course was a significant departure from the consensus of Reformation and Counter-Reformation theology.[18]

On this basis they opposed all claims to infallibility. Sceptics were arguing that being consistently rational led to the conclusion that we do not know anything at all. Montaigne and others had used the argument to conclude that we should accept the authority of the Catholic church. Falkland and Chillingworth replied that we should not accept authority as it is, but question it. If the church were infallible, they argued, we could not know this to be the case unless the information were provided by some higher standard of knowledge; but in that case the higher standard would replace the church as the highest authority. If there is an infallible church it is not self-evidently the Roman Catholic church. If we knew it to be the Roman Catholic church there would remain questions about its authority; just as scripture needs an interpreter, so do papal decrees. There would still be no guarantee that it could ensure salvation. To base the church's authority on tradition would be to claim infallibility on the basis of a fallible source. It was true that reason could not assure troubled souls that they were *certainly* not destined for hell, but certainty was not necessary. What is most important, the Great Tew theologians often argued, is not what we believe but *how* we believe. To arrive at one's beliefs through the exercise of reason is more pleasing to God than whether one arrives at the right answer.[19] As Chillingworth put it,

> To ask pardon of simple and purely involuntary errors is tacitly to imply, that God is angry with us for them, and that were to impute to him the strange tyranny of requiring brick when he gives no straw; of expecting to gather where he strived not, to reap, where he sowed not; of being offended with us for not

doing what he knows we cannot do.[20]

These alternative responses to uncertainty still face us. If we are not sure, should we make an act of commitment or should we keep our convictions in proportion to the evidence? The question arises in every sphere of life. Usually we keep our options open except when the need for action demands a decision. In the case of religious belief the need for a decision was fuelled by religious conflicts and the fear of hell. When these concerns became less pressing it became more feasible to withhold commitment.

These theologians offered a gentler Christianity without the desperate need to know the right truths and belong to the right church. The path to these changes was to reaffirm reason and accept uncertainty. Practically, whatever we believe we cannot avoid the need for reasons. This is true even internally, so that we can make sense of our own beliefs. Publicly it is the only way to explain to other people why we believe what we do, and in turn understand why others do not. Once our beliefs have been publicly described and given reasons it then becomes possible for other people to examine them and either accept them or draw attention to their weaknesses. Only when we affirm reason as the means to doing these things does it become possible for our understanding to increase and our differences to be resolved. In the long view this was not a new insight; many of the ancients and medievals knew it well. For a few centuries, however, the dominant view had been to deny it. The theologians of Great Tew, defending it against opposition, analysed it in greater detail and thereby provided posterity with a richer account of reason.

Their theology had weaknesses. The most significant lies in their resolution of Scripture's obscurities. They claimed that the essential doctrines were clearly expressed but limited. Yet they did not offer a list of these essential doctrines, and could not have done so.[21] The idea of a small number of doctrines, agreed by all Christians, as a basis for both salvation and membership of the church, was an attractive way to resolve the disputes of their day and remained influential for a long time. To put it into practice by listing the clear and unclear teachings was another matter; if they had produced a list they would merely have added one more list of obligatory doctrines to the wide range already available and generated yet more controversy.

In the long run their commitment to reason undermined their commitment to church unity. By arguing that what mattered most was not what people believed but how they believed, they allowed diversity of opinion outside the church as well as within it. At one point Chillingworth made a passing comment - radical at the time - that even the faith of Turks and heretics could justify a person in the eyes of God provided that they showed complete obedience towards the requirements of their faith. This argument would later be used to argue against a united church and in favour of tolerating a variety of sects.[22]

The Cambridge Platonists and Latitudinarians

The Cambridge Platonists were active from the 1630s to the 1680s. They inherited much from Great Tew: the centrality of reason, the Protestant conscience as its voice, the limitation of faith to a few fundamentals, the emphasis on moral conduct at the expense of dogma and the criticism of dogmatic disputes.[23] They examined reason still further. It was a God-given faculty: according to Whichcote, 'To go against reason is to go against God... reason is the divine governor of man's life; it is the very voice of God.' Like Augustine and Aquinas they believed that God has planted an order and method in the world, the 'reason in things' which the human mind can apprehend.[24] Whereas Catholics argued that we should put our trust in the church, Luther had appealed to the principle of liberty to argue that we should judge all things according to Scripture. Whichcote went further than Luther, claiming that the use of reason was a fundamental duty, the characteristic virtue of a Protestant.

Their account of reason was rich. As well as responding and analyzing, it also has intuitive power which provides information about the eternal and unchanging natures of things. Reason therefore provides principles which are true independently of human conventions and perspectives, so that anyone who grasps them understands them in the way God does. To describe these eternal principles they wrote of 'common notions', 'radical principles' and 'intelligible ideas and conceptions of things' which were universal and self-evident. Thus they gave the mind a wide range of faculties, integrated by the principle of analytical reason, and an active role in knowing things. Against those who argued that the intuitive power of reason seemed similar to the divine inspiration of the enthusiasts they emphasized its analytical dimension: we should examine our beliefs according to evidence. The experience of truth is one thing, the criteria for judging it another. Among the principles which they believed were revealed to reason were moral laws. Good and evil are not just expressions of God's arbitrary decree or the laws of states, but are real properties corresponding to the nature of things. Everybody possesses an innate knowledge of them and like mathematical axioms they need no proof.[25]

Among these writers are the first detailed rational arguments for the existence of God, providence and immortality which would in time become central themes of natural theology. Even more daringly they reintroduced reason to discussion of the afterlife.[26] Opponents argued that their rich account of reason, by positing more mental faculties, expected us to take a great deal on trust. Nominalists and empiricists did not believe eternal essences of things existed at all; even if they did it was still open to question whether human reason can know them. They defended their position against these attacks in different ways; More, for example, appealed to the classical medieval principle that in order to have faith in reason we need faith in God.[27]

The Cambridge Platonists had immense influence on later Anglican theology. By developing natural theology, identifying reason with faith and even using it to speculate about the afterlife, they established an alliance between faith and reason which later came to dominate English thought.[28]

Their immediate successors were the latitudinarians. Many of them were taught by Cambridge Platonists, and like them emphasized reason and morality in religion, though they were less philosophical and more committed to active service in the church. Since diversity of opinion was inevitable they lobbied for a broad church acceptable to all but atheists and Roman Catholics, whom they considered enemies of the state. The Restoration settlement had defined Anglicanism in such a way as to exclude a large body of dissenting opinion, but it remained possible to hope that it might be made more inclusive. They therefore emphasized the distinction between a small number of essentials and a larger number of non-essentials. They stressed the fallibility of human judgement, for the sake of greater truth as well as public peace. Suspicious of certainty claims, they argued that the true mark of piety was the humble and impartial search for truth. Substantial disagreement about a doctrine or practice indicated that it was unlikely to be fundamental.[29]

Thus one of the movements which came out of the turbulent years following the Reformation was the Anglican attempt to establish a balance of authorities between Scripture, reason and tradition. It remained popular for a long time. Its greatest eighteenth century exponent was Joseph Butler, whose *Analogy of Religion* described reason as 'the only faculty we have wherewith to judge concerning anything, even revelation itself'. Like the Cambridge Platonists he gave it a wide role: it properly judges not only the meaning of scripture but the evidence of revelation and moral norms, and can lead us from knowledge of earthly to spiritual things; but, at the same time, it still has limits.[30]

H R McAdoo writes of a continuity in this tradition from Hooker to the 1890 collection of essays *Lux Mundi*. It was characterized by a 'vivid sense of the present reality of continuity with the past' and 'the necessity of the freedom of reason to differentiate and to assess'.[31] His classic work on it, *The Spirit of Anglicanism*, notes that what was distinctive about it was not a set of doctrines like those of Lutherans and Calvinists, but a method: 'Anglicanism is not committed to believing anything because it is anglican but only because it is true'.[32]

This approach has long been recognized as the classical

Anglican account of authority. There were differences between its exponents - Hales and Chillingworth, for example, agreed with Hooker in placing reason above tradition, while the high churchmen placed tradition above reason - but the threefold appeal became a distinctively Anglican contribution to Christian theology.[33]

Scripture, Reason and Tradition

Here then is a tradition based on affirming not a particular set of doctrines but a way of searching for truth. Compared with the alternatives described in the preceding chapters, it neither rejects reason nor treats it as supreme. Instead it affirms it *together with* Scripture and tradition. The way it holds them together is by denying that any one of them provides complete truth or provides any truth with complete certainty. It is precisely because we cannot rely exclusively on any one of them that we need them all, to provide checks against each other.

Reason is understood widely. It does not simply compute; it provides information. Our minds have been created by a good God who has designed us to understand the world well enough to live good and fulfilling lives in it. In this account reason is given a wholesome function. On the one hand it provides us with the information we need to understand the world around us and the moral norms which apply to our circumstances; on the other, it has limits. The limits are of two types. Firstly we have freedom of will which enables us, if we so choose, to ignore information which does not suit our interests; and secondly we have no reason for supposing that we have, or can acquire, the ability to achieve any new goal which takes our fancy. It is to this extent a cautionary account of reason; it affirms our ability to perform the activities for which we have been designed and it permits us to explore beyond what we have so far understood and achieved, but it does not allow us to assume that our knowledge and abilities are potentially unlimited. God has designed our reasoning powers for some purposes and not others. Doing the shopping for the next door neighbour is more in keeping with its capacities than altering our genes so that men can have babies. This account of reason, because it requires belief in God - and in a particular type of God - is only available to those who so believe. Today it does not provide a neutral framework for rational debate because secular society counts all religious discourse as an optional extra, not part of a shared account of reality. It did not provide a neutral framework in the seventeenth century either, but for the different reason that many people held contrasting beliefs about God. That neutral framework was better provided by Locke's more restricted account of reason. Nevertheless, where classical Anglicanism was accepted its view of reason proved fruitful. It explained how our knowledge does, by and large, accurately express the nature of reality, while also allowing for errors and differences of opinion: we are not designed to know everything, our immoral desires lead us to ignore information and moral norms which we would otherwise have acknowledged, and no one person is free of error. Reason, so described, provided a fruitful basis for handling disagreements not only in religion but also in science and ethics. It is a theory of real but relative knowledge. It is no coincidence that the country which affirmed it most strongly also led the world in science.

Tradition. During the Reformation debates neither Catholics nor Protestants accepted that the true church should ever change; both claimed to uphold the original Christianity and accused their opponents of innovating. Tradition, both sides believed, ought to be an unchanging package. It was an ahistorical view. Equally ahistorical was the early Enlightenment view that knowledge could be established by reason alone without recourse to tradition. By the end of the seventeenth century, however, the idea of historical progress had infiltrated every aspect of European thought. Especially in science, but also in law, international relations and elsewhere it was clear that significant changes were taking place and most of the intellectual classes considered them changes for the better. For theologians sympathetic to these developments it was natural to apply the same idea to the church. There was good reason for so doing. Contrary to earlier Protestant expectations, scholars had established that the early Christians had believed in relics, prayers for the dead, celibacy, fasting, holy oil, the sign of the cross, the veneration of images and consecrated bread and wine. Many English Protestants concluded that theology must have progressed since then.[34]

In addition they were aware of recent developments. Nonpartisan historical scholarship, committed to the search for truth for its own sake, began to flourish towards the end of the seventeenth century. Texts, linguistic apparatus and knowledge of antiquity had improved considerably since the Reformation. It seemed to follow that the people of the late seventeenth and eighteenth centuries were in a position to understand the Bible more accurately than their sixteenth century predecessors.[35] They could therefore reinterpret tradition dynamically. They could deny that it is a supreme authority which simply maintains ancient truths unchanged, without going to the other extreme of rejecting all tradition as a set of unjustifiable dogmas. Instead they could affirm it in a form which is both more modest and more creative. Tradition provides us with wisdom inherited from the past. While we cannot ignore it all and start from scratch, its insights are neither complete nor certain. Every generation has its opportunities to challenge some elements of inherited teaching and add its own insights, thus contributing to a dynamic tradition which changes over time. Tradition, like reason, contributed to the church's understanding but was not infallible.

Scripture. The same trend also applied to the Bible, though it took longer. To describe every text in the Bible as both clear and authoritative had proved an impossible position. To treat its clear teachings as the only ones essential to salvation while allowing differences of opinion on the unclear ones was a tidy arrangement, successful for a time in limiting conflict, but was only credible because nobody established a comprehensive list of clear and unclear teachings.

The root of the problem was the ubiquitous notion of the Bible as a self-contained unity. While the *whole* Bible was either to be accepted as clear and authoritative, or interpreted by the Spirit's illumination of the individual, differences of interpretation were both inevitable and irreconcilable. As long as it was possible to argue that a person who questioned the truth of one biblical text was undermining the authority of the whole Bible, it could not be a source of creative insight; it was more like a mental prison, obliging people to believe what they were told. Gradually that perspective broke down. Some of the reasons were empirical: closer readings of the texts and increasing familiarity with Hebrew and Greek raised questions which the unitary theory could not answer. Other reasons were theoretical: reason was needed, first to understand what biblical texts meant, then to distinguish between the clear texts essential to salvation and the unclear ones, then to argue - as Locke did - for the truth of the Bible and Christianity. The rational arguments for Christianity, especially the debates over miracles and prophecies, demanded close attention to specific texts and at the same time raised questions about the presuppositions scholars brought to them. To treat every text as God's reason-transcending revelation, worded exactly as God intended, proved an impossible position to maintain. To defend Christianity at all it was necessary to allow different judgements to be made of different biblical texts.

Scripture, therefore, came to be affirmed in a manner comparable to reason and tradition: it was an essential source of insights, but it did not provide a complete account of religious truth and no single text could be accepted as absolutely certain. It needed to be set in balance with reason and tradition. This conclusion opened the door to two developments, natural theology and critical biblical scholarship. Both resulted not only from increasing confidence in reason but also from closer attention to biblical texts.

Natural theology

One reason for the popularity of natural theology in the Enlightenment period was that it appeals to reasoning processes which are universally available. Just as seventeenth century lawyers and philosophers reaffirmed reason because they hoped it would provide a universally acceptable basis for resolving conflict, natural theologians hoped that reason could provide a universally agreed basis for seeking religious truth. This led them to take a positive view of the faith of non-Christians.

From their earliest days Christian preachers had claimed that Christ was Lord of the earth and expected their message to reach every nation. The conversion of Constantine made this expectation seem more feasible. From then on, for over a thousand years, most western Christians had very little awareness of the world outside Christendom, and except in Spain very little contact with non-Christians. It was easy to assume that Christianity spanned most of the world, and that to reject it was a conscious choice by a determined few. One of the collects for Good Friday in the Church of England's 1662 Prayer Book pleads that God may 'have mercy on all Jews, Turks, Infidels, and Heretics, and take from them all ignorance, hardness of heart, and contempt of thy word', thus presupposing that non-Christians have deliberately chosen a dissident stance.

This view became indefensible as knowledge of other parts of the world increased. From the 1680s onwards Christians could hear what Moslems, Confucians, Zoroastrians and American Indians had to say about their faiths rather than depending on inherited Christian critiques. As Europeans became more aware of the size of the world and the minority position of Christianity, the traditional doctrine that all non-Christians would be consigned to hell took on a new significance. Over and above the question of whether Protestants or Catholics would be damned, hell became the fate of the overwhelming majority of humanity, most of whom had not even heard of Christianity or the Bible.

This is a good example of how old doctrines gain new meanings in changed circumstances. Even today, church historians often describe the followers of Luther, Calvin and the Counter-Reformation as 'orthodox' in contrast to the natural theologians. However, once Christians had become aware of the vast number of non-Christians, it was impossible to maintain traditional doctrines unchanged. One side upheld the sentence of eternal hell for all non-Christians, at the expense of turning Christianity into an exclusive minority sect and God into a local deity willing to write off most of the world's population. The other side retained the universal possibility of salvation by permitting salvation to non-Christians. If we ask which view upheld the tradition, the answer must be that both sides upheld one element at the expense of another. Those who claim that the former group were maintaining the tradition, and were therefore 'orthodox', are simply interpreting a changing tradition from one perspective rather than another. The edges were proving fuzzier than tradition had led them to expect. Some, perceiving the threat, were determined to preserve the uniqueness of Christianity and rid it of all non-Christian influences. Their project presupposed that there had indeed been an original Christianity unaffected by other religions. As they developed their case, though, it became clear that many central Christian themes owed their origins to external influences. Augustine had used Platonist ideas. The second century apologists had used *logos* language in a pre-Christian sense, implying that all truth was of God. Findings like these generated a lively debate at the beginning of the eighteenth century.[36]

The alternative was to conclude that divine justice could not possibly condemn those who had not heard of Christianity. On this account the only way to retain the view that God punishes unbelievers in hell - a remarkably persistent doctrine - was to change the criteria to make them universally available. This meant denying that the Bible was essential, and seeking the norms of true religion in what could be known by everyone.

The first influential exponent of this idea was Edward Herbert, Lord Cherbury. Although he died in 1648 his ideas were more characteristic of the later seventeenth and early eighteenth centuries. He believed that God's supreme attribute is goodness; God desires to act for humanity's benefit and therefore must 'provide for all, in doing which he must be just, merciful and liberal'. The means to salvation must therefore be available to all. No single religion can claim to be the only way. Furthermore, it must have been always available; since the histories of Egypt, India and China predated the Bible, salvation must have been available even before biblical times.[37]

He therefore argued that there must be some universally available ways of comprehending and obeying God. He proposed that since the beginning of time everybody has had the intuitive capacity to know the truths necessary for salvation. He listed five: that there is one supreme God; that God ought to be worshipped; that the true way to honour God is to practice virtue; that we ought to be sorry for our sins and repent of them; and that divine goodness dispenses rewards and punishments both in this life and after it. If there is universal consent on these 'common notions' it does not, as he knew, make them true; but he argued that universality is a sign that God has implanted them in our minds. He therefore argued that salvation, and the common notions, were available in other religions.[38]

If true religion is universally available in this way it should be possible to compare the different religions with each other by reference to the common notions. Thus Christianity is relativized in a way which remains with us: it is one religion among many. Here Herbert neatly, and correctly, inverted the tradition. To Reformation and Counter-Reformation theologians Christianity was unique because its doctrines and practices were *not* derived from any natural human religious sense, but instead were directly revealed by God. With his awareness that other religions make similar claims to direct revelation, he relativized precisely those elements of Christianity which had seemed most unique. It was the claims to divine revelation which made Christianity just one more religion alongside all the others. If any one religion was to stand out from the others as unique, it must be the one based on what God has made available to all.[39]

Biblical scholarship
Others paid close attention to biblical texts, either in order to defend Christianity or to attack it. As their studies raised more and more challenges to the accuracy of biblical statements it became increasingly difficult to maintain that the truth or falsity of one text

implied the truth or falsity of the whole Bible.

One issue was the age of the world. By examining the biblical genealogies sixteenth century scholars calculated that it had been created at about 4000 BC. The Egyptians and Chaldeans claimed that their history extended beyond that time. At first it was possible to reject these claims, but the discoveries of new lands, new peoples and new histories forced them to think again. There was also increasing concern, throughout the eighteenth century and even more in the nineteenth, about biblical texts which seemed immoral. The God of the Old Testament condoned slaughter and sacrifice and seemed arbitrary and unjust. Everlasting torment in hell, and the need to appease God's wrath with the death of Christ, disturbed many. While some rejected Christianity, others hoped Scripture could be reinterpreted.

Critical scholarship could only flourish where there was freedom of thought. It was led by English scholars in the eighteenth century, Germans in the nineteenth. In general the English laid down the basic principles but the Germans revealed its potential with their detailed historical and linguistic work.

In practice the founding texts of all traditions, religious and non-religious alike, eventually prove problematic. Living traditions reinterpret them. Every reinterpretation is designed to overcome the problems of its day, but eventually becomes problematic itself. To heap interpretation upon interpretation is to lose touch with the original meaning. This is especially problematic when students are so strongly committed to the view that the texts are relevant, that they are determined to attribute to them meanings which make them relevant. Critical scholarship therefore makes a distinction between establishing the original meaning of a text and judging what value it may have for us today. The original meaning is what was meant by the human authors in their social and historical context. To establish it is an empirical matter. Only after the meanings of texts have been understood in their own terms do scholars look for patterns and general principles about the nature of the Bible as a whole. Rather than imposing onto the Bible an external set of harmonizing general principles, therefore, critical scholars begin with what the texts say and only later reflect on what general principles emerge from them. After the meanings have been established it then becomes appropriate to ask whether and how the texts are authoritative for us today.

This is not to deny that alternative readings of biblical texts may prove fruitful. In literary studies it is often observed that readers can draw from texts significant meanings which were not part of the authors' intentions, and the idea has been borrowed for hermeneutical approaches to biblical interpretation. The implication is that God may speak to Christians today through biblical texts even though the insights they receive from the texts are not what the authors had intended to say. This of course is true; but the personal insights so received, however valuable they may be, cannot legitimately be presented more generally as though they were what the Bible teaches. If what the Bible says is to be *authoritative* for Christian communities today, its authority cannot be based on whatever anyone takes it to mean; it needs to be rooted in what the authors intended to convey.

Scholars anticipate that biblical texts were written for reasons which can be compared with the motives for writing today. For example we know how easy it is for those who benefit from the economic status quo to believe that it enshrines eternal moral values, and conversely how those who feel oppressed often appeal to God's commands as a way of denouncing the ruling classes. When we find biblical texts expressing views of either of these types, we feel we understand. However we are also aware of the differences. Because we do not have iron age smallholder lifestyles we do not apply most of their laws to ourselves, and because we do not believe that patterns of worship can influence plagues, droughts and wars we do not maintain their worshipping practices. Recognizing both the similarities and the differences, it becomes possible to affirm the intentions behind a biblical text without necessarily believing we should follow its instructions today. If we decide that it does have authority for us, we do so after due consideration of what it says and why, not simply because it is in the Bible.

By distinguishing between the question of what a text means and the very different question of what value it may have for us today, critical scholarship enables us to make different judgements about different texts. We do not need to treat all texts as equally authoritative. Some texts express what was wisdom in a particular place and time but not always and everywhere. The texts which seem immoral to us may indeed express immoralities; they may have been included in the Bible because they formed part of a work which was valued for other reasons. Some pairs of texts contradict each other, but both may have been included in the Bible because both were judged of value. By breaking open the enforced unity of the Bible and using scholarly skills to consider each text on its merits, critical scholars are prepared to judge them accurate or inaccurate, and of local or universal significance, without presuming that by judging one text they are also passing judgement on the whole. In this way they have been able to solve the problems of biblical interpretation which seventeenth century Anglicans could not solve.

They also make it possible to affirm both the Bible and natural theology at once. When we assess the significance of particular biblical texts, some of the thoughts we bring to the process come from natural theology. Conversely, when we assess the judgements of natural theology, some of the ideas we bring to it are those we learned from the Bible. Each contributes to a shared dialogue because both are of value but neither insists on having the last word.

Critical scholarship uses tools of interpretation which can only be used well by trained experts. To accept its judgements, we neither entrust biblical interpretation to a church leadership committed to preserving its teachings unchanged, nor expect every believer to read and understand the Bible for themselves. Instead, our understanding of the Bible is guided by these experts. This brings our religious understanding into line with our understanding of other aspects of our lives: when we are seeking guidance in preparation for making a decision, we seek it from those with professional expertise. We do not expect their knowledge to be either complete or certain, and we may seek two or three expert opinions before making a decision; but we value their expertise because they know more about the subject than we do. In the same way critical scholarship expects not that the community of biblical scholars have a collection of certainties, but that they know more than the rest of us do. Over time as different theories are proposed, examined and accepted or rejected, the amount and accuracy of their knowledge increases. We value it not because any of it is beyond question but because it is our best source of information.

Coherentist religion

In this chapter I have described a tradition which defends a coherentist theology in the face of rival foundationalisms. For Catholics the authority of the church trumps all else. For the Reformers Scripture trumps all else. For early Enlightenment philosophers reason trumps all else. These foundationalisms have two weakness in common. Firstly, by exalting their trump suit to the rank of supreme authority on all matters, they have little use for the others. The others can only be affirmed to the extent that they support it. Secondly, by definition a supreme authority can only be judged or challenged by itself. It becomes an unalterable monolith, an autocrat. It was the genius of the Anglican tradition to affirm the authority of Scripture, reason and tradition as all essential contributors to the Christian search for truth and holiness. It was only possible to do so by recognizing the limits of all three. We need them all because they are all fallible.

Many argue that we should add a fourth element, experience, thereby allowing a place for the insights of the enthusiasts as well. Many Anglicans in the seventeenth and eighteenth centuries were so horrified by the chaos engendered by some of the enthusiasts' claims that they bent over backwards to resist it. Nevertheless in principle there is a strong case for affirming religious experience, both individual and communal, both private and in the setting of worship. Firstly, a dynamic account of tradition ought to incorporate it as a contributor to its understanding. The medieval mystics, for example, have had immense influence. Secondly, those who affirm a rich account of reason can accept that people may gain insights through mental processes of the type we might describe as spiritual or religious experiences. Within a coherentist framework it is necessary, of course, to reflect on the proposed insights in the light of what is already believed before judging whether to accept them. This, in the long run, is the role of the developing tradition.

Whether one classifies experience as part of reason or tradition or counts it as a fourth element is perhaps unimportant. However I am attracted to the triad because it draws attention to a wider pattern. All developing fields of study contain a dialectical relationship between tradition and new research. If every generation began from scratch, with no tradition to provide resources, knowledge would remain limited. Conversely, traditions live and develop because of reason's challenges. Thus every subject of study holds both rational processes and a developing tradition in creative tension. In addition to these two, however, there is a third element which we may describe as the subject's *roots*. Some examples are obvious: Marxists describe their tradition as beginning with the ideas of Marx, psychoanalysts with Freud, sociologists with Comte, Islam with Mohammed. Within that subject area, this is the point at which the story of their tradition begins. In each case we may ask 'Why here? What happened *at this point* to make sense of the idea that a new tradition began here?' Each tradition offers its answers, usually with great pride. When economists date modern economics to eighteenth century writers like Adam Smith they are making claims for what is distinctive about Smith's writings. It is what *differentiates* Smith from the earlier Catholic church's teachings on just prices and wages, or their objections to lending money at interest, which makes the study of modern economics *begin* with writers like Smith.

The story of the beginning of each tradition, therefore, is told in a way which reveals that tradition's commitments. It stresses the importance of a particular turning-point: one set of ideas was abandoned, another affirmed. To locate the roots of the tradition at that point is to claim that what was abandoned needed to be abandoned and what was affirmed needed to be affirmed. In this sense Scripture stands, for Christians, as the roots of our tradition. It is the starting-point for our story. The analogy only holds, though, for a coherentist account of Christianity, not a foundationalist one. Marxists do not say of Marx, or Freudians of Freud, that their founder's writings were complete or infallible. In fact they claim the very opposite: that they were *fruitful*. By setting out new ideas they enabled a tradition to flourish which would, in time, far exceed what the founder proposed. It is this fruitfulness which characterizes the beginning of a new tradition. By rejecting one approach and proposing another, the innovator hits on something which produces a succession of new insights building on each other.

It is even possible for the original insight to be subsequently refuted by its own tradition while still being recognized as an essential starting-point. An illustration might be early modern science's rejection of unobservables. It was a common belief in the sixteenth and early seventeenth centuries that invisible angels and demons could influence physical events. Scientists needed to reject it for two reasons. One was that because they could not be observed it was impossible to study how they operated. The other was that since they had free will they were unpredictable. Early modern scientists therefore denied that either unobservables or undetermined agents could have any impact on physical processes. Twentieth century physics, however, abandoned the principles of both observability and determinism. There are differences: they now describe the unobserved and the indeterminate in different ways, and there is no indication that they are likely to reaffirm the existence of demons and angels. Nevertheless it is a continuing, developing tradition which denied unobservables then but accepts them now; it remains the case that principles which at one stage were essential to the development of the tradition have subsequently been abandoned.

A coherentist perspective allows for a close similarity between the role the Bible plays in Christianity and the roots of developing traditions in the sense I have described. To explore it further one might ask how the Bible illustrates the rejection of a dying tradition and the commencement of a new one. Different coherentists might do this in different ways. A traditional Jewish account of the Hebrew scriptures might emphasize its monotheism. Those heavily influenced by Paul might emphasize freedom from laws. In either case what would be important about the Bible is not that its information is complete or certain, but that its approach, its ideas and insights, are fruitful. Its fruitfulness is most clearly shown in those instances where it has enabled Christianity to generate, over the course of its subsequent history, new and helpful insights which were not contained within the Bible itself. One practical example of this process might be the current consensus that those who are true to the Bible ought to oppose the practice of slavery even though Scripture itself permits it. In the same way some argue that another example is the growing conviction that homosexuality is not immoral.

My proposed interpretation of the triad is not of course essential to coherentist religion. Scripture, reason and tradition, with or without experience, are not fixed lists of our sources of information. They express, rather, a continuing process of interaction between a countless number of sources; indeed, what most distinguishes coherentism from foundationalism is its refusal to settle for a fixed list at all. Instead it values information from any source while retaining the right to judge its reliability.

The coherentist account of religious belief which I have described in this chapter is both humbler and more creative than foundationalist alternatives. Humbler, because nothing is guaranteed. We may be wrong. More creative, because we may have been wrong yesterday, and today we may discover why; or yesterday's new insight may lead to another insight today. It is that combination of affirming reason but not expecting certainty which is also able to affirm, as Aquinas did, that by examining what we do know we are led to discover other things which we did not know; or as Whichcote put it, 'we must have a reason for that which we believe above our reason'.[40] The beliefs we hold with confidence provide a basis for exploring new possibilities; and as we explore them we distinguish between the convincing and the unconvincing, between those which fit our experience of life and those which do not.

It is therefore only available to those who are prepared to let go of certainty. It is not the purpose of this book to propose psychological reasons for particular beliefs - there are many ways to explain why some people feel more strongly than others the need for certainty - but without doubt everlasting hell, when feared, generates a strong desire for it. One seventeenth century Anglican, Jeremy Taylor, expressed his surprise 'that men should be greedy to find out inevitable ways of being damned', and that they should try to 'invent reasons to make it seem just'.[41] To those who are not so afraid a gentler, more open-ended, coherentist faith is possible.

This coherentist approach to religious belief, which I have illustrated using the Anglican tradition, I shall describe as 'coherentist liberalism'. It depends on a high level of trust: that reality can be understood, that our minds are capable of understanding it, that we can learn from the past but are not limited by it, that we may have a role in contributing to the tradition, and that we will not be punished in the afterlife if we hold erroneous beliefs. It is characteristic of a confident society. When that confidence is lacking, it becomes much harder to maintain. In the next chapters I shall describe how declining confidence led to a reactionary search for past certainties.

CHAPTER 6

DUALIST FAITH COHABITS WITH

MODERN REASON

The universe is a giant machine. It consists of nothing but atoms pushing each other according to eternal and unbreakable laws of nature. Every event is determined by a cause, and the cause was determined by another cause. There is no God. The human soul is nothing but the mind, the mind is nothing but brain processes and brain processes are nothing but parts of the physical universe. All our ideas, our hopes and fears, our values and moral judgements are meaningless by-products of chemical processes in our brains. Such was the picture of reality to which science seemed to be heading in the late eighteenth century and throughout the nineteenth.

Twentieth century science has turned the tables. With its vastly more complex account of reality it has opened up various dimensions of the unobservable and indeterminate which have made it once again possible to believe that human values and freedom have nothing to fear from science. Throughout the nineteenth century, however, the picture looked bleak.

It was one result of Enlightenment reason. There is no doubt that Enlightenment philosophy has made an immense contribution to modern western culture. It has provided methods which are now taken for granted by nearly all branches of knowledge. Nobody seriously wishes to jettison them all. Nevertheless it had its weaknesses. For present purposes two are significant.

First, the pursuit of certainty had narrowed the definition of reason to rational deduction and empirical observation. Determined to resist the excessive claims of many enthusiasts, proponents of reason were suspicious of knowledge claims based on emotion, intuition or feeling. It was an over-reaction. In the nineteenth century, while positivists continued to insist that nothing else could be known, others saw the need for a wider account of knowledge. The emotions, intuitions and feelings of individuals do often provide information which can be usefully shared with other people even though it cannot be empirically verified. An obvious example is pain. We can never experience another person's pain, but we do not jump to the conclusion that they do not have any. What was needed was to recognize the positive achievements of Enlightenment reason in general but adapt it by allowing that we can gain knowledge from other people's descriptions of their inner experiences.

Once this extension is accepted religious experience can be acknowledged. Worshippers engage in activities which express their emotions and intuitions. These activities renew the sense of relationship with the divine and, they sometimes claim, enable them to know things which would not otherwise be known. As with pain, it should be possible to accept individual stories into the public domain. This is not to say they should be accepted uncritically; people can describe their inner feelings in misleading ways, and many find it difficult to distinguish their experiences from the interpretations they put on them. However inner feelings, like other truth-claims, can be generally valued and affirmed as part of human experience.

The other significant weakness was that by reacting against excessive claims for authority Enlightenment reason rejected tradition as a source of knowledge and sought instead to begin with a clean slate. Nineteenth century thinkers abandoned the clean slate and reaffirmed tradition. They were right to do so. In practice, no subject of study expects its students to begin by accepting only what they can themselves derive from first principles. Students are invariably initiated into a tradition. Recognizing this fact, the dominant nineteenth century approach was that tradition has an essential part to play in the long-term development of knowledge, but also needs to change in response to rational criticism.

These were adaptations, not rejections, of Enlightenment reason. In general nineteenth century thought built on the progress made by Enlightenment theory but recognized significant weaknesses and adapted accordingly. In the religious revivals, however, and *only* in matters of religion, we find a more extreme reaction, so hostile to modern reason that it was determined to reestablish reason-defying accounts of knowledge and tradition. This was by no means true of all. Some responded to the scientific challenge constructively. They doubted that the threat to religion was as great as it seemed, and expected science and religion to interact with each other constructively in a common search for truth. This meant judging scientific claims according to the evidence for each one rather than taking a single stance towards science as a whole, and expecting scientists to return the compliment. This response is in keeping with the coherentist liberalism described in the last chapter; a unified reality with a unified search for truth expects empirical data and rational analysis to inform each other but without guaranteed certainties in either science or religion. In the long term its optimism was vindicated; apart from the remaining positivists few expect that science will, or even can, disprove religious belief.

Far more common in the nineteenth century, however, was the widespread fear that religious faith would be disproved. It produced various defensive reactions against science. Perhaps the best known is the Romantic movement, from which the nineteenth century religious revivals borrowed heavily. I shall classify the religious reactions into three types. They oversimplify and there are fuzzy edges, but I hope the classification will indicate how the range of options then available produced the types of religion with which we are familiar today.

The first was to accept secular knowledge, abandon all attempts to challenge it, and restrict religion to matters which were beyond the reach of science. This meant accepting the new and humbler role which secularism permitted religion, limited to its own sphere and forbidden to trespass outside it. Non-religious secularists might, and still do, treat this as a method for denying that religion has any real knowledge or value and therefore dispensing with it; but religions which accept this role can insist on the reality of many religious phenomena which cannot be explained by science, and focus their attention on them.

The second response was to resist the claims of science - and secular reason in general - in the name of upholding the truth of divine revelation on all matters. If science could claim to offer empirical facts more certain than religious beliefs, religion could respond that divinely revealed facts are more certain than scientific theories. Scientists might seem successful but that would be because God was deceiving them, for example by putting fossils into rocks to mislead them about the age of the earth.[1] Most people today accept that this rejection of science was mistaken. However, some of the claims being made on its behalf were also mistaken. Affirming a spiritual dimension to reality seemed to many, supporters and opponents alike, to be only possible by rejecting science.[2]

The third response was to seize on the radical postmodern critiques of all knowledge in order to relativize the claims of science and secularism and assert the right to hold counter-rational beliefs or to adopt one's own system of rationality.

All of these responses have their defenders today. They overlap; secularism does not speak with one voice, and those who resist one of its elements often willingly accept another. Reactionary movements are usually very aware of the innovations they are opposing but less aware of the innovations they are accepting. This chapter will describe the first option and the next two will describe the second and third respectively.

The overall effect of these changes was to give western Christianity a very different character. Theologians today often describe the theology of the eighteenth century as arid.[3] Although there is truth in the criticism, one reason why they find it so is that their own assumptions about the nature of religion have been formed by the nineteenth century reactions. Hobbes, Locke and Kant offered accounts of reality and human knowledge of it which were both theological and philosophical, and had immense influence on eighteenth and nineteenth century thought. They are often taught in philosophy courses today, though usually stripped of their theological elements. Theologians, though, rarely show interest in them; the theology of those days was too closely related to issues from which it has now retreated. Nineteenth century theologians speak a language which is far more familiar in religious circles today; to a large extent, western religion now lives in the age which began in the nineteenth century. If eighteenth century theology seems arid to us, ours would probably seem to them to have lost its point.

Modern dualist religion
By far the most popular of these three reactions was the dualist one. Modern secular accounts of knowledge are characteristically 'compartmentalist'; instead of a hierarchy of the sciences with theology at the top, as Aquinas had proposed, they allocate each subject to its own 'compartment' with its own expertise without specifying hierarchical relationships. This structure enabled the defenders of religion to revive dualism and describe religion as one such compartment.

The theologian most closely associated with this development is Friedrich Schleiermacher, who has often been described as the 'father of modern theology', or at least of modern liberal theology. Faced with the prospect that both reason and biblical criticism were undermining religious belief rather than defending it, he looked inward for the source of religious authority. Like Kant he denied that religious doctrines can be established by rational or empirical methods, but unlike him he also refused to identify the essence of religion with morality.[4]

> In order to take possession of its own domain, religion renounces herewith all claims to whatever belongs to those others and gives back everything that has been forced upon it. It does not wish to determine and explain the universe according to its nature as does metaphysics; it does not desire to continue the universe's development and perfect it by the

power of freedom and the divine free choice of a human being
as does morals. Religion's essence is neither thinking nor
acting, but intuition and feeling... Religion maintains its own
sphere and its own character only by completely removing
itself from the sphere and character of speculation as well as
from that of praxis.[5]

Schleiermacher's central concept in his *Speeches on Religion* is that
religion can only really be understood from within. He urges those
who want truly to understand the nature of religion to 'transport
yourself into the interior of a pious soul and seek to understand its
inspiration...fix your regard on the inward emotions and disposi-
tions.' He believed that religious 'feeling' was the essence of
religion. In his later major work *The Christian Faith* he defined this
feeling as 'the consciousness of absolute dependence, or, which is
the same thing, of being in relation with God'. Like the enthusiasts
of an earlier age he claimed that individuals can relate to the divine
in a way which is not mediated through reason. He differed from
them by refusing to restrict it to Christians, arguing instead that it
is available to all as part of human nature. Nor did he consider it
contrary to reason; like many of his contemporaries he retained the
central role of reason in public discourse about religion, while
recognizing that religious beliefs and practices are caused by
individual experiences as well as rational deliberation. True
religion, he emphasized, should be understood in terms of the
individual's sense of the divine. Traditional doctrines should be
tested against the religious experience of the contemporary
Christian community.[6]

Another theologian to affirm the distinctiveness of religion was
Albert Ritschl. Ritschl extended the anthropocentrism already
present in Lutheranism. For Luther the central doctrines of
Christianity had been about the human soul's relation to God; the
world of nature was at best a neutral backdrop to the drama of
salvation. For Ritschl nature was not just a backdrop but a threat;
if humans were part of it, we were determined machines. Religion
therefore centred on the freedom which enabled humans to

transcend nature: 'In religious cognition the idea of God is dependent on the presupposition that man opposes himself to the world of nature, and secures his position, in or over it, by faith in God'.[7]

Others developed these interpretations further. Whereas the earlier enthusiasts had claimed religious experience as evidence of personal salvation, in the late nineteenth century it was more a matter of defending religious belief as a whole against materialistic atheism. Henry Scott Holland argued that faith is comparable to the 'primary intuitions' of seeing, willing, and loving: 'It is deeper and more elemental than them all: and therefore still less than they can it admit of translation into other conditions than its own... Belief is only intelligible by believing'.[8] Auguste Sabatier argued that faith is 'an independent, original, psychological act';[9] it is 'God consciously felt in the heart, the inward revelation of God and his habitation in us'.[10] Later Rudolf Otto described awareness of the holy as 'a category of interpretation and valuation peculiar to the sphere of religion', and ineffable 'in the sense that it completely eludes apprehension in terms of concepts'.[11]

In the churches, and in popular belief, the religious revivals were expressed by an upsurge of interest in spiritual phenomena. This produced a wide range of beliefs and practices. In some churches there were more visions of angels, saints and Mary. Others saw more ghosts. Spiritualists were in greater demand with their visions and messages from the dead. Inner spiritual experience became more important. Especially for evangelicals, the individual's religious experience was central,[12] and for many of them the conversion experience marked initiation into the ranks of the elect. Speaking in tongues was revived.[13]

Protestants and Catholics alike increasingly expected divine intervention. Expectations of the second coming, conversion experiences and miracles all expressed a conviction that God could, and did, intervene. The divine interventions proposed by Newton and Locke had been rare events of universal significance; in the nineteenth century God became busier. Early in the century the papacy insisted on accepting some most improbable miracles and legends, including the apostolic foundation of the principal French bishopricks.[14] Some evangelical founders of missionary societies were so sure that Christians should trust God to provide for their needs that they considered it a matter of principle to send out missionaries without any support except a commitment to pray for them.[15]

Lives of personal holiness were encouraged. There was a revival of monastic orders. The Oxford Movement preached obedience, devotion, fasting and mortification.[16] The clergy were professionalized. Among evangelicals the idea of the holy life was expressed in a variety of ways; perhaps the most popular, the Holiness movement which began in the 1870s, taught that in addition to the conversion experience a second decisive experience would grant victory over sin and freedom from temptation.[17] Ritualism and pentecostalism, later developments out of the Oxford and Holiness movements respectively, in their different ways aimed to give worshippers an inward reassurance of their relationship with God through spiritually fulfilling worship.

Tradition was reaffirmed. In the last chapter I described how Anglicans affirmed tradition as part of a developing process. In nineteenth century religion the dominant trend was to affirm it in *opposition* to theories of progress. Religious traditions were increasingly seen as unchanging, and therefore not open to challenge or modification. This led to stronger affirmations of dogma, and therefore infallibility.

This was true across the theological spectrum. In the first half of the nineteenth century a major feature of evangelicalism was its social concern. Evangelicals were perhaps best known for their campaigns against the slave trade, but they were active on many fronts. Later this commitment weakened. Bebbington suggests that this reflects the declining influence of Enlightenment thought. The later Enlightenment had developed the conviction that humanity as a whole was progressing to a better state, and secular society continued to believe it throughout the nineteenth century. Evangelicals at first expected progress to march in step with the advance of Christianity, as human effort brought about a new and better world order and sinful social structures were reformed. However as, during the nineteenth century, they increasingly reacted against Enlightenment ideas of progress and depicted religion as separate from society, they preferred to contrast the glories of their own faith with the godless world outside.[18] The emphases on personal holiness, inward spiritual experience and worship became in effect alternatives to social concern. Many evangelicals came to believe that in order for a Christian to help a non-Christian live a better life it would first be necessary to convert them to the Christian faith. Social concern should either be avoided altogether as a distraction from conversion or should concentrate on matters of personal responsibility like drunkenness, gambling and observance of the sabbath.[19]

This trend was accentuated by the increasingly popular belief that the second coming would take place soon. Those influenced by Enlightenment theories of progress had often believed that Christ would return after a period of success for the church through preaching the gospel. This view came to be called 'postmillennialism'; the alternative, 'premillennialism', expected the second coming imminently and was so called because Christ would come before the thousand-year reign mentioned in Revelation. Earlier millennarian movements had expressed the desperate hopes of the economically oppressed; this one was a reaction against Enlightenment progressivism, a distinctively religious phenomenon with no stake in political change.[20]

The search for distinctively religious sources of dogma and infallibility were, for evangelicals, focused on the Bible. Before the 1820s evangelical leaders were aware that it contained errors and contradictions and found ways to account for them, but thereafter the doctrines of inerrancy and verbal inspiration became more popular.[21] They were not, though, accepted by all evangelicals; in effect the pressures of secularism led some to defy modern reason while others sought to reconcile their faith with it.

The same tensions can be seen in the history of the Oxford Movement. At first it revived tradition as dogma. Rejecting the Latitudinarian belief in theological progress, Newman, Pusey and

Keble sought to re-establish the notion of an unchanging, reason-transcending body of doctrine, citing the Vincentian Canon's appeal to what was believed everywhere, always and by everyone. They condemned Protestants for subtracting from it and Roman Catholics for adding to it.[22] In Tract 85 Newman listed many inconsistencies and incredible narratives in the Bible and on this basis argued that only commitment to an infallible church could enable one to accept it. In his search for certainty within the church he was gradually led to the view that it could only be found within Roman Catholicism.[23] There, to account for the church's new doctrines he used the analogy of the unfolding flower. Recently articulated doctrines had been there all along in embryonic form, hidden and gradually developing: 'it had to be this way, pre-determined in apostolic truth'.[24] In 1860 Mark Pattison's contribution to *Essays and Reviews* noted the gradual disintegration of the Anglican synthesis of Scripture, reason and tradition as Tractarians and evangelicals exalted one element at the expense of the others in order once again to claim certainty.[25]

Later in the nineteenth century, however, the Oxford Movement changed its emphasis. Newman himself had always maintained a respect for reason, as is shown in his *University Sermons* of 1843, and his *Grammar of Assent* (1870), written in his Catholic days, remains one of the finest rational arguments for Christian theism. Similarly Charles Gore led the second generation of Tractarians to recognize the need to reconcile the church's doctrines with modern knowledge. With other scholars in the 'Holy Party' he produced *Lux Mundi* (1890), a set of essays which affirmed biblical criticism and evolutionary science and sought a new harmony between Scripture, tradition and reason.

Trends in Roman Catholicism were heavily dependent on the papacy. For most of the nineteenth century it sought to suppress liberalism, which it associated with the French Revolution. The 1832 encyclical *Mirari vos* condemned Catholics who supported democracy and liberty of conscience. In 1864 the *Syllabus of Errors* rejected all forms of modernity and denied that 'the Roman pontiff can and ought to reconcile himself and reach agreement with progress, liberalism and modern civilization'. The succession of Leo XIII in 1878 raised hopes for change, particularly because one his first acts was to make Newman a cardinal. In 1879 he issued an encyclical, *Aeterni Patris*, which made the teachings of Aquinas mandatory for the whole church - thus suppressing alternatives - but had the advantage of urging Catholic scholars to turn away from the narrow scholasticism which often characterized seminary text books and rediscover the writings of Aquinas himself. For some the hopes for change gave rise to a sense of liberation and paved the way for a diffuse movement later described as Catholic Modernism.

However in 1893 Leo issued another encyclical, *Providentissimus Deus*, which insisted on the complete inerrancy of the Bible, rejected critical studies and decreed it sacrilegious to suggest that traditional teaching required any modification or revision at all.[26] His successor Pius X went even further; describing Modernism as a subversive movement he condemned it and required all priests to swear an oath against it. His 1907 encyclical *Pascendi* described Modernism as the 'synthesis of all heresies';[27] Modernists, he claimed, 'lay the axe not to the branches and shoots, but to the very root, that is, to the faith and its deepest fires... so that there is no part of Catholic truth from which they hold their hand, none that they do not strive to corrupt.'[28] Later though there was a degree of liberalization, culminating in Vatican II.

Across the theological spectrum, therefore, a division developed which would in time produce the polarization between liberals and conservatives which we have today. On the one hand new learning produced new challenges and many, like the inheritors of the liberal tradition described in the last chapter, were concerned to respond constructively to them. On the other, those who saw science in general as a threat to Christianity wanted the churches to define themselves over against it. This latter response produced an increasing dogmatism, among Protestants and Catholics alike, which emphasized the authority of distinctively religious authorities and thereby reaffirmed dualism.

Dualism in effect redefined the role of churches. They began to perceive their success in terms of numbers of people who attended worship. The British census of 1851 generated much concern by announcing that a large proportion of the British population, possibly 38%, attended no church at all. Societies were formed to evangelize them and many new churches were built.[29] These anxieties are so familiar today that they may seem natural. At the time they were new. The religious debates of the sixteenth and seventeenth centuries had been motivated by conflicting theories of truth; what mattered was what one believed and whether one was saved, not statistics about church attendance. The Age of Reason had found ways to reconcile differences of opinion, reduced the fear of hell and increased religious tolerance, thus permitting people the option of exempting themselves from their Sunday duties. From the perspective of the nineteenth century revivals this was a sign of decline. An immense amount of effort was put into mission work. In some churches everlasting damnation once again became a popular theme, and Protestants and Catholics alike were determined to rescue the heathen from it.[30] Nineteenth century churches and chapels invested in libraries, games rooms, coffee rooms, recreation grounds, harvest homes and choir suppers, not as direct means to conversion but as techniques for persuading people to attend services. The 'All Welcome' sign is a product of this age.[31]

Other changes accompanied it. In the nineteenth century it became normal for women to outnumber men in church. In the case of some occupations there were practical reasons, but the phenomenon was too widespread to be explained by these. It may be that religion was increasingly being seen as part of the mythical world of childhood, and therefore more appropriate to women as guardians of the young.[32] Whatever the reason, it indicates deep changes to people's attitudes to churchgoing, and is still with us.

These among the most noticeable features of the nineteenth century religious revivals. They have a common feature: they emphasized distinctively spiritual phenomena and created a rich world of distinctively religious beliefs and activities. Many of them were of great value for other purposes as well, but they all expressed that determination to affirm spiritual realities beyond the reach of secular science. They thereby shifted the nature of modern Christianity decisively towards the new, more constrained role which secularism had allocated to religion. Far from being society's way of expressing how life's many phenomena fit together in a coherent account of reality, it had become just one of those phenomena, a compartment alongside the others, restricted to its own expertise.[33] Its doctrines and practices therefore became the centre of religious attention. Worship and prayer became more important. Miracles, and sightings of angels or the Virgin Mary, became victories in the struggle against godlessness.

It was a more private understanding of religion. Until the seventeenth century it had been God who gave humans our bodies, our minds, the world around us and good governments, so religious debate had had a public character. Locke, however, had argued that religious belief is primarily an individual matter; churches were voluntary associations for the purposes of prayer and worship, so states should allow variations of belief as long as they involved no political commitment. The nineteenth century religious revivals succeeded by accepting this new role. The Bible was interpreted anew: in the seventeenth century it had told kings how to govern, through its histories of Israel's kings; in the nineteenth it primarily contained resources for the spiritual life. Whereas in the seventeenth century the biggest religious disagreements had caused wars over how the state should be governed, by the end of the nineteenth they caused court cases over candles on the altar.

Dualism and liberalism

How does this revived dualism relate to liberal and conservative theologies today? Commentators often describe its theological expressions, especially Schleiermacher's, as liberal. This label derives from the fundamentalism debates of the 1920s, and of course from a fundamentalist perspective it is indeed liberal in the sense that it accepts secular authority on physical matters.

However, many of the religious phenomena I have described would today be associated with conservatives rather than liberals. Especially where fundamentalism is still influential, as it is in parts of the USA today, liberals often value dualism as a way of resisting religious claims about matters such as evolution or the age of the earth. It seems like a mid-point between atheism on the one hand and fundamentalism on the other. To take this view is to agree with Schleiermacher that a great deal of human experience lies outside what secular materialism can explain, but also to agree with him that religion should stay within its own sphere, refusing to claim expertise on matters outside religion.

From a coherentist perspective, however, it is not a mid-point at all. It is a lurch from one extreme view - that religious authority always takes priority over secular sources of knowledge - to the opposite extreme, that religious authority has nothing at all to offer to secular knowledge. Fundamentalism and dualism are in this sense mirror images of each other. They both account for religious beliefs and practices - and whatever religious phenomena there may be - by means of foundationalist packages of doctrines. The difference between the two is significant enough - fundamentalism claims supremacy over secular knowledge while dualism only asks to live a quiet life in one of its pockets - but they are both defensive foundationalist reactions against secularism, concerned to protect their own certainties against the atheist threat.

In practice much of the time there is no noticeable difference between coherentist and dualist religious claims. Most people rarely if ever analyze the philosophical structures of their opinions, let alone reflect on how they underpin their religious beliefs. For practical purposes we often make use of a *de facto* qualified compartmentalism. We accept that different people have different kinds of expertise, and whether we ask the vicar or the plumber depends on whether we want to know about life after death or how to make the radiator work. Furthermore compartmentalism fits the way universities operate and it is natural for academic theologians, like other academics, to draw boundaries around their expertise.

Nevertheless there remains a distinction between the two, and often it becomes significant. Many of the religious phenomena described above can be interpreted in contrasting ways. An example would be a personal religious experience. Secular atheism denies that it is a truth-revealing experience at all. Dualism interprets it as an event in the religious realm; in a reality which is mainly secular, there remains a religious compartment where these things happen. The subject of the experience is, so to speak, branded with the mark of religion and perhaps becomes 'a religious person'. Coherentist liberals may also affirm it, but without locating it in a specially religious compartment. Anybody may have a religious experience, and it does not follow that they will suddenly become churchgoers.

Another example would be faith healing. Secular reductionists often deny that it is possible at all, though perhaps allowing for a placebo effect. Dualists interpret it as interaction with spiritual forces beyond the realm of science. Some of them argue that only Christian faith healing can possibly be successful; if a non-Christian healing appears to succeed it must be the work of the devil plotting to capture another soul. A coherentist interpretation would be, again, less dramatic: there may be any number of processes at work which science has not yet discovered, and if they exist they are part of God's creation irrespective of whether science will one day understand them.

The more reactionary phenomena of the religious revivals noted above were also the most distinctively dualistic, even when their intention was to resist dualism. In the case of the Vatican's determination to oppose modernity, for example, commentators have often noted that the more Roman Catholicism distinguished itself from secularism the more it marked itself out as an autonomous institution characterized by its specifically religious expertise, thereby accepting the position granted to it by secularism. Much the same is true of evangelical revivals of Reformation doctrines: the imminent second coming, for example, had been publicly debated as part of mainstream culture in the early seventeenth century but had become a counter-cultural claim in the nineteenth, only affirmed by dualists in their distinctively religious realm.

What I wish to challenge, therefore, is the argument that in order to resist dogmatic supremacy claims by religious leaders on scientific matters, we should go to the other extreme of denying that religion can contribute anything at all to public knowledge of non-spiritual matters. This denial is the central claim of dualism. Secularization, being a reaction against the religious disputes of the Reformation era, established a taboo on talk of the divine; explanations of the way things are in the world are now expected not to make any reference to it. If they do, they are judged to be religious statements and *therefore* not part of ordinary discourse about reality. What makes dualism appear attractive is that it leaves the secular account largely intact and restricts itself to defending a spiritual realm *within* that godless account of reality as a whole.

In order to do so, however, it needs to make sure that its spiritual realm is beyond the reach of science so that religious phenomena cannot be scientifically explained away in non-religious ways. It therefore needs to establish strict boundaries between the religious and the non-religious. It is these strict boundaries which make religious doctrines irrelevant even if they are true. We may think of this boundary-setting as the end point of a gradual decline of theological influence. In the Middle Ages church leaders could lay down rules about just wages and prices and when rulers might or might not go to war, and were influential even though they were often disobeyed. From the religious wars onwards, secularization granted one aspect of society after another its freedom from religious authority, until paradoxically religion itself, faced with the threat of atheism, needed to protect its own realm by insisting that it did not impinge on others.

This is the tradition on which politicians and social commentators are drawing when they condemn religious leaders for 'interfering in politics'. Economics provides a good example. In the Middle Ages it was primarily seen as a branch of ethics, as it taught that money should change hands in accordance with the moral rules. Modern economics, from the eighteenth century onwards, has been understood as a technical matter, an expertise with respect to the economic laws of nature. From this perspective to impose ethical restraints on economic activity is often perceived as a category mistake and economically harmful. For a religious leader to make ethical judgements about economics is to accentuate the category mistake; religious leaders should stick to their own religious expertise.

In this way dualism successfully resists fundamentalism, but at the expense of making religion appear irrelevant outside its own inward-looking world. It is therefore quite unsatisfactory to Christians and other religious believers whose faith inspires them to engage in campaigns about poverty, racism, war, global warming or any issue at all which engages with the physical world or physical human life. These campaigns and the organizations which support them constitute a major element of religious life today and persist in being religiously motivated regardless of the declining fortunes of churchgoing. Coherentist liberalism and fundamentalism both have ways to account for these kinds of religious activism. Dualism, with its strict boundary between the religious and the non-religious, does not. It can only affirm a religious campaign if it is devoted to an issue which belongs within the distinctive realm of religion. It can accept a campaign against abortion if it understands abortion as a religious issue - that is, as an issue which belongs in the realm of religion and should therefore be decided on religious grounds. Similarly with homosexuality: dualism requires that it is either a religious issue - in which case it should be decided by religious authority - or it is a non-religious issue, in which case medical and psychological research prevails - but not both.

Dualism necessarily operates in this manner because it was designed precisely for this purpose. Faced with the persistent tendency of religious authorities to impose dogmas and suppress alternative views, in the Middle Ages it carved out a sphere of empirical research which was not subject to church censorship. In subsequent centuries for the same reason it provided other disciplines with the same escape route from religious dogma, eventually leaving religion in a disconnected world of its own. Disconnected religion, however, does not describe the beliefs religious people do in fact have. Dualism offered a solution to a real problem, but it has turned out to be the wrong solution.

Another weakness of dualism is its similarity to the 'God of the gaps'. Just as Newton tried to show that God must exist in order to account for occasional adjustments to the positions of the planets, but was later refuted, so also it is possible that science may produce non-religious accounts of religious phenomena. For example, if there is a 'religion gene', does this mean that religious belief is better explained by the existence of the gene than by the existence of God? From a coherentist point of view the religion gene, like evolution, can simply be God's way of doing things. From a dualist perspective it is a threat: the whole point of dualism is to affirm realities which cannot be explained by science.

Dualism and the meanings of doctrines

A practical disadvantage of dualism is its tendency to change the meanings of religious doctrines. To illustrate the point I shall refer to George Lindbeck's influential classification. Lindbeck's position is decidedly postmodernist but I include it here because it illustrates so well what happens to doctrines in a dualist framework. His proposal stems from his work with ecumenical dialogue between Christian denominations, where conflicting doctrines are barriers to unity. He proposes three types of theory of doctrine. The 'cognitive' type expects doctrines to be truth claims about objective realities. This, he says, 'was the approach of traditional orthodoxies (as well as of many heterodoxies)'. The second is 'experiential-expressive'. This type does not expect doctrines to be informative. Instead they function as symbols of inner feelings, attitudes or existential orientations; the type 'highlights the resemblances of religions to aesthetic enterprises and is particularly congenial to the liberal theologies influenced by the Continental developments that began with Schleiermacher'. The third is 'cultural-linguistic'. Noting that church doctrines are often most prominent neither for their truth claims nor for their ability to express the religious experience of Christians, but as authoritative rules of discourse for a particular church, he argues that this should be seen as their *only* function. Just as the contradictory rules 'drive on the left' and 'drive on the right' are both obligatory but apply in different countries, so contradictory doctrines regulate different churches. This 'rule theory' of doctrine means that doctrinal propositions like the Nicene Creed do not make truth claims; they only set rules for churches.[34]

I shall make two responses to Lindbeck's proposal. The first is that it describes very well what doctrines have come to mean to many Christians today. The second is that it reveals how far they have degenerated from their original meanings.

The early church engaged in passionate debate about its doctrines because they explained what Christians believed and why they believed them. They had explanatory value. The later medieval and Reformation churches accepted inherited doctrines as true because they had been inherited, but debated the meanings of many of them because, far from still having explanatory value, they were difficult to understand. In the middle of the nineteenth century similar doctrines were presented to the faithful as essential beliefs regardless of whether they could be understood, let alone whether they explained anything. They had become nothing but badges of orthodoxy. It is said that when the English dean, Arthur Stanley, suggested to the Prime Minister that the Athanasian creed should be omitted from the English prayer book, Disraeli replied 'Mr. Dean, no dogmas, no deans'.[35]

Characteristically doctrines are developed at times when they are valued because they explain something. Later they are decreed as official positions, which enables them to survive long after they have ceased to have any explanatory value. Later again other movements revive them, possibly because they once again serve their original purpose but more often for some other reason; perhaps they are simply part of a package of doctrines which the movement wishes to revive. Today traditional Christianity, Catholic and Protestant alike, contains a great many doctrines which most people find unhelpful at best and absurd at worst. The fact that it is so top-heavy with them is one of the main reasons why many spiritual seekers today are discouraged from taking Christianity seriously.

The idea of distinguishing between the first two types - doctrines which make truth claims and doctrines which express attitudes and experiences - has proved popular. To philosophers it legitimates the view that religion lives in a world of its own, making statements only about spiritual beings or inner feelings. To conservative theologians it is a way of sidelining liberals on the ground that they do not really believe Christian doctrines at all.[36] Thus Alister McGrath, arguing that doctrine makes truth claims, agrees with Lindbeck's critique of the experiential-expressivist theory citing David Tracy as an experiential-expressivist, though he denies that Schleiermacher would have counted as one.[37] On this basis secular philosophers and conservative theologians can agree that liberal theology is akin to atheism.[38]

Theologically I believe it is a false dichotomy. Neither type serves much purpose at all unless it is combined with the other. Doctrines which only provide true propositions, and do not engage with contemporary attitudes and experiences, are merely statements of the irrelevant and therefore have no religious value. Conversely, statements which only express the attitudes and experiences of contemporary individuals are passing ephemera. They do not express doctrines until they are treated as expressions of truth-claims which persist in a tradition. To offer a simple example, to say 'I had a dreadful day yesterday; why does God allow it?' is no more experiential-expressive than 'I had a dreadful day yesterday; my tooth hurts.' It does, however, raise cognitive questions about religious truth. The religious question is significant precisely because it is asking for a cognitive framework within which to interpret experience.

The 'experiential-expressive' element of doctrines needs to be present if they are to have value for believers today. Here lies a problem which is mainly associated with liberals, although many conservatives struggle with it as well. The problem is that many inherited doctrines simply do not relate at all to the experiences and understandings of most people today. Those who wish to make sense of their religious beliefs are faced with a choice between abandoning traditional doctrines and giving them new meanings. Thus Nancey Murphy writes that 'the liberals began with the point that religious language cannot be directly about God but must be mediated - it must be, in the first instance, about how God appears in human subjectivity. The biblical narratives cannot be literally about God's doings; the real meaning must be about something else.'[39]

This is a genuine dilemma for religious believers today. Either they maintain traditional doctrines without exploring their contemporary relevance, or they seek to give significance to traditional doctrines by reinterpreting them. Reinterpretations which succeed in being helpful may be very far removed from the intentions of those who first propounded them. They may miss the original point altogether and they may do so deliberately.

Nevertheless, for those who are already committed to a Christian church doctrines which have lost their relevance continue to have two functions. One relates to the afterlife. Many believe in the Resurrection and the Atonement, not at all because it helps them to make sense of their lives, but because the knowledge is needed for *salvation*. In an age when so many people spend their youth learning information for which they have no need except to gain qualifications, perhaps it is not difficult to understand how the function of Christian doctrine can easily degenerate into a kind of revising for an examination.

The other is Lindbeck's 'cultural-linguistic' account of doctrines: they provide rules rather than truth. They are often used in this way as badges of orthodoxy. I am orthodox, or mainstream, or sound, because I believe in the Virgin Birth; if you do not, I mentally preen myself. I am a better Christian than you. Similarly with homosexuality and women priests; as the religious press reveals every week, those who wear the badge consider themselves better Christians, truer upholders of tradition, than those who do not.

Used in these ways, doctrines do not need to explain anything. The converse is that they do not themselves need to be explained. If I believe in the Resurrection because assenting to it is the means to salvation or church membership, I do not need to worry about exactly what happened and how, or the difference between Paul's account and Luke's account; I simply accept that it happened. If a doctrine does not seem to make sense, no matter. Nobody needs to make sense of it. It can be classified as a mystery. Once a doctrine reaches the stage where the only reason for believing it is that those who do not so believe are not considered true Christians, what it means has no relevance.

When nineteenth century religious leaders, Catholic and Protestant alike, reached back into history to revive old doctrines of their traditions, the long-term effect was to reduce the significance of religious belief. By reaffirming that the biblical miracles really did happen, for example, they were not at all doing the same thing as their seventeenth and eighteenth century predecessors. Far from taking part in society's public debate about what could or could not have happened, they were defiantly rejecting society's public debate, speaking a private language of their own and digging new holes in which to bury Christianity.[40]

Believers who understand a traditional doctrine in this 'cultural-linguistic' way do not merely forget the explanatory value it once had; they prevent it. This is because by treating it as a badge of orthodoxy they oblige members of the relevant churches to assent to it, at least in public. If, for example, the members of a church are strongly expected to believe in the Virgin Birth, the expectation inhibits not just discussions about whether the doctrine is true, but also more general explorations of what it might mean. People become reluctant to express their own ideas in case they are out of step with required belief. In these circumstances it is hardly surprising that who do not feel a need to identify with the church's badges of orthodoxy lose all interest in whether the doctrines are true.

Characteristically it is the administrators of church organizations who value a doctrine's cultural-linguistic function most highly. From their point of view it is most helpful if doctrines can be summarized in a succinct set of words, so that people can be given a simple yes-or-no choice: Do you believe in the Virgin Birth? Do you believe Jesus is your personal Lord and Saviour? Do you oppose homosexuality? Doctrines become tribal affirmations or slogans. To those more concerned about truth and explanatory value these questions are pretty meaningless; any doctrine worth believing will generate discussion of its changing significance in varying circumstances, and will need to be re-stated accordingly.

Lindbeck's analysis shows what happens to doctrines within a dualistic framework. None of his three types provides, on its own, a good reason for believing a doctrine. A good reason would be that it both is true and helpfully explains something; that is, it should fit the first two of his types. The third is a by-product of these two, not an independent reason for belief. Religious denominations do not set themselves up for other reasons and then decide to choose some doctrines by which to distinguish themselves; the doctrines come first and the denominations follow.

The long-term effect of these changes is described by Reardon:

Protestant religious teaching, apart from certain more or less restricted enclaves within the main Protestant communions, or in the obscurer sects on their fringes, has moved away from the positions held by the great reformers themselves and so uncompromisingly defined in its classic confessions of faith. In fact it is no exaggeration to assert that the central doctrines of historic Protestantism - original sin, atonement, justification *sola fide*, predestination, the verbal inspiration of scripture - not to mention those which the reformers received from antiquity through their Catholic inheritance and themselves fully endorsed - the dogmas of the Trinity and the person of Christ - all of them stressing the sovereignty and prevenience of God and the incapacity and dependence of man, are now almost unintelligible without the aid of an extended historical commentary.[41]

Why, then, do religious traditions - unlike other traditions - become so top-heavy with outdated doctrines? Why do they not abandon doctrines which no longer serve their original purpose? Usually, behind the resistance to formal change lies the idea of certainty. When the nineteenth century churches reaffirmed the doctrines of the Reformation and Counter-Reformation they felt the need for an authority strong enough to resist the rising tide of atheism. Both Bible and pope were decreed infallible. To claim that a doctrine is certain to be true is, also, to oppose any change to it. It is the foundationalist presuppositions behind religious traditions which make every generation feel it does not have the right to jettison outdated doctrines.

I therefore see coherentist liberalism as a better means to seeking religious truth. Because it denies that we can have absolute certainty it is prepared to reconsider the doctrinal statements of past ages. It should be possible for doctrines which are losing their explanatory value to be adapted or rejected, so that at any one time the ones being affirmed are meaningful and nobody feels obliged to assent to embarrassing relics of a bygone age.

It also dispenses with the need for sharp boundaries between the religious and the secular, making it once again possible to consider whether the physical has spiritual significance. Neither inherited Christian doctrine nor religion-free secular reason can on its own provide an adequate basis for society's attempts to seek greater understanding of reality as a whole, but both have contributions to make.

Whereas dualism protects its religious realm while otherwise leaving secularism alone, coherentism engages positively with modern secular understandings of reality, affirming some aspects but also claiming that it needs to recognize a spiritual dimension to reality as a whole. The flaw in non-religious accounts of reality does not just relate to one compartment, but is endemic. Coherentism is thus a constructive but critical supporter of secular culture.

Dualism focuses on a distinctively religious realm where it values spiritual realities beyond the reach of science. It therefore looks for evidence for them, and makes much of the evidence it finds. Coherentist liberalism is prepared to find religious significance pretty well anywhere. It therefore does not focus so much on specifically religious places and activities, and is less interested in whether an apparently religious phenomenon can be explained scientifically. It may believe in, and value, some of the religious phenomena mentioned earlier in this chapter, but it does not depend on them so much. It is not just religion which witnesses to God, but reality as a whole.

CHAPTER 7

FUNDAMENTALIST CERTAINTY DEFIES
SCIENTIFIC THEORY

'Fundamentalism' is a problem word. It comes from *The Fundamentals,* a set of twelve volumes published from Chicago, probably between 1909 and 1915. They were critical of Darwinism and biblical criticism which, they argued, did not take account of the special divine authority of Scripture. Only in the 1920s when the debate between fundamentalists and liberals was at its height did they come to be treated as significant documents.

Currently the word is used in different ways. In the USA many conservative evangelicals call themselves fundamentalists; in the UK the word has negative connotations, so many conservative evangelicals take pains to distinguish their position from fundamentalism. The word is also used of militant Islamic groups.[1] I have no wish to defend or oppose particular uses of the word, but I shall use it here to describe the Christian movement which is most popular in the USA and which is described there as fundamentalism. Some fundamentalists are dualists, but my present interest in it is in how it offers an alternative to dualism. It is a more thoroughgoing attempt to reject secularism, one which insists that divine revelation is supreme not only on matters of faith but on all matters.

When the medieval scholastics and the Reformers accepted the truth of the Bible they were primarily concerned with doctrines. Historical and scientific information was of less interest, and they usually accepted it uncritically because they had few other reliable sources of information. Fundamentalism insists more strongly on the Bible's accuracy in scientific and historical matters and thereby reacts against contemporary scientific and historical studies.

Most commentators trace its philosophical roots to eighteenth century Scottish Common Sense Realism. Thomas Reid, the founder of this school, responded to the growing realization that Locke's theory of ideas could not guarantee certainty about empirical knowledge. To defend certainty he argued that what our minds perceive is not merely the ideas of objects but the objects themselves. In the same vein he reverted to Bacon's theory of induction according to which scientists should derive laws of nature directly from collections of empirical data without developing hypotheses. God, Reid believed, has given us principles of common sense which enable us to know with certainty what we observe empirically.[2]

These objects of knowledge are 'facts'. Barbara Shapiro has traced the development of the modern concept of 'fact' from the 1660s. Before then, facts were events, something done. To prove that they had been done required evidence. After that time a 'fact' was an event which no longer needed evidence; its truth had been established and could be taken for granted. The concept proved useful in the empirical sciences where it could denote statements which had been empirically established and could therefore be known with certainty. Later Reid borrowed the idea, arguing that 'what can fairly be deduced from facts duly observed, or sufficiently attested, is genuine and pure; it is the voice of God, and no fiction of human imagination.' For Reid, not only observed events but also the laws of nature were facts. All else was conjecture, hypothesis and theory.[3]

Among philosophers the theory did not survive Kant's assault. Kant distinguished between 'phenomena', things as they seem to us, and 'noumena', things as they are in themselves, arguing that there is always a difference between the two because we always process our information. However one of Reid's successors, James Beattie, used the theory to defend the Bible against critical scholarship. Beattie argued that since the sense impressions are generally reliable, so is testimony based on them. We can therefore rely on the testimony of the biblical authors. Although transcribers might have introduced errors into texts he was confident that the apostles were unbiased and only reported what they had heard and seen. Their reports of miracles and prophecies could not have been mistaken. God has designed the Bible to provide evidence which will convince people of every rank. It is only sophisticated reasoning and false philosophy which hinders acceptance of its truth. Recognizing that some doctrines are beyond our understanding he argued that the appropriate response is simply to accept them.[4]

In this way Beattie combined Reformation claims about the authority of the Bible with modern claims to certainty in empirical studies. His successors applied Bacon's inductive method to the Bible, seeing it as their job to collect and classify biblical 'facts'. They contrasted these facts with the mere hypotheses of critical biblical scholars.[5]

The first classic text applying this theory was Louis Gaussen's *Theopneustia* (1841). Gaussen's foundational first principle was that God had inspired the writing of the Bible. From this he deduced the Bible's qualities, and these in turn provided resources for deducing the nature of reality. In the process he established some principles which remain central to fundamentalism. 'Plenary inspiration' asserts that all the parts of the Bible are equally inspired by God; 'verbal inspiration' that God inspired the words, not just the ideas, of Scripture; and 'inerrancy' that God so guided the biblical authors as to preserve them from all errors and omissions.[6]

The most influential theorists of biblical inerrancy were the 'Old Princeton' theologians Charles Hodge, Benjamin Warfield and J Gresham Machen, writing at the end of the nineteenth century and the beginning of the twentieth. Hodge expresses fundamentalism's philosophy very clearly in the first few pages of his *Systematic Theology*. Just as nature provides the basic facts for scientists, who must accept whatever results their experiments produce, so also the Bible provides the basic facts for theologians, who must accept whatever it says. Biblical inspiration extends to 'everything which any sacred writer asserts to be true', including 'statements of facts, whether scientific, historical, or geographical'. Theologians should therefore collect the facts God has revealed in the Bible, accept them as certain, and combine them to develop general principles.[7]

The doctrine of inerrancy was therefore essential to their theology. They defended it in two different ways. Hodge defended it deductively; because it is inspired by the Holy Spirit, it is 'free from all error whether of doctrine, fact, or precept'. Its authors were 'the organs of God for the infallible communication of his mind and will', so that 'what they said God said'.[8] He knew of minor errors, but felt able to dismiss them:

> No sane man would deny that the Parthenon was built of marble, even if here and there a speck of sandstone should be detected in its structure. Not less unreasonable is to deny the inspiration of such a book as the Bible, because one sacred writer says that on a given occasion twenty-four, and another says that twenty-three thousand, men were slain. Surely a Christian may be allowed to tread such objections under his feet.[9]

Warfield reversed the order of argumentation. Instead of beginning with the doctrine of inspiration and deducing factual accuracy, he argued that we should begin inductively, reading Scripture and noting its authenticity, historical credibility and general trustworthiness. In this way we will be led to conclude that it must have been divinely inspired. However, this argument is at risk from empirical evidence of errors in Scripture. Even Hodge's limited admission of minor factual errors became impossible to Warfield; it was essential to his case that the Bible should contain no errors at all.[10]

Warfield accepted that a proved error in Scripture would undermine his doctrine, but insisted on such high standards of proof as to render it impossible. It would be necessary to prove that the error existed in the original autograph (the manuscript originally written by the biblical author), there should be no uncertainty about the text's meaning and the statement in question must be proved erroneous with absolute certainty.[11] Here lies a weakness: to insist that all biblical statements should be taken as true unless disproved in this way is hardly consistent with reading the Bible and noticing that all its statements are in fact true.

In Old Princeton, then, we can see a reaction against both critical scholarship of the Bible and nineteenth century accounts of science. Their account of the Bible's authority combined doctrinal principles inherited from the Reformation with an empiricist interpretation of biblical 'facts'. As so often happens a reactionary movement, in opposing one novelty, creates another.

These theological ideas were popularized by evangelical movements, particularly the holiness movement and premillennialism. Premillennialism depended on accepting the relevant biblical prophecies. There were two main approaches to interpreting them. One was the 'historicist' one, which read in the books of Revelation and Daniel prophecies of events which had already taken place. This movement was therefore interested in showing how public events were fufilments of prophecies. To make the dates fit the theory an essential premise was that prophetic days should be interpreted as years. Many expected the second coming around 1866, and when it did not arrive, reviewed their calculations. Others rejected interest in public concerns and believed the biblical prophecies were foretelling supernatural events yet to take place. Believers would be caught up in the air to meet Christ in the 'rapture'. This would be followed by the 'great tribulation' prophesied in Revelation. Finally Christ and his saints would come to reign over the earth. This view is often called 'dispensationalism' because it distinguishes between different dispensations, or periods of divine dealings with humanity. The state of affairs in the world, they believed, could only get worse until the second coming; they therefore opposed proposals for social improvement. The intense mood of anticipation led to a denunciatory tone, condemning all who disagreed. Historicists faced difficulties with literal interpretations of the Bible, as the historical fulfilments never matched the biblical prophecies with the literal accuracy they would have liked. Dispensationalists were free of this problem and could afford to affirm literalism more strongly.[12]

Encouraged by these movements, fundamentalism reached a peak in the USA in the early 1920s. The debates with liberals were at their most intense then and some fundamentalist organizations were very militant. The most celebrated event was the Scopes trial. In 1925 the State of Tennessee prosecuted John Scopes for teaching evolution. It was basic to the prosecution's case that true science rests on facts whereas evolution is mere hypothesis, 'millions of guesses strung together'.[13] Although the prosecution won the case the trial convinced public opinion that fundamentalism was not intellectually credible.[14]

It was at this time that American fundamentalism developed some of the features for which it is best known today: its tendency to split into competing factions, its separatism - some groups lived completely separate lives with their own dress codes - and its belligerent condemnations of other Christians. They could justify these practices by appealing to the older Calvinistic zeal to root out error and preserve doctrinal purity. Later, counter-reactions led to yet more fundamentalist organizations seeking closer co-operation with other evangelicals in order to maximize effectiveness in campaigns. British fundamentalism was less extreme than American, largely because Keswick conventions emphasized emotion at the expense of reason.[15] British defenders of inerrancy like James Packer and John Wenham have been more flexible than their American counterparts.[16]

Fundamentalist doctrine today

The foundationalist character of fundamentalism makes the Bible's inerrancy essential to its case. Scripture is the initial principle from which all other truth claims can be deduced as 'facts', so fundamentalists need to be able to take for granted that its words are certain to be accurate. Proof-texting, though not accepted by all, remains common: since the whole Bible is a single, unified document, inspired by God throughout, it should be possible to combine any two texts and derive legitimate conclusions from them.[17]

The main practical difficulty is that fundamentalists have failed to find a satisfactory method for dispensing with all the errors and inconsistencies in the Bible. Americans have produced many different theories of inerrancy and continue to debate them intensely. One question is the extent to which biblical texts may be interpreted figuratively rather than literally. Some are more willing than others to allow figurative interpretations, though the characteristic approach is to interpret non-literally only when a literal reading would imply error. Critics argue that this shows their position to be untenable; if literalism were true it would be applicable in every case. The lack of a satisfactory defence continues to generate new theories. Because of the variety of meanings inerrancy now has, many British evangelicals have abandoned the term.[18]

During the twentieth century conservative scholars became more sympathetic to critical scholarship. Today many engage in it but remain conservatives in that they reach conservative conclusions. James Barr has examined this trend. As a biblical scholar himself he welcomes the move towards accepting critical tools, but distinguishes between two ways conservative evangelicals use them. Those who reach conservative conclusions because they think the evidence points to them are using critical scholarship appropriately; when scholars like F F Bruce and J D G Dunn fail to insist on conservative conclusions they disappoint conservative evangelicals but they gain respect among scholars.[19] Others on the other hand are committed to establishing conservative results in advance of their scholarly investigations, and to that end use critical scholarship selectively. These scholars, Barr argues, are in fact operating as fundamentalists even if they do not believe the term describes their position. Harris illustrates Barr's case with Alister McGrath's attempt to distance his own position from fundamentalism by arguing that 'fundamentalism is totally hostile to the notion of biblical criticism, in any form', whereas evangelicalism 'accepts the principle of biblical criticism (although insisting that it be applied responsibly)'. If 'applied responsibly' means 'used to reach only conservative conclusions', then it would appear that McGrath's scholarship is fundamentalist; if not, he should be genuinely open to accepting whatever conclusions the evidence indicates.[20]

Given the centrality of inerrancy fundamentalists are often called upon to explain how God ensured that the biblical authors wrote the correct words. Inerrancy is best defended by 'mechanical dictation' in which the human authors' minds played no part in selecting them. Most, however, believe this denies the humanity of the authors. They must have believed in what they were writing, from the perspective of their own social settings and their personal concerns. However, the greater the role of the human authors the greater the danger that the words they wrote were not those of God. To avoid this danger many have argued for 'double authorship'; while the authors, as Stott puts it, 'were researching and reflecting, and writing in a manner that was appropriate to them, the Holy Spirit was carrying them forward to express what was intended by him'.[21] Opponents of this theory argue that God would thereby have deceived the authors, subjecting them to divine inspiration without their knowledge.

Many inerrantists resist the attempt to clarify the issue. A common way of doing this is to appeal to Baconian induction: just as Baconianism restricts scientists to observing and classifying phenomena and forbids them to speculate about hidden causes, so students of the Bible should concentrate on what the words say without speculating about the process of divine inspiration.[22] Critics argue that fundamentalism distorts scripture by imposing its own tradition of interpretation on it. Because of its strong emphasis on biblical inerrancy it has developed a hostility to modern theology and critical biblical study, and this has caused it to produce its own theological system. Barr argues that, despite all the claims to the supreme authority of the Bible, the core of fundamentalism is not the Bible, but a particular kind of religion which fundamentalists associate with accepting biblical authority and which they impose upon the Bible, thereby misinterpreting it.[23]

Evidence for Barr's argument lies in the strong commitment to doctrines which are not in the Bible. Substitutionary atonement, the Fall and the Trinity are commonly defended by fundamentalists. However they accept them in their classical formulations, which were not developed until long after the Bible was written. Barr adds that fundamentalists borrow these and other doctrines from older Protestant orthodoxies in a piecemeal fashion, with little regard for their explanatory value, and treat them as tests of orthodoxy, to be believed simply because this is what the fundamentalist tradition in question believes.[24]

Being a foundationalist system claiming certainty, fundamentalism demands total assent. *Every* biblical text is to be taken as inerrant. Commentators have often noted its 'domino mentality': question one text and the authority of every text is put in doubt.[25] This has led to exclusivism, especially in the USA. Universal agreement about the 'the clear teaching of Scripture' in every text is of course impossible. As in the Reformation debates, within the theory the only way to account for differences of opinion is to conclude that those who disagree with one's own opinion are not submitting to Scripture and therefore are not true Christians.[26] It is a psychologically brittle situation. It naturally produces strong disapproval of those who interpret Scripture differently; but the stronger the hostility, the greater the disorientation when disagreements arise within one's own sect. A trusted friend disagrees with one point, leaves - or is expelled - and suddenly becomes one of the denounced opponents. Inevitably this brittleness often produces a militant hostility to other Christians. Even where the sectarian ethos is much weaker, conservative evangelicals often function as a sect within a sect by rigorously ensuring that ministers in their denomination who do not share their distinctive stance are not invited to preach.[27]

The claim that the Bible is authoritative on all matters, not just matters of faith, lies behind the fundamentalist challenges to secular education in the USA. If God is the author of both the Bible and true science, they argue, the two can never contradict each other. True science therefore accepts Scripture as authoritative; when they appear to disagree we can be sure that scientists will eventually find that they were in error.[28] Americans who take this view often make scientific claims which astonish non-fundamentalists. Thus Willie Criswell, a Southern Baptist, wrote in 1982 that Hebrews 11:3, 'God made this world out of things that are not seen', is 'the finest statement of the atomic theory you will ever read in your life'. Harold Lindsell wrote in 1976 that Job 38:7, where 'the morning stars are said to sing together', should be taken literally, since 'scientists now tell us that in the air there is music that comes from the stars'. Harris reports that the camera crew in Pat Robertson's Christian Broadcasting Network discussed the possibility of situating television cameras in Jerusalem to televise the second coming, and even considered how to avoid the glare of Christ's radiance.[29]

Fundamentalists do sometimes revise their interpretations of the Bible to fit scientific information. 'Creation scientists' - opponents of evolution - oppose revision most strongly, usually by dismissing new discoveries as 'mere hypotheses'. They sometimes argue that evolution is no less a religion than Christianity, sometimes that 'creation science' is no less scientific than evolution.[30]

James Barr's critiques have generated extensive debate about the distinction between evangelicals and fundamentalists. This is especially significant in the UK, where many conservative evangelicals reject the fundamentalist label. Much of the debate is about subjective interpretations of Scripture. Evangelicals have often understood their relationship with God as personal, so that when God speaks to them through the Bible the experience is an inward one. Fundamentalists, on the other hand, insist on the objectivity of Scripture. Scripture challenges human ways of thinking and should not be subject to them; its meaning lies in the texts, not in the way they are interpreted. They therefore accuse evangelicals who emphasize inwardness of making a similar error to biblical scholars, interpreting the Bible according to their own scheme instead of accepting it as it is. This makes the doctrine of perspicuity still attractive to fundamentalists: Scripture has a 'plain sense' comprehensible to 'the plain man', and since biblical scholars are in error when they claim privileged understanding of it, the same must also be true for evangelicals who grant authority to their subjective experiences.[31] It is this emphasis on rationality, objectivity and 'facts', at the expense of a more personal and spontaneous faith, which non-fundamentalist evangelicals most often oppose.[32]

One of Barr's most hotly debated criticisms is that many evangelicals who deny that they are fundamentalists do in fact treat the Bible in a fundamentalist manner. Self-designated fundamentalists often agree with him and complain that other evangelicals caricature fundamentalism in order to exaggerate the differences; in particular they complain that they are falsely accused of being anti-intellectual. One of Barr's illustrations is that because he does not believe the Bible to be inerrant, evangelicals describe him as believing it is errant. He replies that to present the options in these terms is to betray a fundamentalist presupposition - that the only way to interpret the Bible is as a collection of facts which are either true or false. Interestingly, John Stott replied to Barr's critique: 'It is not dishonest in the face of apparent discrepancies, to suspend judgement and continue looking for harmony rather than declare Scripture to be erroneous. On the contrary it is an expression of our Christian integrity'.[33] Harris comments that Stott here, while claiming not to be a fundamentalist, expresses precisely the stance which characterizes fundamentalism: that the most important claim for the Bible is that it contains no errors, and that non-evangelicals aim to uncover errors in it.[34]

This brief account of fundamentalism leaves out some who call themselves fundamentalists and includes some who do not. Nevertheless the word generally refers to a recognizable tradition with distinct features. Unlike earlier Protestant theories of biblical inerrancy it focuses on the Bible's historical and scientific statements. Unlike dualism it rejects the findings of modern science when they conflict with biblical statements. It thereby aims to retain a more unified account of both the Bible and the physical universe. The Bible is supremely authoritative on all matters, not just matters of faith; fundamentalists have no need to draw a line distinguishing between the spiritual realm and the rest of reality, or between those biblical statements which are authoritative and those which are not. Physical reality can be known through science, but wherever Scripture describes it, Scripture cannot be in error.

If the central claims seem simple their application is not. The persistent debates between fundamentalists reveal that they cannot agree on an account of physical reality which is both empirically defensible and compatible with all relevant biblical texts. This failure is caused by a weakness in its philosophical basis. We have seen how it combines two principles. One inherits the Reformation principle of the supreme authority of the Bible and insists that its statements are inerrant. The other applies Bacon's theory of induction to biblical texts in order to establish facts about historical and scientific matters.

The combination of these two derives from Common Sense Realism. This philosophy argued that the five senses provide us with knowledge which we perceive directly and can know with certainty. Fundamentalism reapplies the idea to the Bible, so that whatever we read there we can know with certainty. This, though, is quite a different matter. According to Bacon one observes the world in order to find out facts about the world. Fundamentalists argue that they are being inductive, and therefore scientific, when in the same way they observe the Bible in order to find out facts about the world. They are not. Observing the Bible will produce facts about the Bible, not facts about the world. This properly inductive method is used by critical biblical scholars, who look for information about the Bible - like who wrote each book, when and for what purpose - but distinguish these findings from questions about whether biblical statements are true. Fundamentalists, by treating biblical texts as inerrant facts about the world, are imposing onto the Bible a theoretical principle of inerrancy which induction cannot justify.

Many fundamentalists, including Warfield, have tried to avoid this conclusion by arguing that the Bible's inerrancy can be established inductively; that is, by reading the Bible we notice that it is inerrant. This theory is still defended, but is clearly inadequate; in fact by Warfield's time a great many people had abandoned their faith in the accuracy of the Bible, if not Christianity altogether, precisely because when they read it they found not just many errors but also immoralities.[35] Even if they had not done so Warfield's argument would have been weak, as it presupposed that personal reading has the authority to judge the accuracy of the Bible and therefore has greater authority.

Fundamentalist theory claims to be scientific by appealing to Baconian induction. Bacon believed that, by collecting and classifying data, scientists would be able to accumulate facts which would be known with certainty. He therefore rejected the procedure of devising and testing hypotheses, as it would not be possible to establish certainty this way. His theory produced a sharp distinction between 'facts', which were known with certainty, and mere 'hypotheses' or 'opinions' which were not. In practice hypotheses are too useful to be rejected. Scientists do not work with Bacon's distinction. Everything is hypothesis, and there is a sliding scale from those still to be tested to those so well established that we can take them as true. Often whether a hypothesis can be taken as true depends on the use to which it is being put; for some purposes a significant possibility of error is acceptable, while for others it is not.

Fundamentalism, however, demands complete certainty. When fundamentalists today claim that their theories are scientifically based, the scientific basis turns out to be an outdated Baconianism which practising scientists rarely find adequate. Instead of recognizing the inadequacy of their position, however, they often use it to gain a rhetorical advantage. The science of which they disapprove - like evolution - is, they claim, mere hypothesis, while their alternative accounts are based on fact. Although it is nothing but a rhetorical trick it is often persuasive; those who claim to know certainties easily score over those who believe all knowledge is relative. 'What I know, I know for certain; by your own admission you don't know whether your opinions are true' is no more than an easy debating point but it often convinces.

Science has moved on a long way since the early days of fundamentalism. Contrary to fundamentalism's claims the Bible has not proved a fruitful source of scientific information. Nor have fundamentalists shown much interest in using biblical texts to challenge new theories. Their campaigns continue to focus on the issues which were prevalent a hundred years ago - evolution, the age of the earth, the six-day creation. Biblical scholarship has also moved on, shedding new light on biblical texts, so that critics like Barr and Barton complain that fundamentalists who claim to give so much authority to the Bible ought to pay more attention to what it actually says and means.[36] From the perspective of critical scholarship this gives fundamentalism an air of being stuck in the past. A century ago Warfield genuinely believed that the original autographs of the Bible would be discovered and would turn out to be free of error. Today nobody expects that they will ever be found; but discussions about them continue to play an important part in fundamentalist biblical analysis.

Fundamentalists often reply to these criticisms by arguing that only those with a proper respect for the Bible's authority can understand what it really is and therefore correctly interpret what it is saying.[37] Recent defences of fundamentalist readings of the Bible have therefore appealed to the postmodern claim that there is no neutral vantage point, free of presuppositions, from which the text can be objectively interpreted, and that fundamentalist presuppositions are as legitimate as liberal ones. I shall discuss this further in the next chapter.

We have seen how fundamentalism has its roots in a foundationalist account of unified truth which believed that the reasoning processes of religion are the same as those for science. Nineteenth and early twentieth century inerrantists expected that the rational and empirical processes used in science could be applied to the Bible to reveal that it is both inerrant and informative. They could afford to affirm reason all the way because they expected it to vindicate their beliefs. Their successors today cannot do this. Their two principles, of biblical inerrancy and inductive Bible reading, conflict with each other. Characteristically they continue to affirm that the truth of Scripture needs to be authenticated by reason because people need good reasons for accepting it. On the other hand, once it is accepted, reason is to submit to it. James Packer, for example, contrasts submission to the Bible with subjectivism. Subjectivism, as he describes it, springs from the principle that the final authority for faith and life is the verdict of one's own reason, conscience or religious sentiment. By contrast, evangelicals accept the Bible as 'finally authoritative'. Thus he paints a picture of a debate between two contrasting foundationalisms. John Stott makes a similar case.[38] This is to resolve the tension by means of a two-stage process. In the first reason is the supreme authority and it establishes the inerrancy of the Bible. In the second the Bible is the supreme authority, and sets limits to reason. Packer's argument is, in a way, similar to Descartes' 'cogito', in which he appealed to reason to prove the existence of God and then appealed to God to justify the reliability of his reasoning. Critics of Descartes point out that it is a circular argument. Packer's case is not so much circular as self-refuting: reason establishes the truth of Scripture, and then Scripture establishes that reason is *not* reliable.

Fundamentalist evangelism is characterized by the commitment to certainty. If I feel absolutely certain that I am right, and you disagree with me, I am bound to conclude that you must be certainly wrong. It follows that I have nothing to learn from you. However much trouble you take to explain in painstaking detail why you take a different view, I do not listen to you with a learning ear. Instead I watch out for weaknesses in your argument, to pounce on them. At the end my expectations are realized: I have not learned anything from you. Thus evangelists need to be confident that they know everything they need to know, and it follows from the logic of the theory - though they do not put it like this - that they should see it as their duty to do all of the talking and none of the listening. If others argue back, and point out the weaknesses in the argument, this can be used as further evidence that 'the wisdom of this world' only leads people astray. For a fundamentalist to take seriously what the non-fundamentalist says in reply, *and think about it*, is not only discouraged; it is the most dangerous risk of all, the devil at hand waiting for the opportunity to tempt them away from the true faith.

At Sheffield University in the 1980s the main Christian Union meetings regularly appealed for volunteers to evangelize members of the public on the following Saturday evening. There were three standard venues, two in the city centre and one outside the University Students' Union. Students often volunteered to do a turn in the city centre. It was much harder to persuade them to volunteer for the Students' Union. I discussed this with some of them and the reason was clear enough: at the Students' Union they might meet their friends. Without the conceptual tools to articulate the problem, students were aware that they were being asked *to do something one would not do to a friend*. For people in their late teens or early twenties to approach complete strangers perhaps two or three times their age, expecting to have an important message worth sharing, takes some courage. One needs genuine conviction that one belongs to a small minority of true Christians who alone know truths essential for salvation. When they played this role, therefore, they preferred to engage with people they were unlikely to meet again.

Because the artificiality of certainty-driven evangelism is felt by the evangelist, unconsciously if not consciously, training often provides techniques to cope with it. The result is that the fundamentalist evangelist often gives the impression of having a role similar to that of the commercial sales representative. Both are trained to sell the product by whatever means of persuasion work. The absolute perfection of the product is never to be questioned. If doubts come from the customer, they are not to be taken seriously: a patter must be learned to deal with every question.

Herein lies one of the main reasons for the present day decline of interest in Christianity. Fundamentalism, like dualism, attempts to show that Christianity is true and meaningful. Dualism seeks to do it by establishing a spiritual sphere inaccessible to science, fundamentalism by claiming the relevance and reliability of the Bible on all matters. Those innovations once seemed suitable solutions to the problems of their own day. The problems of our day are different: the credibility of God's existence has increased but the credibility of the churches' dogmas has decreased. The new roles these movements have given to religion may attract those who are already sympathetic to Christianity, but they make it harder for those who were not already sympathetic to see the point of it.

Fundamentalism, like dualism but to a much stronger degree, generates a polarization between its supporters and opponents. Now that most people accept that public reason and knowledge, without any reference to religion, have the power to enlighten and benefit society, fundamentalism defies it and earns a reputation for opposing reason altogether. While attracting some to Christianity it drives much larger numbers away. Its failure to have a positive effect on society as a whole is indicated by the fact that the terms 'humanism', 'rationalism' and 'free thinker' have come to refer to opponents of religious belief.

CHAPTER 8

POSTMODERN FAITH CHOOSES ITS OWN REASON

In the last two chapters I have described two types of defensive religious response to the threat of atheism when it was at its most extreme. One accepted the secular understanding of the physical universe but asserted the reality of a spiritual realm beyond the reach of science; the other accepted the importance of scientific facts but asserted the supremacy of the Bible on scientific matters. In this chapter I turn to a third response which rejects secular and modern accounts of reality even more radically.

It is often described as postmodernist. Postmodernism has a wide range of meanings. In art and architecture, where the word was first used, it describes what followed a distinct 'modernist' movement. In the contexts of culture, philosophy and theology the 'modernism' against which postmodernism reacts is variously described but usually refers to some combination of Enlightenment thought and the nineteenth century developments of secularism.

Characteristically postmodernists describe modernism as offering knowledge with certainty, and absolute - universal and timeless - standards and values. Many postmodern critiques are along the lines discussed in the last few chapters. On the whole religious liberals accept that we do not have certainty, either in secular or religious matters, while conservatives seize on the uncertainties of secular knowledge in order to assert their religious beliefs against it. I shall focus in this chapter on different elements of postmodernism, metanarratives and the question of commensurability.

Jean-François Lyotard's critique of metanarratives is a major theme of postmodernism. I described in Chapter 4 how Christianity was replaced by reason as Europe's dominant metanarrative. Postmodernists argue that we should have no metanarratives at all. Modern science, Lyotard argues, tells a story of how Enlightenment thinkers overcame ignorance and superstition and thereby made us all healthier and richer. When we reinterpret it, not as a universally true metanarrative, but as one 'local narrative' among many, then we can redescribe it as 'the story white Europeans tell about the natural world' and it loses its prestige. In replacing metanarratives with local narratives he aimed to establish political justice for those who are excluded by the universalizing rationalism of Enlightenment thought.

Similarly in ethics; postmodernists often complain that universal and objective ethical standards are used as tools of oppression. Feminists argue that modernism favours a male perspective, liberationists that it favours the ruling classes. In each case the argument is that modernism excludes the 'different' and 'other' from consideration. The 'other' can argue 'Your account of reality, truth and goodness is just one of many: mine is just as valid as yours'.[1]

Whereas Enlightenment philosophers valued reason as a set of universally accepted norms for resolving conflict, postmodernists challenge the notion of universal reason. A major contributor to the debate is Alasdair MacIntyre's *Whose Justice? Which Rationality?* This study examines the way traditions of thought develop their concepts of justice and rationality, and respond to challenges, from the ancient Greeks through Augustine and Aquinas to Enlightenment 'liberalism'. MacIntyre argues that Enlightenment liberalism, though it began as an attempt to dispense with tradition and establish knowledge by universally valid methods, has in fact become just one more tradition among others.[2]

If there is no universally true system of rationality capable of judging between contrasting traditions, the question arises as to how different traditions, with different accounts of rationality, can relate to each other. MacIntyre argues that each tradition thinks it is more rational than other traditions because it accepts its own account of rationality. Sometimes, however, a tradition finds that it does not have the resources to solve its own problems but an alternative tradition does. When this happens one tradition may be subsumed into another, or two merge to form a new one. His favoured example is the way Aquinas reconciled the Augustinian and Aristotelian traditions.[3]

Other postmodernists go further to claim that in the absence of a universal rationality different traditions are simply incommensurable with each other and therefore cannot learn from each other or merge into each other. Only those inside a tradition can fully understand it. Thus John Milbank, replying to MacIntyre, argues

> If a tradition has *really* collapsed, then this must mean that its criteria - which are part of its very woof and warp - have split asunder... What triumphs is simply the persuasive power of a new narrative... Decisive shifts within traditions, or from one tradition to another, have to be interpreted as essentially 'rhetorical victories'.[4]

Claims like this draw support from recent theories in the philosophy of science, especially Thomas Kuhn's claim that science does not always develop in a linear and gradual manner but sometimes undergoes switches from one paradigm to another, so that there is no single paradigm which accounts for all scientific development.[5]

In these theories, then, the Enlightenment search for a universally valid system of rationality is replaced by a range of incommensurable traditions, each with its own rationality. Because there is no universal rationality capable of passing judgements on the different rationalities of traditions, it is impossible to resolve the disagreements.

Postmodernists vary widely not only in their critiques of modernism but also in the alternatives they recommend. The most common classification is into three types. 'Post-liberals' do not want to replace modernity's standards with alternatives, but instead affirm and defend the 'postmodern condition' without them. 'Pre-modernists' welcome the collapse of modernist standards in order to appeal to earlier theories. 'Neo-liberals' agree with some critiques of modernism but believe it can adapt to take them into account. The distinctions are often unclear as modernism is variously described, but the first is the most distinctively postmodern. Lakeland, describing it, suggests that 'The postmodern sensibility... is nonsequential, noneschatological, nonutopian, nonsystematic, nonfoundational, and, ultimately, nonpolitical. The postmodern human being wants a lot but expects little. The emotional range is narrow, between mild depression at one end and a whimsical insouciance at the other.'[6] The sociologist Steve Bruce describes the new religious movements and New Age spirituality as characteristic of postliberalism because they are liberal, tolerant, relativistic, consumer-driven and eclectic.[7]

Postmodern religion
Theologians react to postmodernism in a variety of different ways. Liberals often adopt a 'neo-liberal' stance, rejecting some elements of modernism while defending and adapting others as I have done in this book. Conservatives often defend their traditions by taking a 'pre-modern' stance; they are encouraged by the collapse of modernism because they see it as an opportunity to reaffirm an older tradition. It is the Christian tradition, not secular modernism, which should provide Christians with their understanding of reality. Thus the New Testament scholar Richard Hays writes that 'the hermeneutical primacy of the New Testament is an axiom for the life of the Christian community: tradition, reason and experience must find their places within the world narrated by the New Testament witnesses'.[8]

Others again present themselves as postliberals in order to defend conservative religious positions. Arguing that religion, like the feminine and the economically oppressed, is one of the margin-alized elements of secular modernity which can be reaffirmed in the postmodern world, they conclude that believers can appeal beyond secular reason, for example to the prophetic and mystical.[9] Once it is accepted that there is no neutral rationality with which to judge between traditions, a commitment to Christianity is as justified as any other.[10] Thus Hunsinger argues for Barthianism, claiming to do so from a postliberal position.[11] However, postliberalism is usually understood as a position which rejects metanarratives and universalizing truth claims; it only affirms Christianity to the extent that one can dip into it while also dipping into other traditions. What underpins these conservative defences of Christianity is not the eclecticism and relativism which characterizes postliberalism, but simply the appeal to incommensurability. I think it is better to interpret these positions as premodernist.

The argument, then, is that we must reject metanarratives. Because there is no objectively true universal system of rationality with the authority to judge between competing traditions, they are incommensurable with each other. Nobody has a detached observer's stance, outside all traditions, from which they can legitimately judge that one tradition is better or more rational than another. Instead, everybody lives within a tradition. The only tools we have for reflecting on reality and reason are the ones provided by our own tradition, so we inevitably understand reality and rationality in the way our tradition describes them.

Two things follow. Firstly, because there is no universal system of rationality, there is no neutral vantage point from which one can rationally judge which tradition to choose. To choose to belong to one tradition rather than another must therefore be a non-rational choice, whether the tradition chosen is a religious one or not. Christian conservatives can therefore argue that to make a non-rational choice to become a Christian, live within the Christian thought world and perceive the whole of reality from the perspective of Christian doctrine and worship, is as legitimate as any other choice.

Secondly, because each system of rationality is internal to a particular tradition, it is inevitable that what makes sense from the perspective of one tradition does not make sense from another. Members of one tradition, with their patterns of observing, understanding and deducing formed by that tradition, cannot really understand the accounts of reality produced by other traditions. The only people who can understand a particular religious tradition are its committed members.[12] Rational dialogue between believers and unbelievers is impossible, so Christians and non-Christians cannot convert each other by rational means.[13]

The fundamentalism described in the last chapter makes demands on believers which cannot be justified in the terms of modern secular rationality. In this sense it pushes in the direction of incommensurability. It is not surprising, therefore, that incommensurabilist theories appeared in religion before the discourse of postmodernism developed.

An early account is the neo-Calvinism developed at the end of the nineteenth century by Abraham Kuyper and others. Kuyper was writing at the same time as Warfield but rejected his empiricist approach. He argued that worldviews and presuppositions are more basic than facts and propositions, and presuppositions are affected by the presence or absence of the regenerating work of the Holy Spirit. Faith, therefore, has the power to determine how one perceives evidence: not only theology, but also natural science, rests on faith. Belief and unbelief, therefore, each has its own scientific system, with its own faith.

Kuyper therefore argued for a sharper distinction between the regenerate and the unregenerate. The constitution of the unregenerate is damaged by sin, which causes a 'darkening of our consciousness' and an estrangement from the cosmos, though it does not remove the ability to think logically. The regenerate have different presuppositions and therefore a different world-view. Because the two systems of thought are so different there is no common understanding to which Christians can appeal in presenting evidence or constructing arguments in favour of belief. Rational argument cannot vindicate Christianity; the fundamental principle of one's life-system can only be changed by God.[14]

This theology has had immense influence on conservative evangelicals, including many fundamentalists. However as the logic of fundamentalism is very different, tensions arise. Harris' study of Campus Crusade in the USA illustrates what happens when the systems are combined. With its background in fundamentalism Campus Crusade challenged hearers to recognize the evidence in support of its claims for the Bible. On the other hand, if there is no common rationality between true evangelical Christians and non-Christians, there should be little point in trying to convince people of the truth of Christianity. The result was a mixture of contradictory ideas. Evangelists were trained to offer rational defences of Christianity, but they were also taught that whether they were successful would depend on other factors: 'No one is won into the Kingdom of God by being beaten in an argument'.[15] They should pray for God to give the speaker the right words, cause suitable people to attend and prepare their hearts. Personal testimonies of conversions emphasized the role of religious experience rather than evidence and argumentation. This led to an emphasis on preparing conditions for individuals to have emotional experiences which could then be interpreted as conversion experiences. Practices of this type remain popular today; much evangelical preaching and charismatic worship is described, by supporters and critics alike, as designed to produce such an experience. Supporters may see the process as the proper means of evangelism while critics condemn it as emotional manipulation.[16] In effect fundamentalist theory legitimated the attempt to convert unbelievers rationally while the theory of incommensurability legitimated the wide variety of non-rational activities.

Karl Barth's immensely influential theology has also been described by many scholars as incommensurabilist. Barth initially reacted against his teachers, especially Harnack, when they supported German imperialism in the First World War. It seemed to him that they were virtually identifying Christianity with contemporary German society; against them, he emphasized the difference between God's Word and German 'culture Christianity'. He continued to press the point between the wars when the German emphasis on the spirit of nation, people and land, as though they were the epitome of Christianity, paved the way to Nazism. He therefore argued that contemporary culture cannot teach us anything about true Christianity. He was at his most radical in the early part of his career. Later he modified his position, but his earlier writings have remained far more influential and it is these with which I am concerned here.[17]

Barth proposed to reject all rational arguments for Christianity. Arguments use the thought-forms of their own society and to use them in defence of faith, he believed, makes human reason a higher authority than revelation.[18] Non-Christian philosophy, he believed, was 'the classical point for the invasion of alien powers, the injection of metaphysical systems which are secretly in conflict with the Bible and the church'.[19] Instead he insisted that God is totally *other*: altogether unlike us and beyond our powers of understanding.[20] In order to relate to God at all we depend entirely on a divine act of self-revelation through the Word. Our minds cannot understand God, but God's truth 'always throws a bridge over a crevasse'. It is 'the light shining out of darkness', always a miracle.[21] He emphasized that revelation cannot be justified on the basis of something else; to do so would imply that there is a higher authority. On the contrary God's revelation is

a court from which there can be no possible appeal to a higher court. Its reality and truth do not rest on a superior reality and truth. They do not have to be actualized or validated as reality from this or any other point. They are not measured by the reality and truth found at this other point. They are not to be compared with any such nor judged and understood as reality and truth by reference to such. On the contrary, God's revelation has its reality and truth wholly and in every respect... within itself.[22]

Natural theology, he argued, works the wrong way round. It proceeds by beginning with ourselves and from there seeking to understand Jesus. Instead we should come to understand ourselves on the basis of understanding Jesus.[23]

The supremacy of God's Word was a major theme. Barth criticized liberal scholars for presupposing the modern scientific world-view and judging the Bible on that basis. Once a doctrine is understood in its cultural setting, he complained, it always seems possible to find it no longer relevant. The nineteenth century 'quest of the historical Jesus' had made faith depend on the results of historical investigation. When we read in the Bible about things like miracles which do not fit the presuppositions of modern science, liberals allow modern beliefs to judge the Bible. It should be the other way round; the Bible should pass judgement on modern culture.[24]

Barth's theology has been subjected to a great deal of criticism, including some from Barth himself in his later years. Calvin and Warfield argued that by reading the Bible we can see for ourselves that it is authoritative: Barth did not allow human reason even this role, leaving us with no way of knowing that it *is* revelation. To use postmodern terminology, therefore, his account is one in which accepting God's Word is incommensurable with rejecting it; before we accept it, it would appear, we have no way of judging whether there is any divine revelation, let alone whether it is to be found in the Bible, the Qur'an or any other document.

Barth believed that the Word of God is revealed in the Bible but did not equate it with the Bible, denying that he was a fundamentalist. His theology makes selections from it. Critical scholars also select, but explain the basis and reasons for their selections. Barth did not provide such reasons; instead he presented his theory as *the* Christian revelation. Critics reply that rather than describing God's Word, at best he has only provided his own version of it.[25]

A practical illustration of his incommensurabilist position is a conversation he is reported to have had in 1935. He told an Indian Christian, D T Niles, that 'other religions are just unbelief'. Niles asked him how many Hindus he had met, and he replied 'Not one'. Niles then asked 'How then do you know that Hinduism is unbelief?' Barth replied '*A priori!*' The answer accurately expresses Barth's position, together with its weakness. The idea that non-Christian religions are unbelief was the logical conclusion to his theory, a deduction which he made without taking account of real non-Christians and what they in fact believe.[26] Conversely, to recognize Hindus as believers would be to reject his theory.

This determination to reject all natural theology and argue that true Christian belief is completely different from, and incommensurable with, all other beliefs, remains common among Barth's disciples today. An example is an argument by Tim Gorringe, who describes natural theology as 'a prime example of the truth of Marx's dictum that the ruling ideas of any age are always those of its ruling class, so that what is "natural" turns out to be the values which guarantee the *status quo*'. To illustrate his point he attributes the oppression in Nazi Germany and Apartheid South Africa to natural theology which, he tells us, 'begins from the perceived fact that we are not all equal, and builds on this'. Against this, he argues, 'beginning from revelation, which is to say from Christ, we understand all human beings as equal, as sisters and brothers of the Son of Man, sharing with him the image of God'.[27]

This argument illustrates the Barthian approach, but also its weaknesses. First let us consider his illustrations. Afrikaaner racism was strongly influenced by the experiences of the early settlers and accentuated by the Great Trek. The Dutch Reformed Church had forbidden its ministers to take part, so the Trekkers were led by devout lay Calvinists. They took with them their family bibles, and had little else to read. As de Gruchy describes it,

> The theological interpreters of the events that were to shape Afrikaaner tradition indelibly were not trained by the Dutch or Scottish faculties of Calvinist theology, but by their own experience and their reading of the sacred book. As they journeyed, the pages came alive with meaning and relevance. The exodus of the people of Israel and their testing in the wilderness were happening again. Any obstacle along the way to the promised land had to be overcome, by sheer grit and by the gun. Any doubt of divine providence was not only unthinkable, but blasphemy, a harbinger of disaster.[28]

This is as good an example as one can find of a society which was so cut off from other societies that their patterns of thought, and interpretations of their own situation, were heavily influenced by their reading of the Bible. If any community was well placed to turn its back on natural theology and base its way of life on the Bible, it was this one. Surrounded by potential enemies, they read the passages in the Old Testament where God commanded the Israelites to kill their enemies and conquer the land, and they believed God was calling them to do the same. They were every bit as committed to divine revelation through the Bible as Gorringe could have wished them to be. Gorringe's argument here is not in fact an attack on natural theology at all; it is one more example of one conservative tradition accusing another of being liberal because it interprets the Bible in a different way.

By contrast early twentieth century German society had a wide range of intellectual resources available to it, and it is impossible to rule out influence by any one of them. Barth accused Harnack and the theologians of his day of being influenced by German imperialism and in turn contributing to it. Students of the rise of Nazism, however, tend to attribute the development of its ideas to very different sources;[29] if any one person's ideas dominated it must surely be Nietzsche who was altogether opposed to Christianity.

Secondly, Gorringe equates Barth's critique with that of Marx. However it was Barth, not Marx, who was determined to distinguish between natural and revealed theology; the object of Marx's critique was religion in general. It is no doubt often true that the dominant ideas in a society are those of its ruling class, and that the ruling class draws on the ideologies of the dominant religion; but to the extent that this is true it vindicates Marx's argument, not Barth's. To justify his position Gorringe would have to show that the ruling classes derive their values from natural theology but not from revealed theology.

It is certainly true that many leading scientists in the late nineteenth and early twentieth centuries applied the theory of evolution in such a way as to conclude that white Europeans had progressed further than other human races and could therefore benefit those other races by ruling them. It is also true that liberals were more willing than conservatives to accept the theories of contemporary scientists, including evolution. At the time, therefore, it was possible to believe that rule by a superior race would benefit Africans. However the only connection with natural theology was that natural theology made it possible to speculate about the matter, whereas conservatives were more inclined to reject contemporary science altogether.

Thirdly, Gorringe illustrates natural theology with the argument that inequalities exist and therefore must be God's will. Such an argument would indeed be an example of natural theology; but it is such bad natural theology that it can hardly represent its type. Applied consistently it could describe anything at all as God's will, provided only that it has happened. No natural theologian argues in this way. Occasionally the idea appears; in the British debate on fox hunting in the early 2000s, for example, some argued that hunting is natural and therefore morally acceptable, but they were not influential.

Finally, Gorringe's revelation-based argument for equality has precious little historical justification. The biblical themes of the image of God and the brotherhood of Christ can indeed be used as arguments for equality, but they have not been so used until recently. Here Gorringe's argument, like Barth's, is hampered by an over-simple classification of all ideas into two types: everything is either revealed by God or comes under the heading of natural theology. With a classification like this it is inevitable that they describe every religious idea they disagree with as natural theology. It would be more realistic to suspect that both Gorringe's disapproval of Apartheid and Nazism, and his commitment to equality, owe a great deal to natural theology. Prior to the Enlightenment the only universal human equality which most church leaders taught was equality in a sinfulness which deserved eternal damnation; it was the inequalities, between the righteous and the unrighteous and between the saved and the damned, to which preachers drew attention. Modern concepts of equality have their conceptual roots in both the enthusiasm of the Reformation era and Enlightenment natural law theory. These two movements were so closely related to each other that it would be impossible to untangle them and conclude that the views we hold today derive from one but not the other.

This is characteristic of the way traditions develop. Christian interpretations of the biblical tradition are too closely intertwined with natural theology for the ideas we hold today to be labelled as deriving from one but not the other. Conversely secular political theory with its commitment to human rights and equalities is indebted not only to Enlightenment reason but also to its Christian inheritance. This is as coherentism would expect. We often find it helpful to divide what we think we know into different categories for different purposes, but if they all contribute to a unified account of knowledge we should expect the categories to have fuzzy edges. Just as the biblical authors often appealed to natural theology, so do Christians today - even when they intend not to.

Kuyper and Barth were writing before the development of postmodernist theory. The claim that we have to choose non-rationally between a variety of incommensurable traditions, each with its own rationality, had not yet been developed. They were working with the concept of only two options, true Christianity on the one hand and unbelief on the other. In both cases versions of Christianity which did not fit their theory were treated as tantamount to unbelief. Because they rejected the existence of an overarching system of reason within which one could argue for or against Christianity, they both treated becoming a Christian as a nonrational decision. In this sense they were, in the language of postmodernism, incommensurabilists.

More recently, and from a very different Christian tradition, comes John Milbank's self-consciously postmodernist defence of incommensurability in his influential *Theology and Social Theory* (1990).[30] Milbank complains that MacIntyre's account of traditions described above 'tries to demonstrate, from a detached point of view, that tradition-governed inquiry *in general* is rational, and makes objective progress', whereas for Milbank 'the only possible response to nihilism is to affirm one's allegiance to a particular tradition, and derive an ontology from the implicit assumptions of its narrative forms.'[31] While MacIntyre seeks to replace modern liberalism with a return to ancient virtue, Milbank proposes to replace it with Christianity.[32] It is central to his case that the claims of Christianity are not to be explained or justified on the basis of something else which is more foundational.[33] The Christian worldview is itself foundational and interprets all else: 'A certain history, culminating at a certain point, and continued in the practice of the Church, interprets and "locates" all other history. It "reads" all other history as most fundamentally anticipation, or sinful refusal of, salvation.'[34]

Milbank does occasionally make objective claims for Christianity: that it is distinctive in supernaturalizing 'the good';[35] and that, far from being 'merely one more perspective', it is uniquely different.[36] More generally, however, he sticks to his principle of incommensurability, so that there are no good reasons for changing from one tradition to another. Criticizing MacIntyre for trying to argue against secular reason, he claims that secular reason 'is only a *mythos,* and therefore cannot be refuted, but only out-narrated, if we can *persuade* people - for reasons of "literary taste" - that Christianity offers a much better story'.[37] Thus he recommends the doctrine of the Incarnation because of the 'inherent attractiveness of the picture of God thence provided'.[38]

Narrative and rhetoric replace argument. He believes this is characteristic of earlier Christian tradition: 'The Fathers and the scholastics understood the beliefs grounding their ethics as matters of persuasion, or of faith. These positions of faith could not be dialectically inferred or called into question but were, rather, "rhetorically" instilled'.[39] Explanation, and even understanding, are he believes aspects of the modern secular reason which he proposes to replace with 'the single mode of narrative knowledge'.[40] Since 'textuality is the condition of all culture', narrating is more basic than explaining or understanding. So 'to understand or to explain a social phenomenon is simply to narrate it'.[41]

In these ways a diverse range of theologians make claims for incommensurability. Christianity, as they describe it, makes sense within Christian rationality but not within non-Christian rationality; and as there is no overarching rationality, no metanarrative which can judge between Christianity and its alternatives, the decision to accept or reject Christianity cannot be a rational one. Kuyper, Barth and conservative Christian postmodernists urge their adherents to accept, non-rationally, their own narrative as a complete, coherent and authoritative account of reality with its own system of rationality. They know it conflicts with the dominant secular account of reality, and they respond by denying that there is any neutral vantage point from which one can judge the secular narrative superior to the Christian one.

The need for metanarratives

I shall respond to these arguments from the perspective of a coherentist liberalism, as described in Chapter 5, which believes that we need both metanarratives and commensurability, even though our accounts of them are never perfect.

Metanarratives provide societies with a framework for understanding the relationship between its different aspects, and judging what moral norms are appropriate for engaging with them. Characteristically, as we grow up we ask where we ourselves and our families come from before we ask where our city or country comes from, and only later still do we ask where the world comes from. As our horizons broaden and we engage with a wider range of people and things, we need broader frameworks within which to reflect on how we relate to them and how we ought to behave towards them. A century ago, for example, most of our weekly shopping would be accountable in terms of local explanations: the butter came from the farm in the next village, the vegetables from the field the other side of the river, we do not buy from Mr Mitchell because we disapprove of his lifestyle. Now, in the global economy, the equivalent account is on a planetary scale: food is grown in one country, packaged in another using tin from a third, and flown from continent to continent in aeroplanes created in others again. The equivalent to not buying from Mr Mitchell is an immensely complicated analysis of fair trade, conditions of employment, air miles and much else, which we can only understand in the simplified form of statistics provided by specialists. In general, local narratives provide adequate explanations for issues which are contained within the local, but global issues need global narratives.

Metanarratives are needed not only to explain relationships but also to set the terms for moral judgements. One reason for rejecting metanarratives is that they impose universal moral rules on all people; if there are only local narratives, what is wrong in one place may not be wrong in another. However to argue against metanarratives for this reason is to confuse two separate issues. It is indeed the case that in the absence of metanarratives one would not expect the same moral rules to apply to everybody. However if there is a true metanarrative with an overarching account of morality, it does not necessarily stipulate that the same actions are right or wrong for all people. It is possible to argue that homosexuality or abortion is immoral for all people at all times, and as this is a universalizing claim it must presuppose a metanarrative; but it is also possible to believe, from the perspective of a different metanarrative which affirms diversity more strongly, that these actions are permissible in some situations but not in others, or that it is a universal truth that these judgements can only be made within the context of each particular situation. Conclusions like these are just as compatible with metanarratives.

Local narratives affirm the existence of different 'local' moral authorities, each of which can only provide a limited account of right and wrong. This leads to two questions. One is: on what ground do I accept its authority? What legitimates the account of right and wrong which I have accepted? The other is: when two moral authorities conflict, how do we decide which to accept? Any authoritative answer to either of these questions must appeal to objective standards and therefore a metanarrative. For example, I noted above that postmodernists who consider themselves oppressed often describe their society's moral standards as merely the interests of the ruling classes; they argue instead that their own standards are equally valid. This argument is so weak as to be self-defeating. As Stephen Clark observes, those who reject objective standards can indeed claim that the stance of the oppressed is valid, but 'those already in authority (with access to more power) will be delighted to support that claim, since their opponents will have thrown away the one best tool of revolution: the appeal to something of more weight than they'.[42]

The story of how societies have recognized the need for universal moral norms is the history of natural law. Its earliest European expression is often taken to be Sophocles' *Antigone*, which explores whether there is a higher moral obligation than the obligation to obey the ruler of the state. More recent expressions are the natural rights asserted by the eighteenth century American and French revolutionaries and the Universal Declaration of Human Rights of 1948. This tradition of natural law, with its nation-transcending universal norms, legitimates international authorities like the United Nations and provides agreed frameworks for resolving international conflicts.

The postmodernist theologians who appeal to incommensurability to justify Christianity are accustomed to a society in which the dominant metanarrative is secular. They therefore welcome the attack on metanarratives in general in order to establish a legitimate place for religion. This leaves us with the impression that we have only two options: on the one hand a true metanarrative which must be secular, and on the other a variety of local narratives with a finger vigorously pointing - non-rationally - to the Christian one. It is an unsatisfactory position. Firstly, as Reader observes, it is self-contradictory to argue for Christianity as a tradition with its own distinct rationality, by appealing to postmodern arguments which are themselves external to the Christian tradition.[43] Secondly if, as postmodernists argue, there is no neutral rationality, and therefore to choose Christianity or any of its alternatives is simply a matter of taste, then there is no case for commitment; the appropriate response is to settle for the uncommitted postmodern lifestyle, dipping into Christianity, Buddhism and Tarot cards according to circumstances or as the mood takes us but withholding any long-term commitment.

The irony of this situation is that the secular metanarrative against which postmodernist theologians are reacting is historically a descendant of biblical monotheism, albeit with God taken out. Many accounts of ancient polytheism accounted for the nature of reality and ethics by appeal to a variety of gods in conflict with each other, thereby providing a conceptual framework for incommensurability: whether a piece of land belonged to this tribe or that, and whether a particular activity was to be encouraged or condemned, depended on which god one worshipped. The ancient Hebrew scriptures, in the editions which have come down to us, affirm monotheism at the expense of polytheism and thereby present a metanarrative in which there are supreme objective standards. They offer truths about reality and ethics which are established by a single, omnipotent, omniscient and good God who has made the universe accordingly. The purpose of our creation is *shalom*, a word which encompasses peace, harmony and well-being. There is therefore an underlying unity and harmony of reality. One implication is that all people should be able to live together in harmony provided we accept limits to our freedom, and these limits are to be discovered rather than invented. This is a metanarrative; it not only asserts the existence of universal objective truths about reality, reason and ethics, but also defends their authority by explaining their origin as intrinsic to the way the universe has been made.[44]

The dominant forms of early Christianity retained this perspective. To the conviction that the whole world was made by one God with one purpose they added that Jesus is the Lord not only of a small religious movement but of the whole world. Viewing the world like this naturally led to other universalizing claims like the essential unity of the human race. This perspective continued into medieval thought: Jews, Christians and Moslems alike believed in a supreme God in whose mind complete knowledge and goodness resided. No one human had a God's eye view of reality-as-a-whole; but God did, and this justified the conviction that although we cannot see for ourselves that truth and goodness are self-consistent realities in harmony with each other, they are. The faithful, while unable to attain a God's eye view, could approximate to it not only through reason and learning but also through prayer and meditation.

In time, however, the Christian appeal to a single metanarrative rooted in a God's eye view broke down under the pressure of competing versions and was succeeded by a reason-based alternative. It was only very gradually that this successor dispensed with God, and therefore with that God's eye view which guaranteed the unity of reality. If the only understandings of reality are human understandings, whether or not a unified view of reality is both possible and true becomes a matter of uncertainty. Perhaps there is no self-consistent account of reality; perhaps there is no set of moral norms which would enable us to live together in harmony. When, therefore, postmodern conservative Christians attempt to defend their faith tradition by rejecting metanarratives, the best they can do is to salvage some elements of Christianity at the expense of at least one of its major themes.

If we really were faced with competing incommensurable traditions it is difficult to see how we could avoid a return to the conflicts of the Reformation era. We would, after all, be back to a situation where contrasting accounts of reality were asserted against each other in the absence of any rational way to resolve the disagreements. This would mean, for example, that there was no way to resolve the current debate about homosexuality. The only possible conclusion would be to follow Milbank's advice and simply grant victory to whichever orators can 'out-narrate' their opponents; but if this is the only criterion for success there is no reason to suppose that any agreement will last beyond the next airing of the debate.

However there are good reasons for suspecting that this is by no means the case. Here I note four. Firstly, as MacIntyre notes, treating church doctrines as incommensurable with other rationalities makes them essentially conservative because each one is unalterable.[45] In practice, however, every religious tradition generates internal reflection and debate; if it did not, all its members would hold identical views. In practice the only members of a religious tradition who accept all its doctrines without question are the ones who are not interested in them.

Others spot inconsistencies or introduce ideas from outside it. Most of us adapt our faith commitments in the light of new information. We describe ourselves as belonging to a particular tradition while at the same time disagreeing with some elements of it. Paul Murray comments: 'As a glance around the congregation in any large urban parish church reveals, questions as to whether the Church should be open to the world, and if so how, are made somewhat irrelevant by the realisation that the world in all its diversity is already present within the Church'.[46] Most doctrines are better explained inductively, as the best available theory, rather than deductively as the only possible conclusion from foundationalist first principles.

Secondly, members of a tradition do find it possible to explain its worldview to others to a greater or lesser extent. When Milbank claimed that the early Christian theologians and the medieval scholastics had promoted Christianity only through rhetoric, without using reason, he misdescribed them; although they often used rhetoric, they also used the rational tools available to them. Liberals argue that although things do look different from different standpoints, they are not so different that dialogue is difficult or impossible.

Thirdly, Christianity is not an all-encompassing tradition. Central to the incommensurability thesis is sharp dividing lines between one tradition and another; as we have seen, according to the theory one is either within a tradition and committed to it or outside it and unable to understand it. However postmodernist theologians are often unclear about what constitutes a tradition. Kuyper, Barth and Milbank all argued that there is one Christian tradition, incommensurable with alternatives, but each provided his own account of it. If Christianity can be described in these different ways it would appear that it does not have sharp boundaries so well established as to justify the incommensurability claim. To add to the uncertainty, other postmodernists like Lindbeck describe Christianity as containing a number of contrasting traditions, each incommensurable with the others.[47] Just as the idea of a sharp distinction between clear and unclear biblical statements suited the Great Tew theologians and the Latitudinarians, but only because nobody produced lists of the clear and unclear texts, so also the idea of a single self-consistent Christian tradition incommensurable with other traditions only seems convincing as long as postmodernists do not attempt to agree on a definition of this incommensurable Christianity. In practice whether we count Christianity as one tradition or many, and whether we set its boundaries where Kuyper, Barth, or Milbank proposes, it will remain the case that every Christian holds beliefs and presuppositions which come from elsewhere; otherwise, for example, they would be unable to use any new technology. Indeed, no tradition at all is so all-encompassing as to provide its members with *all* their presuppositions and perspectives. Traditions always have fuzzy edges, and this makes it possible to belong to more than one at a time.

Fourthly, not only Christianity but all its denominations do over time change their practices and doctrines. Some expend a great deal of effort on denying that they change, but historians are well aware that they do. Outside religious discourse this is well known. For example, when Tony Blair became leader of the UK Labour Party in 1994 he proposed to repeal Clause Four of the party's constitution. His opponents could have insisted that since he did not agree with the constitution he should not be a member of the party at all. They did not take this line. They knew it would have smacked of pedantry. We live in an age of countless organizations, each with its own constitution and founding principles. Most people, when they they feel inclined to join one, do not read all its foundational documents and check that they can assent to every item; on the contrary, most people are willing to join an organization when they agree with its main thrust even though they may disagree with some of its principles. The fact that they do join makes it possible for the organization to change with the times and survive.

I suggest that a more realistic account of commensurability is that it varies along a spectrum. Some of our rational processes, and the things we believe, are only shared by our compatriots or the members of our religious denomination. Others are shared across the continent in which we live, but not by most people at the far side of the world. Others again are shared by all societies in the world. The variation in rationalities and beliefs depends on a number of factors, only one of which is the tradition of rationality in which we have been brought up. Others include personality and experience. We can communicate to varying extents with people from radically different traditions, and more easily on some matters than others. The idea that we cannot communicate at all across traditions is more of a deduction from a postmodernist theory than an observation of what happens in normal life.

If, as I have argued, we need a metanarrative, it does not need to be of the kind which forbids mention of the divine in its accounts of reality. A 'complete' metanarrative would perhaps provide a framework within which it was possible to develop theories to account for everything that exists and all ethical norms. Every metanarrative humanity devises, however, has its limitations and thereby hides some aspects of reality from view. One of the limits of secular modernity's metanarrative is its rule that all language of the divine is to be irrelevant outside the distinctive social phenomenon of religion. We have seen why this rule was imposed, and in practice it is unlikely to be lifted as long as there remain influential groups of religious foundationalists, like opponents of evolution or homosexuality, determined to impose their views on others on the ground that they know the truth with a certainty which trumps what other people believe.

A better metanarrative would provide a framework for relating secular culture, science, institutional religion and the search for spiritual understanding to each other in such a way that they do not conflict with each other. For many centuries the physical and spiritual aspects of reality have been split apart, each allocated their own realm and their own rationality. Our metanarrative needs to bring them back together so that both contribute to a unified search for truth. Equally important, it needs to accept the limits to human knowledge and be humble enough to adapt in response to new insights.

CHAPTER 9

CONSERVATIVES AND THE

FOUNDATIONS OF CERTAINTY

Over the course of nearly two thousand years what Christianity stands for has varied immensely. There were different traditions from the start. In the Bible and the early church defenders of particular points of view would appeal to divine revelation and natural reason without any sense that the two were in opposition to each other. By doing this they reflected the normal pattern; ancient and medieval societies developed their understanding of reality in a unified way using theories about God and empirical observations of the world to inform each other without recognizing any theoretical problem in doing so.

About halfway through Christian history, however, a pattern began to develop in which reason and faith favoured opposite sides in a succession of debates. The question of how they relate to each other became a problem. To solve it, a theory developed that they *ought* to be kept separate from each other. Once the two had been split apart and each given its respective function, the nature of both faith and reason changed. The Reformation and Counter-Reformation accentuated the claims of reason-free faith and early modern scientists accentuated the claims of faith-free reason.

It was possible to avoid the polarization, and I have shown how the Church of England did. 'Classical Anglicanism' flourished from the second half of the seventeenth century until around the middle of the nineteenth. By this time the separation of the physical and spiritual realms seemed to many to be heading for a complete victory for secular science and the refutation of all religious belief. Anxious defenders of Christianity wanted more assertive claims for religious certainties, and reverted to the more extreme positions of the Reformation and Counter-Reformation. They could not, however, turn the clock back. Science had revealed its potential; to reject it was no longer a constructive contribution to society's search for knowledge, more a defiant reaction against it.

I have described three forms which this reaction has taken. Most institutional churches have functioned within a dualist theory of reality, more or less restricting religion to non-physical matters. Others have retained a unified account of reality while giving the Bible precedence over scientific research, especially in the USA. Others again have opted for postmodern and non-realist theories which deny that there can be a coherent public account of reality at all.

Christianity thus continues to vary widely. Any attempt to classify its different versions is bound to obscure more than it reveals, but I hope the classification I have offered will be of some service in understanding the present polarization between conservatives and liberals. Many churchgoers describe themselves as conservatives or liberals with reference only to personal experience or specific issues, and may be conservatives on one issue but liberals on another. Others describe themselves as conservatives or liberals for social, political or economic reasons. The concern of this book is with the background to current church debates, so the conservatism and liberalism I am interested in is *specifically* religious (concerned with religious rather than political or economic issues) and *generally* religious (concerned with general understandings of why we hold the religious beliefs we do, rather than the views we hold on specific issues). Often the distinction is unclear; many churchgoers, for example, oppose homosexuality without thinking through whether they do so for specifically religious reasons or only because they belong to a society which disapproves of it. Nevertheless the current polarization reveals a radical difference of approach to questions of religious truth, a difference which despite fuzzy dividing lines is remarkably consistent across the range of western Christian versions of conservatism and liberalism.

People who describe themselves as conservatives in this sense generally understand their faith in terms derived from the nineteenth century reactions. This is not to say that their beliefs are no older or newer than the nineteenth century; on the contrary, those traditions themselves borrow from earlier traditions and continue to develop today. Nevertheless, their characteristic approach to religion expresses what those reactions were concerned to establish. They all express a reaction against a secular society which they see as fundamentally anti-Christian. Some reactions are strongly counter-cultural, others less so; but they agree with each other in expecting to find contrasts between Christian values and the dominant values of their society. While liberals accuse them of selecting homosexuality as the issue of the day because it is most likely to unite evangelicals who are usually too fissiparous, conservatives accuse liberals of only supporting homosexuals because they blow with the wind, accepting the norms of contemporary society instead of upholding Christian teaching.

Nearly all counter-cultural conservatives accept the chief features of modern society. Other counter-cultural movements may inspire people to make dramatic sacrifices - to live self-sufficient lifestyles on smallholdings or refuse to pay their taxes and go to prison for it - but religious conservatives usually bear no programme for radical social change. They do not lead the campaigns against economic globalization, poverty or climate change. They drive cars, fly in aeroplanes and play the lottery or the stock market just like non-Christians of their own social and economic class. Their religious convictions produce a disapproval of society restricted to selected features only. When secular society rejects their truth claims, this counts as evidence that secular modernity simply does not have the tools to accept their distinctively Christian insights. It reinforces the belief that Christianity runs counter to all natural human reasoning. It therefore encourages them in the conviction that conservative Christians alone hold a trump card - revelation - which enables them to perceive reality in a way which is not available to secular society.

Revelation *overrides* natural human ways of knowing things. It leads to a sympathy for dogmas, truth claims which cannot be defended or justified by empirical or rational examination but are presented as divine gifts to be accepted just as they are.

People who call themselves liberals - in the sense I have described - generally understand their faith in terms derived from the Enlightenment and contemporary secular thought. Again this is not to deny that their views have roots in older traditions, but it is the approaches described in Chapters 4 and 5 which characterize their thought. Their understanding of knowledge and reality is more in tune with their host society. Even if they oppose the prevailing political and economic structures, as they often do, they respect society's reasoning processes and knowledge claims and use them to argue their case. Conservatives accuse them of thereby abandoning Christian standards. Liberals reply that conservatives themselves do not defend every biblical command; they ignore most, and select for attention a few which in reality express the dominant concerns of a passing generation. Liberals are therefore more sympathetic to natural theology. Truth in matters of religion, as in all else, comes through processes which are generally available to all humans, whatever their religious tradition. They are suspicious of claims to special divine revelation and intervention: the Bible, the church's tradition, stories of miracles and individual claims to divine guidance all need to be examined by the community through its normal processes of judgement before being accepted.

The root difference between the two, then, derives from their different sources of information: on the one hand information which comes directly from God and is received and accepted by a limited number of people, and on the other the wide range of processes which are available to human beings in general: the five senses, logic, memory, imagination, intuition, instinct, a sense of the presence of God and whatever else they may consider a potential means to understanding.

Underlying the debates, then, is the question of how we know things. Can we humans gain true knowledge about the nature of reality by reason? The extreme answers do not characterize either liberals or conservatives. Positivists and enthusiasts for new technology often answer with an unqualified yes. I described this answer in Chapter 4. Its weakness is that it has no way to justify its claims for reason without presupposing reason's reliability in the first place. Before Hume it was given theological justification: at its simplest, a good God would not deceive. Once the appeal to God is rejected all that is left is a circular argument: our reason is reliable because our reason says so. At the opposite extreme is non-realism: we have no justification for presuming that human reason can access the nature of reality at all so perhaps reality, as we perceive it, is just the way our minds classify their experiences.

Leaving aside these extremes, more moderate answers state that reason does give us access to reality, but it is limited. How, then, do we distinguish between the things we do know and the things we do not? Older, theological answers offer reasons why the gods have given us some powers but not others. According to ancient Hebrew monotheism, the universe and human minds have been designed according to a benign plan to match each other. We do not need complete knowledge of the universe, but we do need some knowledge. This would lead us to expect that our minds have been designed (perhaps through evolution) to know what we need to know. An alternative theological view is that human reason cannot discover the nature of reality, at least in matters of religion if not more generally. However some people are given insights from a divine source. On this account there are two important contrasts. One is between the things we know through reason and the things we know through revelation. The other is between the people who have received revelation and the people who have not.

The debate between religious conservatives and liberals expresses the difference between these two theories about how we know things. Both provide an explanation of our knowledge, and also of our ignorance and errors. Both acknowledge a variety of apparent sources of information; but while one tells us they are all capable of both providing information and misleading us, the other advises us to distinguish between the sources and always give priority to the one which is directly guaranteed by God. This is the difference underlying the current debates within the churches. It is also the difference between religious foundationalism and coherentism.

For the remainder of this chapter, therefore, I shall summarize religious foundationalism and explain why I find it unsatisfactory. In the final chapter I shall describe the coherentist alternative. In practice most Christians do not analyze the philosophical bases of their beliefs and, rather than consistently appealing to one or the other, mix the two - often because they want to reach conservative conclusions on one issue and liberal ones on another. To clarify the issues I shall first describe strict foundationalism, as it is expressed when it is most consistent and permits no compromise. It produces the most extreme positions. It will then become easier to assess more moderate positions.

Foundationalism is based on two principles, a truth which is known with certainty and deductive logic which derives other certainties from it. In religious foundationalism, religious truth (for dualists) or truth on all matters (for non-dualist fundamentalists) is to be accepted from divine revelation. Predominantly, for Christians, this means the Bible. Divine revelation transcends reason, cannot be judged by it, and is therefore to be accepted even if it contradicts it. Revelation, once known, is known with certainty. The only role for human reason is to deduce one certainty from another. From the perspective of someone who knows a revelation with certainty, a person who disagrees with it must certainly be wrong. Foundationalism therefore paints knowledge in black and white: on every relevant question there is a right answer, and each person either knows it or is ignorant of it.

To allow that there may be more revelations yet to come would be to deny the completeness of the revelation already available and throw the onus onto human reason to judge whether a new idea is indeed a revelation. Foundationalism therefore expects that the only new insights possible are deductions from revelation which earlier generations might have made but did not; as such they are not really innovations at all. Revelation, then, is inherited from the past and eternally valid. For the same reason foundationalism denies that Christians can learn anything of value from other sources of information such as non-Christian faiths; to allow for the possibility would be, again, to treat the Christian revelation as incomplete. It follows that there is no value in seeking to learn from other sources, or in imaginative thinking. If the ethics of homosexuality is a moral issue for Christians, extra-biblical information such as psychological research into homosexual orientation cannot, as a matter of principle, have anything to contribute.

Divine revelation, therefore, is the supreme authority for all times and places. It provides statements of truth and moral commands which are universally and eternally infallible and cannot be repealed. Just as omitting one digit in a long mathematical equation would invalidate the whole equation, to doubt the truth of any one biblical text is to reject the whole foundationalist system. Within this perspective it makes sense to treat the Bible as a collection of facts. To the horror of liberals, conservatives often describe it, and treat it, as a rule book or instruction manual.[1] When faced with a problem one searches for a biblical passage describing how to solve it, and this may involve jumping from one part to another just as one would do with a car manual or computer help file. When one finds a solution one knows it with certainty.

Foundationalist churches transmit doctrine. As the only source of information is revelation, teaching is hierarchical - from the teacher who knows to the learners who listen. The local church may welcome attenders with contrasting beliefs, but positions of leadership need to be restricted to those who accept the church's teaching on all matters. To grant a leadership post to a person who disagrees with one element of revelation - for example, an unrepentant homosexual - would dilute the sense of certainty with which doctrines are taught and therefore undermine the very purpose of the church. By permitting one homosexual bishop they would tacitly permit other church members to be homosexuals. Worse still, by permitting differences of opinion about the biblical teaching on homosexuality they would tacitly permit differences of opinion on other revealed truths as well.

It follows that the group discussion is not a potential source of new truths, only a method for learning those already revealed. They should not invite church members to hear both sides of an argument and make up their own minds as that would be to exalt reason above Scripture. Since a new answer must be a wrong answer, there is no role for creativity. Discussion groups are planned so that they reach predetermined conclusions. The process of deducing one certainty from another does not allow for differences of opinion. If there are members who openly disagree with some elements of the church's teaching the initial response is to explain where they are in error. If they persist the only possible conclusion is that they are not true Christians. The local church must either exclude them altogether or publicly label them as unsound or liberal so as to warn other members not to follow their lead.

In this way foundationalists can deny that the true Christian community is divided over an ethical issue like gay bishops; instead they prefer to describe it as a division between Christians and non-Christians. The implication is that those who disagree with them are not true Christians at all. Conversely, those who in all conscience cannot agree with the views of their church's leaders find that they have no option but to leave. This is why the inheritors of the puritan tradition have such a record for sectarian splits: every disagreement has the potential to provoke one faction to leave the church and set up an alternative. It is a function of sharp boundaries. Every person either is, or is not, a true Christian. Every church either does, or does not, teach true Christianity. The local church service is the central occasion where members reaffirm their identity as Christians, their allegiance to the church and their sense of being different from non-Christians.

The greater the emphasis on being different from other people, the greater the need for evidence. Most of the time foundationalist Christians have lifestyles very similar to those of their neighbours, but it is difficult to retain over time an image of oneself as radically different from others unless there is some evidence for the difference. All through history sectarian groups have developed distinctive practices to mark themselves out from the rest of society. Peter Brown, for example, has shown how many of the early Christians developed sexual renunciation as their distinctive practice.[2] Some groups, like the Quakers, have distinguished themselves in costly ways which were also impressive witnesses for other reasons.

Others are less impressive. The cheapest, easiest way to make a claim to superiority is by condemning an activity which one has no wish to practice oneself. For a church's moral stance to perform this function it needs to position the dividing line where it does in fact separate members from non-members, while at the same time being justified by its doctrines. In the Introduction I mentioned the ethical campaigns by twentieth century religious foundationalists against alcohol, abortion and homosexuality. They fit this pattern well. Each campaign opposed a practice which western society as a whole was increasingly tolerating. Opposition to homosexuality has the advantage that most people do not, and never will, have any desire to practise it. For these people, condemning homosexuality is a cost-free way to present oneself as a strict upholder of moral standards. Those who suffer as a result are the homosexuals. They can be selected as scapegoats without much loss of membership.

This is religious foundationalism in its strict form. It is widely represented in many conservative churches, though other conservatives would consider it too extreme. Its rhetoric dominates the current debate in the Anglican Communion. I now turn to some theoretical and practical reasons why it does not provide an adequate account of religious belief.

Descartes' reason-based foundationalism proceeded by doubting everything, including the reliability of his mental processes, and treating as a first principle the one truth he could not doubt, namely 'I think, therefore I am'. This, he believed, was true with absolute certainty. Critics claim that it was a circular argument, as he could not prove it was certainly true without first presupposing that his rational powers were reliable. Religious foundationalism avoids this weakness by claiming that its first principles are established without any involvement by human reason. However it does so at a cost. If we cannot access divine information by any rational human processes, the question arises as to how we can access it at all.

The Gnostic myths described in Chapter 1 describe the situation well. On the one hand the information being provided is totally alien to everything the human mind can comprehend, but on the other there must be something within the human being which enables us to receive the message and recognize its truth. Their solution was to make a sharp distinction between the normal human soul and the spirit. The soul, created by the evil gods responsible for the physical world, is not able to perceive the true state of reality; the spirit, a spark of the supreme good God, can. Usually the spirit is asleep, or in a state of forgetfulness, but the Gnostic message awakens it. Here, then, is an explanation of why our normal reasoning cannot access knowledge which God wants us to have but a different faculty, usually dormant, can. It is however a polytheistic one.

Within monotheism it is harder to defend. There are three related but different questions. Firstly, why did God initially create us all ignorant but subsequently enlighten a minority? Christians often appeal to the doctrine of the Fall, in which God originally created us with full knowledge but Adam's sin destroyed it. However no such doctrine can provide a satisfactory answer to the question being asked here. Either God deliberately permitted human ignorance or it took place contrary to God's intentions - perhaps because of the devil's machinations - in which case the explanation turns out to be a polytheistic one after all.

Secondly, if we are naturally so ignorant, how can we ever know that a divine revelation is available at all? Whereas the Gnostics proposed that we have acquired two radically contrasting mental faculties from contrasting gods, according to monotheism all our mental faculties are provided by the same God. Again the polytheistic distinction is not available. Throughout the bulk of

Christian history divine revelation was so widely accepted that the question was rarely asked. It is only recently, with the rise of radical challenges to religious belief in general, that it has been raised again.

If we are at all able to transcend our natural knowledge, the mental faculties we already have must contain some element which enables us to do so. For example the atheist who has a religious experience and comes to believe in God may wish to insist that it was not a rational experience at all, but nevertheless will try to give an account of why the experience has led to the belief. A statement like 'I just felt God entering my heart' would make a connection between a particular kind of inner feeling and God's presence. The statement communicates successfully because other people have inner feelings and are sometimes led by them to believe things which they would not otherwise have believed; when they hear the statement they have an idea about what is going on. Even the most dramatic conversion experiences are, in practice, interpreted by natural reasoning processes drawing on previously learned concepts.

Thirdly, even if we accept that there is a reason-transcending divine revelation, the problem remains of finding out what it is. How do we recognize, for example, that the Bible and not the Qur'an is divinely revealed? Again there must be some faculty available. What is it, and why do so many people reach the wrong conclusion? To most early Christians it was a matter for rational debate. However, Augustine in his later years emphasized God's initiative at the expense of human freedom, and this later became a common theme in Christian thought. To deny human freedom and attribute revelation entirely to God's initiative is to present us with an elitism: the knowers, who have received the revelation, are radically different from other people by virtue of their knowledge. Their privileged information is more certainly true than anything other people may claim to know. Those in the know appear to be, and are tempted to perceive themselves as, God's favourites.

I now turn to the practical difficulties with religious founda-tionalism. Most of them relate to the claim to certainty and its corollary, the sharp distinction between those who are right and those who are wrong.

Firstly, there is no place for disagreement. When two true Christians honestly and conscientiously interpret a biblical text in contrasting ways, biblical foundationalism resists the conclusion that the Bible is either unclear or inconsistent. It therefore resorts to other explanations. Perhaps one's opponent is making a deductive error which can be pointed out. If this does not settle the matter, he or she must not be a true Christian - confused or dishonest, perhaps, or possessed by the devil. This is the reason why the leaders of the current campaign against homosexuality persistently refuse to countenance the possibility of open and honest debate about whether homosexuality is indeed immoral. From their point of view they are defending the only legitimate Christian view. Historically this refusal to engage in open debate as equals has been a major cause of conflict, especially within some branches of Calvinism where accusations of dishonesty or Satanic possession have been common. Foundationalists often express themselves in terms which others judge as bigotry; and if a bigot is, as the Concise Oxford Dictionary defines it, 'a person who is prejudiced in their views and intolerant of the opinions of others', then the judgement is often a fair one.

Foundationalists often insist that believing certain doctrines is essential to being a Christian or belonging to a particular church. Usually, as we have seen, theories become essential beliefs as a result of controversy; it is precisely because some people do *not* believe them that they acquire the status of official doctrine. Every time a controversy is settled by promoting a doctrine into official teaching, the limits to freedom of belief are restricted further. The long-term effect is that denominations accumulate ever-increasing lists of what their members are supposed to believe. Churchgoers hear about the divinity of Christ, the Trinity and the atonement as answers to questions they never wanted to ask; attacks on, or defences of, prayers for the dead or infant baptism all too often evoke past controversies rather than present ones.

When doctrines are interpreted as divine revelations which

must be accepted without question it becomes difficult to analyze them and they therefore lose their explanatory value. As we have seen, to insist that homosexuality is wrong simply because the Bible says so, and for no other reason, leaves homosexuals in a state of uncertainty. In order to apply the rule they would need to ask questions of the type 'Is this act wrong, and if so is that act wrong?' In practice, of course, there is no shortage of church leaders willing to provide answers; but since the Bible does not provide them, consistent application of the principle that the Bible provides all the answers would lead to the conclusion that there are no answers.

Another product of religious foundationalism is its sharp contrast between the people who know the right answers and the people who do not. When foundationalists feel absolutely certain that they know the right answers even though others disagree, the logical implication is that those others are certainly wrong. They may not articulate their position in this way - in fact they rarely do - but since it is an inescapable implication it tends to be presupposed in their expressions of their beliefs. This produces stilted relationships. There is something fundamentally irreligious about it. All the world's religions teach standards of morality, and all theories of morality reject solipsism. We have to recognize that our mind is not the only one. Other people have minds, with opinions and feelings, like our own. As young children we learn that when we poke a finger into somebody else's eye it hurts them just as it would hurt us. Later we learn - or should - that when we feel absolutely certain that we know something, and other people believe the opposite, we cannot take it for granted that our own sense of certainty trumps everybody else's. Yet this is what, in practice, is being encouraged in religious debate today. It was one thing for medieval Catholics to claim certainty for the church's teaching, assuming that there was only one church and therefore only one route for divine revelation. It is quite another, in today's world full of competing religious theories, to claim that one's own beliefs bear the stamp of divine certainty but those of others do not. Certainty-mongers usually try to avoid the charge of solipsism by claiming in some way that their view is the doctrine of the true church. So argue the opponents of women bishops and gay bishops. Today, though, there are too many claimants to the title of true church for the argument to convince. We are left with the impression that that central moral doctrine of all religions - that we ought to recognize other people as basically like ourselves - is now being undermined by some of the loudest religious voices in western Christianity.

Religious foundationalism as I have described it here expresses the views of some but by no means all conservative Christians. Others will consider the positions I have described as extreme ones. Many conservatives accept an element of foundationalism but do not allow their religious beliefs to be entirely structured by it. We might describe them as 'partial foundationalists'. They may, for example, say that they accept Christian beliefs 'within reason', but at the same time that there are some doctrines which they are not prepared to question. For some, the Resurrection of Jesus is essential, but not much else. For some, opposition to homosexuality is essential.

Philosophers, however, describe foundationalism and coherentism as contrasting options, not as different positions on a spectrum. This is because foundationalist truth claims expect certainty and therefore do not permit shades of grey. Furthermore, whereas Descartes' foundationalism appealed to reason and was therefore open to criticism by rational argument, religious foundationalism appeals to truths which transcend reason and therefore denies that they are open to rational criticism. The central claim of religious foundationalism is that what is known by revelation is known with greater certainty than anything we can know by other means and is not to be judged by those other means.

This is what makes partial foundationalism unsatisfactory. Although it is logically possible to hold some beliefs for foundationalist reasons and others for coherentist reasons, in practice whenever there is conflict between the two the foundationalist argument demands priority. Like a trump suit in a card game, it insists that whenever it is played it wins.

Not only does it demand priority on the issue in question; it also has the more general effect of demoting reason. It treats all coherentist knowledge and understanding as second rate; foundationalism tells us that before accepting any of it we should check it against revelation. An impossible example will illustrate the point. If there were a denomination which believed God had revealed that two plus two make five, the belief would undermine all its mathematical calculations, not just the ones specifically adding two to two. Of course there is no such denomination, but the effect applies whenever a foundationalist bull enters a coherentist china shop. If a revealed doctrine contradicts the conclusions of one of our logical analyses, it makes us ask whether we can trust *any* of our logical analyses, not just that one. Similarly, if it contradicts the detailed scientific observations of something in the physical world, it undermines the validity of *all* our observing.

The practical effect is widespread. Many Christians, when they reflect on issues of debate, may judge that homosexuality does not harm heterosexuals or that women priests can be quite good. These are utilitarian considerations and as such open to evidence either way. When they are challenged by a foundationalist argument, however - that a biblical text forbids women to teach or homosexuals to practise - the situation changes. The foundationalist argument has no interest in utilitarian judgements; weighing up the evidence for the two sides is, from its perspective, irrelevant. It demands to be accepted as the last word on the matter regardless of the practical consequences. It therefore pushes itself to the front of the queue; until a decision is made on whether to accept the foundationalist claim, other considerations have to be put to one side. In this way partial foundationalism is intrinsically unstable. It persistently undermines coherentism and pushes in the direction of consistent foundationalism. Rhetorically, foundationalists can easily triumph in this way as they can present their view as certain and alternative views as riddled with uncertainties.

To summarize, consistent religious foundationalism produces extreme positions which are welcome to some conservatives but rejected by many. More moderate positions, which affirm foundationalism to a limited extent but not on every occasion, produce more widely acceptable doctrines but at the cost of being inconsistent. Foundationalism by its nature insists that it is *the* truth and brooks no dissent.

Among philosophers foundationalism has lost popularity. It exaggerates the degree of certainty we have in the things we know. In practice we think we know things with varying degrees of probability but we are never absolutely certain. Yet it remains popular in matters of religion. We should perhaps ask why. One reason appears to be its power to account for major changes of worldview. Popular publications like *Alpha News* or *The Church of England Newspaper* regularly print stories of people who became Christians and underwent a major change of lifestyle. Characteristically they present a sharp contrast between the old worldview and lifestyle and the later Christian replacement. It is conversions like these which are most likely to leave the subject feeling that nothing in their past life could have prepared them for their conversion so it must be the result of intervention by an alien force, God. Like all human stories, though, these conversions can always be redescribed in different ways. From a liberal Christian perspective it may seem likely that, if human nature contains an element which responds to the divine, people who have been brought up to repress it may well undergo strong emotions and a feeling of radical change when the repression is lifted.

Another reason, perhaps, is group identity. Many churchgoers are not independent thinkers on religious matters but like to feel they identify with a particular church. If it defines itself in terms of particular doctrines, accepting those doctrines becomes part of the identification process. They do not need to be analyzed or understood; they can be accepted as badges of orthodoxy or, to use Lindbeck's term, 'cultural-linguistic symbols'. None of us can become experts on everything, so we all relate to some questions by wanting to feel we know something but without examining all the complications. For many people religious doctrines fit this category, and therefore the most popular answers are the ones presented as simple certainties.

Also important is the role of denominational unity. Religious denominations have many practical reasons for wanting to clarify, and therefore make public statements about, how they relate to other denominations and what limits they set to their own activities. Can we ordain a minister who does not believe in God? Or the Resurrection? Or the baptism of infants? For most church members there is no practical need to distinguish whether these questions are only about the limits to the institution or whether they are also questions of religious truth. Only a minority have such a strong commitment to questions of religious truth that they are prepared to fall out with their friends over it. Those who persist in challenging established doctrines threaten unity. Archbishop Rowan Williams has recently been arguing that unity is important in questions of truth because when denominations split, people stop talking to each other.[3] It is not surprising if, at a time when denominations are faced with a choice between protecting their own unity and encouraging exploration of religious questions, the leaders of church institutions feel most strongly the need to preserve unity. Nevertheless if unity is protected at the expense of discouraging members from asking religious questions, churches are failing to serve their purpose.

Let us now apply this analysis to the current debate within the Anglican Communion. Formally the agenda has been set by successive primates' meetings and the Windsor Report. A central claim is the Windsor Report's assertion:

> The Communion has... made its collective position clear on the issue of ordaining those who are involved in same gender unions; and this has been reiterated by the primates through their endorsement of the 1998 Lambeth Conference resolution. By electing and confirming such a candidate in the face of the concerns expressed by the wider Communion, the Episcopal Church (USA) has caused deep offence to many faithful Anglican Christians both in its own church and in other parts of the Communion.[4]

To justify its claim that the Communion has 'made its collective position clear' it cites the 1998 Lambeth Conference Resolution 1.10. That resolution rejects homosexual practice as 'incompatible with Scripture'. This is the basis on which the Report presumes that there is no longer any cause for continued debate about the ethics of homosexuality. The way the Report and the primates' statements have admonished the North American churches makes it clear that they consider the matter settled: as far as Anglicanism is concerned, in their view, homosexuality is immoral.

Just like the Nicene Creed and the Thirty-Nine Articles, the effect of this statement is to restrict the range of views permitted to members of the church; and, just like them, the views imposed are *not* the 'collective position' of the church as a whole; if they had been, neither debate nor resolution would have been necessary. Outside the world of bishops' meetings it was quite clear then, and remains clear now, that Anglicanism's collective position on homosexuality is that we disagree with each other.

The Report's statement depends on three presuppositions. Firstly it presupposes that doctrines are established by central hierarchies. In fact the Lambeth Conference consists of bishops, not representatives, and has no constitutional right to legislate for the Communion. In any case a large minority of bishops voted against the resolution. The claim that it settles the matter is at best a misinterpretation of the legal situation, though it is hard to see how the Report's authors could have been so poorly informed.

Secondly it presupposes that formal resolutions, once approved, apply universally. Elsewhere the Windsor Report states that 'It is an ancient canonical principle that what touches all should be decided by all'.[5] Like successive primates' meetings it has treated the New Westminster same-sex blessings and the consecration of an openly gay bishop as universally significant even though each of these innovations applied to only one diocese. For a Nigerian or a Texan to insist that they cannot tolerate a gay bishop in New Hampshire is, clearly, to demand universal uniformity in ethical norms.

Thirdly the Report presupposes that formal resolutions, once approved, are irreversible. Again this is made clear elsewhere. It accepts that Christian doctrines do not have to stay the same for all time; theology can, and does, develop. Agreed methods for making judgements are therefore needed.[6] New developments have in the past been subjected to a process of reception; that is, they are tested by how the faithful receive them.[7] This is in keeping with coherentist liberalism and classical Anglicanism. However it continues:

> The doctrine of reception only makes sense if the proposals concern matters on which the Church has not so far made up its mind. It cannot be applied in the case of actions which are explicitly against the current teaching of the Anglican Communion as a whole, and/or of individual provinces. No province, diocese or parish has the right to introduce a novelty which goes against such teaching and excuse it on the grounds that it has simply been put forward for reception.[8]

This is the basis on which it denies that same sex blessings and the appointment of a gay bishop are legitimate examples of the process of reception: these events, it believes, should not have taken place without a much wider consensus of the worldwide Communion. This principle, however, has not been applied in the past. When proponents of change sought to alter the Church's view on slavery, contraception, divorce, capital punishment and countless other issues, the new proposal was initially 'explicitly against the current teaching of the Anglican Communion as a whole'. In the case of contraception some of the early Lambeth conferences had already condemned its use but a later conference overturned the previous resolutions in order to permit it.

In each of these cases the church had already 'made its collective position clear' before the debate began. This, however, did not stop the innovations being proposed, debated at length, and eventually accepted. It was theoretically possible for foundationalists to argue that the Anglican position on the matter had already been established, that those who disagreed with it should leave the church and that bishops and clergy who disagreed with it, far from being permitted to propose further debate on the matter, should be disciplined. Had this view prevailed at the time, we today looking back on it in retrospect would probably judge it as a petty, and rather absurd, blocking move, not a substantial contribution to the debate. Yet this petty blocking move is precisely what the Windsor Report proposes as the standard response whenever it is proposed to review a decision already made and an international consensus in favour of change has not already been established. Such a principle, far from being consistent with the Anglican tradition, would be a major innovation. If it were accepted it would mean that once the Anglican Communion has reached a decision on any given subject it can never be changed unless the whole Communion agrees to change it.

The Report recognizes the existence of *adiaphora*, matters on which churches and individuals can make up their own mind while still being in communion with each other. There are many adiaphora; even in the middle of the Second World War pacifism was one. The question is whether the ethics of homosexuality counts as one of them or whether it is essential that we all agree about it. The Report offers a criterion for distinguishing essentials from adiaphora: is the issue something which 'a sufficient number of other Christians will find scandalous and offensive, either in the sense that they will be led into acting against their own consciences or that they will be forced, for conscience's sake, to break fellowship with those who go ahead?'[9]

This is without doubt a generous hostage to fortune. What, one wonders, is 'a sufficient number' of objectors? A thousand? A million? How scandalous and offensive do they need to find it, in order to block a change which the rest of the church wants to make? If the Anglican Communion were to agree to this principle it would be an open invitation to the opponents of every decision to mount a campaign against it, thereby showing that 'a sufficient number' were scandalized. The Church of England would certainly not have been able to accept women priests if this principle had been in force in 1992. Countless other changes - new orders of service, adaptations to the arrangements for the pay and pensions of clergy, administrative procedures for churches and vicarages, procedures for implementing new legislation by the state - could all be threatened with a veto by small minorities of determined opponents.

From the perspective of critical biblical scholarship, of course, the statement that homosexual activity is 'incompatible with Scripture' has very little meaning. Literally it means that it is forbidden by one or more biblical texts, and this is certainly true; but if that is all it means it only puts homosexuality on a par with trimming one's beard or ploughing a field in the seventh year. A great deal more would need to be done to justify the claim that it is binding on Christians today. It does not, therefore, speak the language of biblical scholarship. In practice both the statement itself, and the repeated reaffirmations of it in the continuing debate, function as rhetorical affirmations of the conservative evangelical tradition. The unspoken implication, every time it is reaffirmed, is that the conservative evangelical interpretation of the Bible is the only acceptable one.

It seems ironic that as secular thought is increasingly recognizing that we do not have the certainty we used to expect - even, perhaps, in mathematics, let alone the sciences - certainty is being reaffirmed in the Anglican Communion, with a revived foundationalism threatening the more open-ended Anglican tradition. Is this, one wonders, an indication that Anglicanism is redefining itself as a counter-cultural sect, responding to its declining influence by retreating into its own corner, and cuddling up to its traditional doctrines, like comfort blankets, so as not to face up to a changing world?

So far Anglicans have lived without certainty, willing to worship together with people of diverse opinions. If the church does turn itself into a counter-cultural foundationalist sect, as many of its leaders seem to want - or are willing to accept as the price of unity - it will be a different matter. In the short term the church may retain more outward signs of success - money, church buildings, bishops. In the long term, though, it will lose more rapidly the status it is already losing with the ordinary unchurched who have some religious sense, want the church to be there and remain its main source of potential new supporters.

The history of sectarian Calvinism shows us what will happen next. The successful foundationalists, having imposed their views about homosexuality onto the entire Communion, will naturally expect that their views on other issues also should prevail. When the endlessly trumpeted certainties of religious foundationalists on the matter of homosexuality are revealed, as they will be, to be the prejudices of a passing age, they will learn - as they did in the case of alcohol - that the issue on which they have been focusing does not really divide true Christians from false. Most of them, however, will not learn the deeper truth that their own opinions are prone to error just like the opinions of those with whom they disagree. They will not abandon their sense of certainty. Instead they will move on to another controversy, and in time another again after that, carrying with them from issue to issue their conviction that their opinion is the only true Christian one and using whatever tools are available to suppress the views of others. Anglicanism, which has retained its unity for centuries, will find itself splitting, splitting and splitting again.

It has often been observed that a precedent was set in the 1993 Act of Synod of the Church of England, which permitted parishes not only to refuse women priests but also to have their own bishops so that their confirmations were not 'tainted'. However politically pragmatic it may have seemed at the time, in the long term it was a major error. By giving approval to the idea of a 'pure' denomination within a denomination it in effect created a split; most Church of England churches are in communion with Methodists and Baptists but not with these other Church of England churches. At the time many critics, including the Group for Rescinding the Act of Synod which continues to campaign against it, warned that not only did it in effect create a split within the Church of England but it also set a precedent for further splits on future issues: if opponents of women priests were to have their own bishops, would not the opponents of other decisions demand *their* own bishops too? Today this is no longer a future prediction; a new generation of alternative bishops are being appointed to serve parishes in the USA which take the view that the only acceptable bishop is one who opposes homosexuality.

As a short-term expedient perhaps permitting alternative sets of bishops may have seemed to some the most politically pragmatic way of avoiding deeper divisions; as a long term method for settling disputes, however, it leads to absurdity. If it were applied consistently we would now need four sets of bishops. One would be for supporters of both women priests and homosexuality; a second for supporters of women priests who oppose homosexuality; a third for supporters of homosexuality who oppose women priests; and a fourth for opponents of both. To take matters further, if differences of opinion are to continue to be resolved by appointing alternative sets of bishops the arithmetic produces a geometrical progression. Just as disagreements on two issues require four sets of bishops, the third disagreement will mean we need eight sets of bishops and the fourth will increase the number to sixteen. Since there is a countless number of issues on which we may in the future disagree with each other, the number of bishops could proliferate until we end up with each of us being our own bishop.

This of course would be an absurdity. In practice it will become clear that the idea of providing alternative sets of bishops, though popular now, cannot survive a continuing succession of disagreements; and since there are always disagreements, better ways of resolving them will have to be found. In the long run we have to choose: *either* we put uniformity above universality and settle for a large number of small churches which keep splitting and realigning; *or* we put universality above uniformity and retain the classical Anglican notion of the church as a big tent within which we can agree to disagree.

Faced with a decision between these two the question at issue is: how certain are we that the opinions we hold are the only legitimate Christian ones? If we are not absolutely certain we have no business to exclude those with whom we disagree. Demanding exclusions, and refusing to belong to the same church as someone who holds opinions contrary to one's own, is only a defensible position if one presupposes that one's own opinions are absolutely certain to be right and therefore those who disagree are absolutely certain to be wrong.

This is the legacy of foundationalism. Outside the realm of religion such extreme claims to certainty are nearly always met with disapproval. They reveal not real knowledge but a psychological defensiveness, an unwillingness to face up to the aspects of reality which lead other people to hold different opinions. The history of religion teaches us, many times over, that those who demand certainty are granted bigotry.

CHAPTER 10

LIBERALS AND THE COHERENCE OF
DEVELOPING FAITH

One strange thing about human beings is how often, and how passionately, we are capable of believing things which are not true. Our knowledge is limited and uncertain. We do not know what the future will do with the knowledge we do have. Our vested interests tempt us to believe what we want to believe. So much knowledge is available that we select what suits us and seems to matter to us. As we are not given a universalizing God's eye view of reality, our main concerns are with what affects us directly. We settle for judgements which satisfy us, often without much regard for their effects on others.

In the last chapter I described how foundationalism functions in religious belief. Some apply it consistently and reach extreme conclusions. Less extreme, partial foundationalism is all-pervasive in Christianity today, but I have argued that it is inconsistent. In this chapter I shall describe what religious faith is like without it, and apply it to the current debate between liberals and conservatives. The philosophical term is coherentism. Whereas foundationalism expects to establish knowledge with certainty, coherentism settles for uncertainty. Perhaps this is the most common reason for disliking it. We like to feel we *really know*; to admit that our knowledge is less than certain requires a degree of maturity.

In coherentism the knowledge we think we have does not derive from a single source and is usually not deduced. Different pieces of information reach us in different ways; through the five senses, through speculating on them, intuition, instinct, the emotions and creative leaps of the imagination. There is not a fixed list of sources. Some possible sources, like telepathy or 'a woman's intuition', are disputed. None of them provides certainty. We therefore value anything which we think may produce information and be a check against other sources. We think we heard something, or remember something, but we are not sure. We read something in a book which contradicts what a teacher told us. We have an intuitive feeling about a particular situation. In each case we make a judgement about the reliability of our information. All these judging processes going on in our minds, usually unconsciously, serve to build up our picture of reality, a web of probabilities which support each other. Any one item may turn out to be wrong but a rich web full of strong connections is likely to persist.

Without certainty all our knowledge is relative. What we think we know is more or less probably true, and the degree of probability we find acceptable varies according to circumstance. While reading the newspaper I think I see, out of the corner of my eye, my toddler grandson walking towards the bookcase. Maybe I look no further; but if there is an open fire next to it I examine the matter more closely. Similarly some people think they know that there is, or is not, a God, but if they do not intend to let the matter affect their lives they may choose not to examine whether they may be mistaken. Because we never reach complete certainty there is always the possibility of learning something new which changes our understanding. The knowledge we think we have may be accurate enough for us now, given our situation and the questions we are asking, without being true for all people at all times.

This type of relativism is not the same as the relativism generated by non-realism. Some people hold the view that the physical reality outside our minds is a creation of our minds, or a 'cosmic porridge', a disorganized chaos which is only set into order by our mental concepts. From this perspective an extreme relativism is appropriate; if our minds create the world's order, my mind may create a different order from yours.[1] Coherentist relativism is consistent with realism; there really are objective truths about reality and sometimes what we think we know correlates with it. Often, though, it does not; either we have made an error or the knowledge we do have is only true within limits.

Herodotus like all ancient Greeks knew that the sun never appears to the north, so on hearing the story of some Phoenician sailors who claimed to have seen it to their north while sailing round Africa, he refused to believe it.[2] His knowledge was good enough for most purposes but not all.

Coherentism tells us that we are all capable of error. Recognizing this is essential to normal dialogue between equals. We speak to others because we think we have true information, but we also listen to them because we may be wrong. It follows that we should always treat other people's views with respect, however much we disagree.

This willingness to accept uncertainty characterizes religious liberals. They do not, like scientific foundationalists, begin with known certainties about the physical world and then choose whether to add onto them a set of less certain beliefs about religion; nor do they, like religious foundationalists, begin with certainties expressed in the Bible and then add onto them whatever information about the physical world is consistent with them. They begin, rather, with real but uncertain evidence for varied pieces of information, and apply to them an attitude of trust - faith that our mental processes represent reality well enough for our purposes. Only God is infallible; however convinced we feel about our doctrines we may turn out to be wrong. Of course the opinions we hold are the ones we believe to be true - otherwise we would change them - but humility and willingness to admit error are just as appropriate to faith as to all else.

Because coherentists welcome information from a wide range of sources they are open to the possibility of divine revelation. Inspired texts, the spiritual guidance of the individual and the wisdom of the church's tradition may all be affirmed as revelation. This does not, however, mean they provide certainties which are eternally and universally true. Like everything else they are mediated to us through our mental concepts and are not, therefore, untouched by human ideas. By the time we can make any sense of our experiences with the divine our interpretative processes have gone to work on them, accounting for them by means of concepts which we had already learned. What we think we are learning from them does not, therefore, override our other sources of information. Revelation is rarely a set of statements to be accepted literally; it is more often an insight to be considered in its context, an idea to be chewed over, a relationship to be valued.

What we take to have been revealed by God, therefore, has a provisional character. Whereas those who believe they have certainty are thereby cutting themselves off from the possibility of learning something new, coherentists are open to new discoveries. God may be leading us into new insights which are not in the Bible and not yet in our tradition. Change is to be expected. Christianity as we understand it today is not what it was hundreds of years ago or in different parts of the world, and there is no reason why it should be. It will continue to change, and we today may have some influence to change it for the better or the worse. To explore the reality of our relationship with the divine can be creative, and even exciting.

The fact that our sources of information vary means that we must judge between them when they conflict. In religion, as in science, there is no fixed set of rules about how these judgements are to be made. Presented with a new piece of information we assess whether to accept it, with what degree of confidence, and how to relate it to other things we think we know. We do so in the light of all the resources available to us. This judgement-making does not just follow guidelines inherited from the past; it also allows a role for creativity. New ideas may arise which do not come from Christian authorities but are nevertheless true. It is entirely proper, for example, to use the insights of modern psychologists to shed light on current debates within the church, even if the psychologists in question are atheists.

It follows that the search for truth in matters of religion is largely a community activity. One of our main sources of information is the people around us. We learn from each other, and different people provide different insights. There is therefore an essential role for public debate, research and reflection. As we engage in these processes disagreements, far from being signs of false teaching, are necessary parts of developing traditions. No two minds carry exactly the same collection of information or have exactly the same combination of faculties. Each of us is good at some things but not so good at others.

Because our own minds are the only ones to which we have direct access we all have an inbuilt self-centredness. A central aim of moral teaching is to overcome this self-centredness and recognize that other people's beliefs, hopes and fears, pleasures and pains are just as real as our own. None of us fully succeeds. What our own eyes have seen seems to us more reliable than what other eyes have seen, and what we have been brought up to presuppose seems to us more obviously true than what others presuppose. Many people find foundationalism attractive because they think that if they have certainty they do not need to take other people's views seriously. Coherentism rubs our noses in the fact that, however confident we are in the truth of our views, we are really just like other people, sometimes right and sometimes wrong.

Respectful dialogue within the believing community is therefore essential to keeping the tradition alive, and involves maintaining communication with people we disagree with. Attempts to convert others does more harm than good unless it avoids manipulative techniques; if I want to convince you that my opinions are true, I must not press arguments which would not also convince me in my best moments. Instead I must tell you the real reasons why I hold them and leave you to judge. Similarly, churches and religious traditions need to retain their awareness of being part of their host society; otherwise they will cut themselves off from many sources of information and lose their ability to relate and convince. In these ways coherentism seeks to spin a unified web of knowledge. This implies close relations with natural theology and raises the question of the relationship between religion and science.

Some people today associate natural theology primarily with the attempted proofs for the existence of God described in Chapter 4. These are foundationalist. I am concerned here with coherentist natural theology which does not expect proofs, but does expect that by using our God-given mental faculties to reflect on our experiences and the world around us we can learn about spiritual as well as physical truths. Such a unified account represents one view in the continuing debate about the relationship of religion to science. It does not distinguish between the two as sharply as dualism does. Of course many matters can be legitimately described, for many purposes, as scientific or religious to the exclusion of the other; but the edges are fuzzy and there is scope for some matters to belong in both categories.[3] A more integrated account benefits both. It permits religion once again to adopt its traditional role of offering interpretations of the whole of reality in ways which make sense of it, bringing our factual knowledge together with our emotions and our senses of purpose, progress, freedom and morality, in an overall account of how and why we have been made and how we should live.

The effect on science is also significant. In Ockham's day reality was divided in such a way as to equate the physical with the observable and the spiritual with the unobservable. Today, not only do neo-pagans reclaim the spiritual nature of the physical environment, but scientists regularly develop hypotheses about the existence of things which cannot be observed, from sub-atomic particles to black holes, without fear of trespassing on the spiritual realm.

Science cannot provide a complete account of reality. Even those who still hope for a 'theory of everything' conceive it narrowly, only as a way of describing what happens and making predictions. I have described three main limitations to science. Firstly it presupposes, but cannot demonstrate, that the world is ordered. How, then, do we account for its order? To say that it is not the result of some intending mind is to say that it is arbitrary. Ian Markham argues that to assume that it is arbitrary is not a satisfactory basis for science:

> If the coherence of reality is arbitrary, then it is possible that either the universe could at any moment cease being orderly or

coherent, or its coherence only extends to certain parts. The major difficulty on this view is that the universe could be intrinsically chaotic and we would not realize it. If, for example, the order is all entirely mind imposed, then the actual state of the universe might be chaotic to a smaller or larger degree. We are left with a fundamental doubt about all claims to truth.[4]

Secondly, science presupposes but cannot demonstrate that human minds have the ability to understand the nature of the world around us. It is possible, as some non-realists believe, that physical reality is an unordered chaos only given an appearance of order by the human mind;[5] or, as some ancient Gnostics believed, that the human mind has been designed to misunderstand the nature of reality.[6] Again, a number of modern theologians argue that in order to defend our ideas of reality against these possibilities we need to do more than merely presume that our minds just happen to be able to understand it by pure arbitrary chance; otherwise we should expect that our luck may run out at any moment.[7]

These presuppositions are not universal common sense; many societies in the past did not accept them and therefore could not develop scientifically. As we saw in Chapter 2 both questions were debated in medieval Europe. The early modern scientists inherited them, not yet as presuppositions but as theories which could be defended on the ground that a good God has created us and the world in these ways. Their successors, from Hume onwards, continued to believe them but rejected the appeal to God. They have so far failed to find an alternative theory to justify them. Order and predictability, and therefore science, still work, but science itself cannot explain why.[8]

Thirdly science, by basing its knowledge claims on measured data gathered through the five senses, only produces information about part of reality. The concepts of intrinsic value, moral good and evil, purpose, progress and human freedom have resisted all attempts at scientific analysis. Two responses are possible: either they are human inventions which do not represent objective reality, or they are aspects of reality which science does not reach.

It is possible to hold the positivist view that what cannot be proved by science does not exist; but if we do we find that the world, and our lives, are strangely empty - so empty, indeed, that even science can no longer be expected to access truth, as we saw in Chapter 4. It is better to conclude that the public search for understanding includes science but also includes non-scientific areas of research which are not second-rate 'opinions' or 'beliefs' but constitute equally genuine attempts to understand the way things are.

Once we abandon the foundationalisms and the certainty-claims, therefore, we can see similarities between science and religion. In both we have practical reasons for wanting to know why and how reality is the way it is. Communities develop answers. Some answers work well and remain unchanged for a long time while others prove unsatisfactory and are replaced or adapted. When a decision needs to be made we commit ourselves to whatever seems the best answer at the time.

Scientists build on what they know in order to ask questions about what they do not know. They are far removed from those opponents of Galileo who argued that since Jupiter's moons could only be seen through the new-fangled invention of the telescope, not by the naked eye, they did not really exist at all.[9] By studying things they can see scientists develop theories about things they cannot see; and once the evidence for them becomes convincing enough they take for granted the existence of these unseen things and use them to postulate the existence of yet more unseen things. Establishing one theory leads to another. Electrons and black holes are many stages removed from anything the naked eye can see. Recently a number of physicists have reflected on how their researches point towards the existence of God.[10]

In the same way religious coherentism, like natural theology, expects that by applying our normal mental faculties to the things around us, what we discover easily may lead us to other, less easy, discoveries. By noticing how we can help or hinder each other, we may learn about how we may help or hinder God's hopes for us. By noticing what it means to love each other and treat each other justly, we are enabled to reflect on what God's love and justice must be like; otherwise terms like 'God's love' and 'God's justice' would be meaningless, as Hume showed. What we learn about God in these ways is not, of course, proved; but coherentists do not expect proof. Just as some evidence points towards string theory but we cannot be certain and there is some counter-evidence, so also some evidence suggests the existence of a good creator God but again we cannot be certain and there is some counter-evidence.

Within a unified account of reality, science continues to explore how the physical processes of the universe operate. The knowledge it fails to establish can perhaps be established by others using different methods, or perhaps is beyond what humans can know at all. Just as good religion recognizes that it cannot answer every question and that some are better answered by science, so also good science recognizes that there are many aspects of our experience which are better explained by religion. Each has its role; what distinguishes the unified account of reality from dualism is that in a unified account the dividing line between science and religion is often fuzzy. The two do not build walls to keep each other out. If the anthropic principle leads physicists to believe in God, or if a religious tradition believes the gap between the rich and the poor is too great, they are not making category mistakes; each proposal can be judged on its merits.

The main practical implication of these fuzzy edges is that we can once again make sense of issues which have both a scientific dimension and a religious one. Economic globalization, for example, is perceived by many as a good thing but is opposed by others. Does the programme to incorporate every one of the world's countries into a western capitalist system benefit everyone or does it benefit some at the expense of others? How do we measure the adverse effects - climate change, dumps of rubbish and toxins, destruction of ecosystems - against the benefits? We know that there are mountains of statistics on these matters, but even they represent only a tiny proportion of the information which would be needed if any serious attempt were made to determine whether the costs will outweigh the benefits. Realistically, judgements like this can only be made on the basis of some deep philosophy about the nature and purpose of human life and the world around us. If we believe our lives and the solar system are the unintended results of impersonal laws of nature, one range of possible judgements will seem credible; if we believe we have been created by a divine being with benign intentions, a rather different range will seem credible. Even if the two ranges overlap the value of globalization may well look different from these different perspectives.

Another example might be the increasing concern about keeping the terminally ill alive. As medical technology advances an increasing number of people in affluent countries are being artificially kept alive against their will. Characteristically, neither the medical staff nor the relatives feel morally justified in suggesting that the patient should be allowed to die. Everybody senses a taboo on proposing that death should be allowed to take place before the available medical technology has been exhausted. The patient may know only too well that he or she will remain in great pain or discomfort until death, but relatives and visitors, anxious to avoid a *faux pas*, often feel the need to express absurdities like 'Of course you won't die'. Because we rarely have an engaged and informed religious awareness confident of reflecting intelligently and openly on issues of life and death and applying them to particular cases, we become anxious to stick to the rules and we find ourselves virtually incapable of engaging in constructive discussion of when would be the right time to let a particular terminally ill person die. Other societies have been able to do this but we cannot; all too often patients are kept alive because, and only because, the technology is available.

These are two examples of issues which are better understood within a unified account of reality than a dualistic one because they contain an essential religious dimension but are not exclusively religious. There are many such issues. Good decision-making demands that the religious and scientific elements are brought together and explored in each other's company. This is only possible in the absence of foundationalism because if either the scientific or the religious contributors present their own contribution as an absolute certainty, creative dialogue becomes impossible.

I now turn to the question of establishing new knowledge. One apparent difference between science and religion is that science has well-established procedures for new research. If new knowledge is also possible in matters of religion, how do we receive it and how do we assess it?

In science researchers characteristically gather evidence, look for patterns, develop a hypothesis to account for them and then look for ways to test the hypothesis. If the tests confirm the hypothesis it is then published: the evidence, the hypothesis, the tests and the conclusions are put in the public domain where others can examine them. It can never be absolutely certainly true - it is always the case that one more test might have disproved it or the tests were performed within too narrow a range of conditions - but if it withstands sufficient examination the community becomes confident that a new discovery has been made.

In these processes there are two distinct elements, gathering data and developing theories. Every research project makes some use of both. If it had no contact with observations of reality it would be pure fiction; if it did no theorizing it would be nothing more than a disconnected collection of statements. For research to work successfully it needs to gather data in ways which do not presuppose the theories being tested. On the other hand if the data enable good theories to be developed, they will in turn suggest types of data to be sought for and new theories to be tested. In every developing science there is a creative spiral in which evidence produces new theories, theories produce ways of looking at the evidence and new ways of looking at evidence produce new projects for gathering data.

Within this overall pattern different research projects vary in the role they play. Some do little more than gather data and tabulate it; at the other extreme, some concentrate on analyzing theories about evidence already gathered. In Chapter 1 I noted that some ancient religious theories were closely driven by specific empirical evidence. Most religious traditions today describe their divinities as more transcendent, so the relationship between empirical evidence and religious theory is less close. Religious beliefs therefore generally tend to be at the more theoretical end of the spectrum. Otherwise the way they change is similar to the way other disciplines change, with an ongoing interaction between inherited tradition and new ideas.

In formal education, for example, school children are taught traditional accounts of each subject without being expected to know about contemporary disagreements between professional researchers. At any one stage what a school teacher is telling pupils, as undisputed fact, may already have been challenged by the latest research. This is characteristic of all developing fields of study: there are roles both for maintaining the tradition and for challenging it. It is not the case either that all knowledge in the subject is inherited from the past, or that practitioners must start from scratch and work it all out for themselves. Instead, reason and tradition interact creatively. New ideas generate new possibilities; established consensus sets limits to which of them can be accepted. We begin by being educated into a tradition, and only when we have mastered it do others credit us with enough expertise to challenge it and perhaps change it.

This tension between general consensus and new research exists in all the professions. For example at any one time the latest findings in medical research often do not correspond with what doctors are offering patients. Doctors expect to give, and patients expect to receive, remedies which are well tried and tested. Nevertheless, far from feeling undermined by new research doctors welcome it, because in time it may make new treatments possible. In the same way criminologists research how offenders should be treated, while judges administer sentences within the laws already passed.

At any given time, then, there is a tension between inherited consensus and new research. It needs to be managed, and this is done by clarifying the different roles of different professionals. We all accept the judgments of authorities on matters about which we ourselves are ignorant. We value the expertise of our doctors, architects and electricians without normally feeling the need to question their judgements. The breadth of knowledge available in our society is only possible because different people specialize in different fields. On the other hand the trust we place in our specialists has conditions. We expect that a highly qualified electrician will usually do a better job of rewiring our house than an unqualified amateur, but we also recognize that possession of qualifications is no guarantee of good work. To maintain their quality we expect our experts to be part of a community of specialists in their area, where they are kept up to date with new developments and required to maintain adequate standards.

Outside the realm of religion, professionals rarely find the tension between inherited consensus and new research difficult to manage. It is only in religion that it regularly appears as a threat. Although church leaders have long complained about the growing gap between academic theology and the teaching which takes place in local churches, in practice the gap shows no sign of getting smaller. Because of the continuing foundationalist commitment to the idea that all truth is inherited from the past, new theories tend to be interpreted as threats to the church's authority.

When Christianity was new different opinions were debated openly. Over the centuries greater numbers of doctrines were formally established as what the church believes, and thereby restricted freedom of expression within the church. Once the inherited tradition had been established as the supreme authority church leaders had a theoretical justification for rejecting all new ideas. For example in the Middle Ages it was still possible for Aquinas, Duns Scotus and Ockham to produce and defend radically contrasting theologies within the same church. The debates were primarily about questions of truth, not about whether their views were within the bounds of permitted Catholic belief. In 1860, by contrast, when seven leading theologians published *Essays and Reviews* urging the importance of biblical and doctrinal criticism, two of them were prosecuted for heresy on the ground that their beliefs were *incompatible with being priests of the Church of England*. The accusation reveals the presupposition that the church's inherited doctrines should constrain the beliefs of its priests. Whenever it does, of course, new learning becomes impossible for them.

On this occasion the Judicial Committee of the Privy Council eventually ruled, in 1864, that they had said nothing contrary to the formularies of the Church of England and that clergy should be free to study the Bible and question traditional doctrine. It endorsed the view, put forward by H B Wilson, that a truly national church must necessarily permit diversity of belief. Thus the law of the state defended the freedom of the clergy against pressure within the church for greater uniformity. Those who opposed the judgement could treat it as one more reason why the church should be free of regulation by the state. It became easier for church leaders to defend their traditions by simple foundationalist appeals to revelation and tradition than by rational debate about the strength of the case for each new theory. Conversely, creative thinkers had less incentive to retain close links with institutional churches which would only ignore or condemn their proposals. Instead of a managed tension between inherited consensus and new research, therefore, the two sides have tended to go their own ways. Kent described the situation in the twentieth century:

> On questions of ethics, especially sexual ethics, theological liberals had powerful social support which helped them, as in the case of the Anglican Church's volte-face on contraception, to obtain important results. But pure theology had only an ecclesiastical environment, it had no other social roots by the 1970s… Liberalism was available to the individual, but it was not available to the institution. And so a certain split had taken place. Certain kinds of religious behaviour belonged to and took place within the environment of the Churches; certain styles of religious thinking had for the moment ceased to belong to the environment of the Churches.[11]

Because modern churches are so poor at accepting new insights they feel threatened by them. When members of a church support changes to inherited doctrine their foundationalist leaders, lacking the means to admit that they may have been wrong, perceive the supporters of change as a threat to the church's unity. If psychological research indicates that homosexuality is part of the genetic make-up of a minority of people, and that suppressing it harms them, those who feel threatened by this challenge to what they believe the church has always taught are strongly motivated to appeal to the foundationalist principle that unchanging doctrine has greater authority than modern science. Hardly surprisingly, church leaders are usually more concerned to maintain the unity of their own church than to examine the truth of the issue under debate. Once this stance is considered acceptable it is not just the issue of the day which will be suppressed, but any new issue which may challenge the tradition in the future. This is a limitation which can only be overcome by recognizing the value of new insights as well as the inherited tradition, without treating either as infallible.

In the last chapter I described the characteristic features of foundationalist churches. I shall now describe the characteristics I would expect to find in churches which express a coherentist approach to religious belief and practice.

They do not have the clear boundaries beloved of foundationalists. They are comfortable with fuzzy edges: rather than distinguishing clearly between members and non-members they accept that some people attend services more often than others, and prefer not to put up barriers against those who are not baptized or are not on the electoral roll.

Nor do they expect true belief in all members. One effect of the Reformation debates was to put the onus on individual believers to work out for themselves what true Christian doctrine was. Foundationalist churches retain it, though usually in weaker forms. Coherentist churches characteristically abandon it. Every healthy society includes people who think about religious questions, but not every person needs to. Sociologists have noted how, especially in rural areas, people who do not attend church services often feel strongly that services should be continue to be held. Like the healthy person who does not need the local doctor but values the fact that there is one, many people do not know what their church teaches but are concerned that it should be there, and that it should provide teaching for those who seek it. A healthy society contains a religious element but does not expect every member to take a great interest in it.

Because new insights can come from any source the coherentist church prefers to hear a wide range of voices; to have 'pure' churches of the carefully selected would be a mistake because it would block our ears. It is better to be inclusive and to hear contrasting ideas expressed in church, so that they can be compared and discussed. Truth emerges not by putting up barriers against error but by knocking them down. If a consensus emerges it is better to value it as it is for as long as it lasts; to turn it into a doctrine to which members are obliged to assent would be to limit free expression.

There is an important role for scholarship. Churches should enable people to keep up to date with new research and ideas which impact on their faith, and assess them using a range of critical tools. Conservatives often accuse liberals of accepting every new idea uncritically; because foundationalism does not accept those critical tools it does not appreciate their significance. Coherentist liberalism avoids telling people exactly what they should believe: instead it provides the tools and invites people to decide for themselves.

Some people know more than others, and some have a legit-imate teaching role. On the other hand, in coherentist churches not even the most learned scholar has the supreme teaching status which foundationalist churches often attribute to their leaders. Everybody has something to learn and something to contribute. Learning, therefore, can take place in any direction, so there is less emphasis on hierarchical teaching from experts and more on shared reflection within the community. It is a more democratic approach.

Because new insights are possible church discussion groups can be genuinely creative. The aim is to help participants think more deeply about the issues, not to reach a predetermined conclusion. It is important that all opinions should be heard with respect; nobody should be left feeling that they asked the wrong question or said something unacceptable. Similarly, if church leaders disagree with each other on significant issues, no harm is done to the church's witness because there is a recognized process for exploring them. If some of our bishops are active homosexuals and other bishops believe homosexuality is immoral, no problems are raised about the unity of the church. The debate enriches the church rather than threatening it.

Coherentist churches are willing to change. Because we never have the whole truth we can only ever make partial judgements about whether our predecessors were mistaken or whether our successors will value what we are doing today. What we do now is always to some extent provisional. So also was what our predecessors did. Like Hooker, coherentists can affirm that the church 'has authority to establish that for an order at one time, which at another it may abolish, and in both do well'.[12]

How, then, does this distinction between foundationalist and coherentist religion relate to the current debates?

Not all conservatives are foundationalists, and not all liberals are coherentists. I have focused on one version of liberalism, drawing on classical Anglicanism and analyzing it as coherentism. Others who consider themselves religious liberals are dualists, or non-realists, or realists about the world who hold a non-realist view of God. To add to the range of possibilities we all often hold contradictory views without realizing it. Nevertheless the current polarization, popularly described in terms of liberals and conservatives, does express increasing resort by conservatives to foundationalism and by liberals to coherentism.

The same applies to churches and theological traditions. Although no theological tradition has been entirely consistent in maintaining either a foundationalist or a coherentist stance, many describe themselves in the language of one or the other. What has distinguished Anglicanism since the seventeenth century is the classical Anglican theology described in Chapter 5, which is coherentist. This theology has not always characterized the Church of England; it was less in evidence in the Tudor period, and since the middle of the nineteenth century large minorities within it, both Catholic and evangelical, have disowned it. In other parts of the world some Anglican churches have had little or no contact with it. Some were founded by missionaries who were unsympathetic to it, or were even motivated to do their mission work by a desire to escape from it.[13] Nevertheless the Anglican Communion stems from the Church of England, and classical Anglican theology is the only theological tradition which can claim to represent the church through the bulk of its history. If there is any way of characterizing what Anglicanism stands for, this is it.

In practice its coherentism has served the church well. Even after it had begun to decline it was influential enough to hold the church together when more foundationalist churches would have split. I have already noted that the Church of England has witnessed many major disagreements and has often changed its view. In the debates about slavery, evolution, women in the ordained ministry, remarriage after divorce, capital punishment and contraception the opponents of change had the lion's share of the biblical texts on their side, but nevertheless the majority Anglican view changed. The changes took time. They were possible because the coherentist influence was strong enough to permit two processes. Firstly, not only the laity but also bishops and clergy were given freedom to disagree in public both with each other and also with the church's traditional view. Secondly, the debate was allowed to continue for as long as it took to discuss each issue on its merits and eventually reach a consensus.

Changes to church teachings are normal, even when they contradict authoritative statements. The Thirty-Nine Articles of the Church of England, for example, include the statement that 'The Laws of the Realm may punish Christian men with death, for heinous and grievous offences'.[14] The 1957 Homicide Act in the UK retained capital punishment for the worst forms of murder and Geoffrey Fisher, the Archbishop of Canterbury, strongly supported it. Only eight years later, though, capital punishment was abolished with the new Archbishop Michael Ramsey and sixteen bishops voting in favour and not a single bishop voting against. The Thirty-Nine Articles had not been amended in the meantime, and still have not been.

With this in mind, let us turn to the question of whether it is acceptable to consecrate an actively gay man to a bishoprick in a church which formally considers homosexuality sinful. I have already argued that the Anglican Communion does not have a formally binding doctrine condemning homosexuality. I now ask: if it did have, where would that leave the consecration of a gay bishop?

By way of analogy let us consider some parallels which are currently less emotive. A local church is committed to opposing infant baptism, both in its constitution and in the views of its members. It would not be sensible for that church to appoint a minister who approved of baptizing infants. Fifty years later all the members have forgotten about the issue except for one couple who would positively like their infant to be baptized. The constitution has not been changed; it just no longer reflects the views of the members. Will it now be permissible to appoint a minister who approves of it? If they do, they will be doing what the Church of England did when it appointed an opponent of capital punishment as Archbishop of Canterbury. Just as Anglicans today consider themselves free to oppose capital punishment if they see fit, many members of Baptist churches consider themselves free to make their own judgements about the appropriateness of infant baptism.

This is as it should be. The institution may decide that it can appoint a leader who disagrees with something in the constitution, or it may decide that it should keep updating the constitution to reflect the views of its members. Whichever choice it makes, what coherentism recommends is that changing opinions should be acknowledged as a normal part of church life. Constructive proce-dures should be in place to ensure that they are permitted but criti-cally assessed. What is not legitimate is the argument that anyone who disagrees with any of the regulations currently in force has no right to belong. Also illegitimate is the attempt - so common in the current controversy - to present a proposal for change as though it were an international crisis.

Such open and honest searching for truth is only possible when church members are free to express opinions at variance with established policy without fear of discrimination. Empathetic and respectful listening to the views of others is only possible if those others are free to express their own beliefs and experiences. Sadly, in the case of the current debate about homosexuality this does not apply. For those who are not homosexuals there is nothing to fear. For those who are, the threats are great - from being refused church appointments to being beaten up on the streets.

Classical Anglican theology has until now remained sufficiently influential to ensure that having a bishop with whom one disagrees is a normal and acceptable part of church life. Evangelicals, Catholics and liberals alike have not expected to agree with their bishop about everything. Even at the height of the debates about slavery many proponents of reform had slave-owning bishops, but they did not issue threats to split the church or demand alternative episcopal oversight.

From the perspective of coherentist liberalism there is no reason why a church should split over the ethics of homosexuality. Homosexuality is but one of many hundreds of ethical issues and churches often change their views on them. Where the current debate innovates is not, therefore, in the proposal to consider homosexuality morally acceptable but in the claim that having a bishop with whom one disagrees is *not* acceptable. This claim derives from foundationalism and is clearly quite contrary to the character of classical Anglican theology. As I argued in the last chapter, in the long run it will be revealed to be utterly unrealistic; it only appears realistic as long as the focus of attention is restricted to a single ethical issue. It is true that some people are asserting that it is such an essential issue for the church that we cannot just agree to differ; but is only an assertion, and a recently invented one at that. No satisfactory case has been made as to why we should all agree about it when we disagree about so many other issues.

To liberals it seems that homosexuality is the central issue of our time only because conservative evangelicals have chosen it as the one most likely to unite evangelicals who otherwise tend to be too fissiparous to unite around a common cause. Liberals and Catholics had no part in giving it so much prominence above other issues. It unites conservatives in Europe and North America because their host society is becoming more tolerant of it. As society changes the moral standards of Christians, as so often happens, follows those of society but with a time lag; in the meantime a moral stance which used to characterize society as a whole can be presented as a distinctively Christian moral norm. For those who believe that God is active outside the church this is only to be expected; there is no reason to expect churches, or Christians, to be first with new insights. On the other hand for those who expect to derive all their truths from Christian revelation it indicates that the new ideas must be contrary to God's will.

At the time of writing there is much speculation about whether the Anglican Communion will or should split, with some arguing that the split has already happened. One group acknowledges the fact that society has become more tolerant of homosexuality and believes that as a responsible part of society it should respect the change. Among them are those who believe homosexuality is not immoral, but also others who believe that since opinions differ a diversity of views should be accepted in the church. In either case they think there is a proper place for churches to adapt their teachings in the light of new insights. Some of them do some campaigning on the issue but most do not. If their view does not prevail they will be disappointed but there will be no major international campaigns, no rival provinces, no consecrations of 'alternative' or 'adequate' bishops to cater for their point of view, no conspiracies to create splits. The institutional church is not so important to them that they are prepared to devote all their energies to it. Some will stay in the church, perhaps muttering - like churchgoers who do not like their new vicar - that one day things will change again. Others will move to a different church if they can find a suitable one. Others again will attend less often or not at all.

Another group also acknowledges that society has become more tolerant of homosexuality, but is determined to oppose it. Its immorality is not up for debate, and those who are opposing the church's opposition to it are undermining the whole church. A church which refuses to make it clear that homosexuality is sinful is not the true church. Better to create a split, so that half a true church survives, than collude with the apostasy being proposed. For people who see Christianity as opposed to society and its values, it is all the more important that there should be true Christian institutions which do not compromise their beliefs. This group has both the commitment to the institutional church and the emotional energy to preserve purity. If offence is caused - if they are accused of bullying and bigotry - well, the Old Testament prophets made themselves unpopular too.

A third group is less concerned about the ethics of homosexuality than the protection of the institutional church. For some this is because of a commitment to Catholic theology, for others because they are in positions of leadership and feel some responsibility to hold the church together. They cannot fully satisfy both the other groups. If they disappoint the conservatives they are threatened with the prospect of a rival administration, and the church may well split irrevocably. It they disappoint the liberals there will be no fireworks, just a slow reduction of support; a churchwarden resigns here, a gay couple stops attending there, but most will carry on supporting the church albeit a little more grudgingly. From the point of view of church leaders taking a pragmatic view of the situation, the solution seems obvious: better to retain the conservatives and let the liberal element quietly decline.

In the long term, however, it will be a different matter. At the end of the last chapter I suggested that if the spirit of foundationalism is allowed to set the tone for the Anglican Communion, far from avoiding a split it will ensure a succession of splits precisely because it will have sanctioned a more intolerant response to differences of opinion. It will also cut off its main source of new members. Black and white certainty claims attract some but repel others. Numerically, the numbers repelled are probably far larger but less noticed. There are statistics to show how the numbers of churchgoers increase and decline, but there are no statistics to show the numbers of people who did not attend any church anyway but are now more strongly opposed to Christianity because of its hostility to gays and lesbians. Yet these people - the generally unchurched, potentially sympathetic but easily put off by hardliners - represent a huge proportion of the population. According to the 2001 census in the UK around two-thirds of the population consider themselves Christians but do not attend church services. In the long run these are the potential new supporters and members of churches. Their beliefs and attitudes vary; but the more church leaders present Christianity as very different and more reactionary, the less attractive most of them will find it.

If history is any guide, over the next ten or twenty years homosexuality will go the way of drinking alcohol. Increasing numbers of opponents will become aware that close friends of theirs, perhaps even members of their family, engage in it. They will refuse to believe that it stands out above all other issues as the defining one for Christians. It will cease to unite them. This will be good news for homosexuals, but not necessarily for other liberals. Foundationalism will move on to its next unifying issue, whatever that may be. This perhaps is the most tragic part of the situation we are in. To split the Anglican Communion over the ethics of homosexuality is no more sensible, or necessary, than splitting it over divorce, contraception, pacifism or many hundreds of other ethical issues. What *would* justify a split would be an inability to agree on how to make decisions. This, unfortunately, is not a fantasy. Behind the debate about homosexuality lies precisely this issue, expressed through the different perspectives of foundationalists and coherentists: do we deduce everything from divine revelation and discount other sources, or do we draw on the widest possible range of sources and allow a place for development and new insights? Is it possible that what the church has taught for the last two, six or nineteen centuries is wrong and it is time to change? Or is it always the church's task to defend the certainties it has inherited?

Until now the Anglican Communion has contained within itself the tools for change in response to new insights. However the gradual growth of foundationalism within it has now reached a point where its supporters feel strong enough to lay claim to the Anglican Communion itself. Many of them have never experienced churches which are not foundationalist - or, if they have, they have been warned against their 'unsound' or 'liberal' teachings and have not engaged constructively with them. The current debate reveals many confident assertions of foundationalism as the only acceptable way to be Anglican. Even the Windsor Report and primates' meetings speak its language. How should coherentist liberals respond?

This is where the difficulty of holding the Communion together is at its greatest. It is nothing to do with homosexuality, everything to do with the excessive certainty-claims of foundationalism. How does a tolerant church tolerate the intolerant? How does an inclusive church include excluders? When a church with a history of inclusiveness and tolerance welcomes into its ranks large numbers of people whose beliefs make them exclusive and intolerant, only two options are available. One is to capitulate to them, and allow them to change the church into an intolerant and exclusive one. This is, at the time of writing, the direction in which the Windsor process seems to be moving. The other is to insist on maintaining the principles of inclusion and tolerance, even at the expense of members who refuse to accept them.

Between these alternatives there is no possibility of compromise. If you are willing to compromise with me but I am not willing to compromise with you, every time we succeed in reaching agreement it can only be because you have given in to me. In the same way the Anglican Communion contains coherentists who admit that their views may be wrong, are prepared to change their minds if persuaded, and even if they are not persuaded are willing to compromise. It also contains foundationalists who are convinced that their views are certainly correct and do not believe alternative views should be permitted. If the Communion's leaders are determined to keep both sides together in the same church, it can only be done by allowing the foundationalists to impose their will on every issue.

I therefore believe that the Anglican Communion should do the exact opposite of what the Windsor process has sought to achieve. It should *protect* diversity of opinion, willingness to accept uncertainty, tolerance and inclusiveness, by *insisting* that they are to be respected and valued as essential parts of a welcoming and developing church. Liberalism does not mean that 'anything goes'; like every other system it needs to be protected against those who attack it. The Anglican Communion does not need to expel those who disagree with diversity of opinion. It can accept them as members, but must impose on them the discipline of respecting Anglicanism: that is to say, refraining from undermining its tolerance, inclusiveness and diversity. Only when people declare - or make it clear by their actions - that they are not prepared to accept this discipline, should we reach the conclusion that Anglicanism is not for them; but when it happens we should not be afraid to do so.

Ultimately, the unity of the church is less important than its ability to help us relate to God. If, as Henry McAdoo observed, 'Anglicanism is not committed to believing anything because it is Anglican but only because it is true',[15] this is all the more reason why the search for truth, in matters of religion as in all else, should be allowed to continue unfettered and the church should see it as its business to encourage it.

The coherentist liberalism I have described here offers the means to engage in this search without putting unnecessary obstacles in the way. Firstly, because it denies that we have absolute certainty it is *undogmatic*. We do not have all the answers so we may be wrong, however strongly we feel. We should not therefore impose our views on others. We engage in dialogue with other Christian traditions, non-Christian faiths and unbelievers partly to share our insights with them but also partly because they may have insights to share with us. To respect the views of others is not only an essential courtesy but a necessary feature of the search for truth.

Secondly, because it denies that all truths have already been established in the past it is *developing*. It looks forward with excitement to discovering new insights using the information, skills, creativity and imagination of the believing community, drawing on the inherited tradition but also willing to contribute to it and update it.

Thirdly, because it takes for granted neither new nor old doctrines, it is *critical*. It brings a questioning mind to both, and therefore values the role of academic scholars who spend their lives seeking new insights into the meanings of biblical texts, the teaching and work of the historical Jesus and the development of Christian doctrines. It is willing to explore new ideas and take as long as is needed to decide which of them are mistakes and which are insights to be retained and valued. In church, no question is the wrong question to ask.

Fourthly, because it does not confine itself to its own religious world and a private spiritual language, it is *public*. It expects to speak the language of its host society. It does not hide its internal debates from public view as though they were cause for shame but explores them openly, inviting others to contribute their own insights.

Finally it is *engaged* - with the world around and the pressing issues of the day. It expects its traditions, beliefs and practices to be relevant not just to its own members but to society in general, as it expresses the theoretical and practical significance of its developing theories about who made us and why. It expects to play a constructive part in public life, contributing to society's ideas and at the same time receiving from it.[16]

We live our lives, and make short-term decisions and long-term commitments, on the basis of the best answers available at the time. The history of religion, like the history of science, contains many stories of blind alleys and ideologically motivated oppression; but it also contains stories of people learning from the wisdom of the past and the events of their own day, producing new insights and helping their society to take one more step towards that complete and certain knowledge which resides only in the mind of God.

NOTES TO INTRODUCTION

[1]The many claims and counter-claims are described in the *Church Times*. The *Church of England Newspaper* describes the debate from a committed conservative perspective, and in greater detail.

[2]These submissions were printed in full on the Anglican Communion's website, http://www.anglicancommunion.org/.

[3]*The Guardian* 15 Jan 2004.

[4]*Church of England Newspaper* 11 March 2005.

[5]*Church of England Newspaper* 29 July 2005.

[6]The Archbishop's statement is entitled *The Challenge and Hope of Being an Anglican Today: A Reflection for the Bishops, Clergy and Faithful of the Anglican Communion*, 27 June 2006. This and the later draft covenant are available on http://www.anglicancommunion.org/.

NOTES TO CHAPTER 1

[1]Byrne, *Natural*, p. 1.

[2]Leviticus 18:22 and 20:13 make it quite clear that sexual activity between two males is the subject of condemnation. 1 Corinthians 6:9 and 1 Timothy 1:10 condemn something, which is usually taken to be homosexuality. Romans 1:26-7 condemns homosexual acts as contrary to nature. The doubtful two are Genesis 19, the 'Sodom' story, and a similar story in Judges 19. In both cases something is condemned, but there is much else in these narratives which deserves condemnation and the majority view among scholars is that the violation of hospitality laws is the focus of disapproval.

[3]Thus the Levitical texts are part of the Holiness Code which lays down rules for Israelites to distinguish themselves from other races, rather than presenting universal ethical norms. The meaning of the Greek word used in the 1 Corinthians and 1 Timothy texts is uncertain. It may refer to male prostitutes, or if it does refer to homosexuality it may be more specific, condemning only the

passive male partner, as was common at the time. The Romans text presupposes that homosexual acts are unnatural; today it is recognized that those with a homosexual orientation find it natural. Additionally, some narrative texts describe relationships which some Hebrew scholars believe are best described as homosexual, even though they do not explicitly state that sexual activity took place. Jennings, *Wound*, explores them. The clearest instances are David's relationship with Jonathan and Ruth's with Naomi. An additional complication is that Christianity's first major internal dispute was about whether Christians should obey the Old Testament laws. According to Acts 15, a council of Christian leaders agreed to impose only four of them on Christians, and the ban on homosexuality was not one.

[4]Cooke, Gillian, and Sheard, Alan, 'Understanding Homosexuality in the 21st Century', *Modern Believing*, 48:1, Jan 2007, pp. 7-14. The Royal College of Psychiatrists' *Submission to the Church of England's Listening Exercise on Human Sexuality* summarizes the research and provides an extensive list of research references. It is available on their website and www.anglicancommunion.org.

[5]For example the Barthian view is expressed by Snaith, Norman, *The Distinctive Ideas of the Old Testament*, Epworth Press, 1944, p. 77; Ringgren, Helmer, *Israelite Religion*, SPCK, 1966, p. 131. Rodd, *Glimpses*, p. 52, offers a critique. Scholars proceed on the basis that they are trying to establish what the human authors intended to convey. If the Bible is to have any authority at all, we need to attribute specific meanings to the texts.

[6]Barton, *Ethics*, pp. 68-76.

[7]*Purity and Danger: An Analysis of Concepts of Pollution and Taboo*, Penguin, 1970.

[8]Barton, *Ethics*, p. 69.

[9]Deuteronomy 4:8, 40; 5:29,33; 6:2-3,18,24-5; 8:1; 12:28.

[10]Lindblom, *Prophecy*, pp. 47-9, 58f. 1 Samuel 9 describes the story of how Saul, looking for his father's donkeys, decides to consult the 'seer'. When approached, the seer - Samuel - announces that God has told him not only to expect Saul's arrival but also to

anoint him as king. Here Samuel is described as having occult knowledge. Prophets with occult skills were usually paid for their services.

[11]Lindblom, *Prophecy*, pp. 216-7; Wiseman, D J in Ackroyd, *Beginnings*, p. 48; Koch, *Prophets I*, p. 27.

[12]Barton, *Ethics*, pp. 61-2; Barton, *Understanding*, pp. 112-4. Isaiah frequently condemns expressions of pride: e.g. 3:16-4:1, 22:15-19 and 31:1-2. Pride itself is not condemned in the Old Testament laws, but the prophet believes it misrepresents the proper order of things (Barton, *Ethics*, p. 63). Elsewhere Isaiah condemns many actions which are forbidden by Old Testament law, but also some which are not, such as drunkenness and excessive feasting (5:22). There is no suggestion that God had forbidden them. Isaiah simply appeals to the moral sense of his hearers - in other words, to natural law. Similarly Rodd, *Glimpses*, pp. 62-63, discusses the repeated complaint in Ezekiel, 'Yet you say, "The way of the Lord is unfair"' (18:25; see also 18:29, 33:17,20). Again the people appeal against God to a standard of fairness which God, in their view, ought to honour.

[13]Koch, *Prophets I*, p. 93.

[14]Genesis 18:23-25.

[15]Rodd *Glimpses*, pp. 44-54.

[16]Barton, *Ethics*, pp. 66-68.

[17]Luke 15:2-4.

[18]Acts 15:20.

[19]Acts 15:12-19.

[20]Respectively, I Corinthians 5-6; 6:1-7; 7; 8; 11:2-16; 11:17-34; 12-14; 14:34-36; 15; 16:1-3.

[21]Hays, *Moral Vision*, pp. 19-36.

[22]E.g. 1 Corinthians 7:10, 9:14, 10:14-32, 14:37.

[23]1 Corinthians 7:12.

[24]1 Corinthians 7:6.

[25]1 Corinthians 11:16.

[26]1 Corinthians 14:34.

[27]Especially Galatians and Romans. It is the basis for the doctrine of justification by faith, a major theme of the Reformation.

[28]E g. 1 Corinthians 7:29-31.

[29]Hebrews 6:1-6; Matthew 5:14-48.

[30]E.g. I Timothy 3:2-5.

[31]Barton, *People*, pp. 29-30; Wiseman, D J in Ackroyd, *Beginnings*, p. 54. For the continuing pattern in the Middle Ages see Levi, *Renaissance*, p. 33.

[32]Barton, *People*, pp. 28-29.

[33]Barton, *Spirit*, pp. 54 & 61; Ackroyd, *Beginnings*, pp. 423-6.

[34]*Dem. ev.* II, 3, 94, quoted by Hanson, R P C in Ackroyd, *Beginnings*, p. 430.

[35]Evans, *Reformation*, pp. 61-2.

[36]Hanson, R P C & Wiles, M F in Ackroyd, *Beginnings*, pp. 437, 461-2 & 474.

[37]*Conf* V, 14, 24, quoted by Bonner, G in Ackroyd, *Beginnings*, pp. 542-3.

[38]*De Doct. Christ*, quoted by Bonner, G in Ackroyd, *Beginnings*, p. 547.

[39]Barrett, C K & Wiles, M F in Ackroyd, *Beginnings*, pp. 378-9 & 480.

[40]Barton, *Spirit*, pp. 74-79; Barton, *People*, pp. 19-20.

[41]Hanson, R P C in Ackroyd, *Beginnings*, p. 436.

[42]Barton, *Ethics*, p. 75.

[43]Barton, *Ethics*, pp. 73-4.

[44]*1 Apol.* 46 & *2 Apol.* 8-10 & 13, quoted by Osborn, E in Esler, *World 1*, pp. 532-3.

[45]Ayers, *Language*, pp. 7-60.

[46]E.g. Pagels, *Gnostic Gospels*.

[47]E.g. Lee, *Gnostics*.

[48]For the bulk of this summary of Gnostic theology I am following Rudolph, *Gnosis*, especially pp. 53-204.

[49]Seventh Hermetic Tractate 2.3, quoted in Rudolph, *Gnosis*, p. 114.

[50]E.g. *The Gospel of Truth* 28-30. Robinson, James M, Ed, *The Nag Hammadi Library*, 3rd Edition, 1990, p. 45.

[51]Rudolph, *Gnosis*, pp. 90-92.

[52]Saggs, *Encounter*, pp. 93-95

NOTES TO CHAPTER 2

[1]Helm, *Understanding*, pp. 27-28 quotes a few texts from Augustine, citing *On Christian Doctrine*, trans. D W Robertson Jr, Indianapolis, Bobbs-Merrill, 1958, p.45. Anselm, *Proslogion*, in Hopkins, J & Richardson, H, *Anselm of Canterbury 1*, London, SCM, 1974, p. 93.

[2]The main differences are that the medieval natural philosophers gathered their empirical data from general observation only, rather than from conducting experiments for the purpose; and they did not attempt to use accurate measuring apparatus. See Grant, *Reason,*, pp. 160-182.

[3]Grant, *Reason,*, pp. 51-58.

[4]Kaiser, *Creation*, pp. 28-9; Grant, *Reason,*, p. 53.

[5]*Life and Letters*, Letter 249, quoted by Grant, *Reason,*, p. 64.

[6]Kaiser, *Creation*, pp. 30-31.

[7]Kaiser, *Creation*, pp. 30-32.

[8]*Summa Theol*. 1 q..a.8, quoted by Evans, *Reformation*, p. 17.

[9]Copleston, *Aquinas*, pp. 59-61.

[10]Byrne, *Natural*, pp. 2-3.

[11]Grant, *Reason,*, pp.12-13.

[12]Leff, *Mediaeval Thought*, pp. 255-261.

[13]Semantically dualism contrasts with 'monism'; but I do not use this word in this book because in religious discourse it usually refers to theories which deny the distinction between God and humans, as pantheists do.

[14]*Sentences* Bk 1, Prologue, 9. See Leff, *Mediaeval Thought*, pp. 280-291.

[15]Beiser, *Sovereignty*, pp. 38-41; Knowles, D in Cunliffe-Jones, *History*, pp. 283-6.

[16]Leff, *Mediaeval Thought*, pp. 291-293.

[17]2 *Sent*. q.15 & 4 *Sent*. qq. 10-11, quoted by Beiser, *Sovereignty*, p. 42. See also McGrath, *Origins*, p. 81.

[18]The clearest examples are where the authors of 1 and 2 Chronicles use but adapt the histories in Samuel and Kings, and where Matthew and Luke use but adapt Mark.

[19]Church House Publishing, 1991

[20]This claim is made countless times in the literature and websites of conservative campaigners. *The Church of England Newspaper* 6 November 2003, p. 3, is one example.

NOTES TO CHAPTER 3

[1]Reardon, *Reformation*, pp. 130-131.

[2]Knaacke, J C F et al, *The Righteousness of God: Luther Studies*, 1883, 1.226.14ff & 26ff, quoted in Reardon, *Reformation*, pp. 80-81.

[3]*Institutes*, 1.6.2. Reardon, *Reformation*, pp. 183-186.

[4]So argued the Council of Constance at the beginning of the fifteenth century, and the Fifth Lateran Council and the Council of Trent in the sixteenth. Evans, *Reformation*, p. 72.

[5]Evans, *Reformation*, p. 75 cites Calvin, Articles of the theologians of Paris, 1544, *Corpus Reformatorum*, Bretschneider, C G et al, Ed, Brunswick, Nova Scotia, 1834, 20 & 35.32-3. For the contrast with the early church see Barton, *Spirit*, p. 52.

[6]Suarez, *De fide*, Disp 3.2.2, quoted by Chadwick, *Bossuet*, pp. 43-4.

[7]Reardon, *Reformation*, pp. 91, 165, 169; Reventlow, *Authority*, p. 76; Beiser, *Sovereignty*, pp. 54-8.

[8]Greenslade, *History*, pp. 14-16.

[9]*The Anglicanism of William Laud*, 1947, pp. 37-40. See Reventlow, *Authority*, pp. 97-98.

[10]McGrath, *Reformation*, pp. 232-3. However Scholder, *Birth*, p. 47, argues that he showed little interest in the question.

[11]McGrath, *Reformation*, pp. 233-4.

[12]J. Dillenberger, *Martin Luther, Selections*, New York: 1961, pp. 14-19, quoted by Reardon, *Reformation*, p. 69.

[13]Reventlow, *Authority*, pp. 31-36.

[14]Reardon, *Reformation*, pp. 90-92 & 165.

[15]Reardon, *Reformation*, p. 69.

[16]McGrath, Alister, *Reformation Thought: An Introduction*, Oxford, Blackwell, 1993 edition, p. 152.

[17]*Institutes*, 1.7.1f, quoted by Reardon, *Reformation*, p. 180.

[18]Greenslade, *History*, pp. 13-14; Reardon, *Reformation*, pp. 105-109. The burial-places are described in Acts 7:16, Genesis 1:13 and Joshua 24:32.

[19]McGrath, *Origins*, pp. 122, 129-32.

[20]Reventlow, *Authority*, p. 166.

[21]For example the 'Covenant for the Church of England' proposed by Chris Sugden et al in December 2006 uses this language.

[22]Byrne, *Natural*, pp. 11-12; Scholder, *Birth*, p. 67.

[23]Evans, *Reformation*, pp. 72-73, quoting Nowell's *Catechism*, p. 115.

[24]Reventlow, *Authority*, p. 82.

[25]McGrath, *Origins*, p. 156.

[26]So argued Bossuet in his *Exposition of the Catholic Doctrine* and *History of the Variations of the Protestant Churches*. Chadwick, *Bossuet*, pp. 5-6, 13-14 & 22-23.

[27]Reardon, *Reformation*, pp. 68-69.

[28]Reardon, *Reformation*, pp. 96-97.

[29]Reardon, *Reformation*, pp. 180-181.

[30]Greenslade, *History*, p. 21.

[31]Knaacke, J C F et al, *The Righteousness of God: Luther Studies*, 1883, 21.466.36.

[32]*Institutes*, 1.8.12. Reardon, *Reformation*, p. 182.

[33]Beiser, *Sovereignty*, pp. 189-192.

[34]Badham, *Challenge*, p. 19. The texts are in Tertullian, *De spectaculis*, ch. 3; Peter Lombard, *Sentences* 4/50/7; and Aquinas, *Summa Theologia* 3.94. a.1.

[35]There was a wide variety of views in the early Church. Many Christians expected a new age in this world, not a new or non-physical life. Whether it would last for ever or for a limited time was another variation.

[36]Augustine, City, 10,32, and see the discussion in Byrne, *Natural*, p. 11.

[37]Augustine's doctrine of original sin was an attempt to explain how this came about.

[38]Levi, *Renaissance*, pp. 54-56, 59.

[39]Luther, *Lectures on Galatians* (1535) (on Gal. 5:3), trans. Jaroslav Pelikan, *Luther's Works*, vol. 27 (St. Louis: Concordia Publishing House, 1964), 13, quoted in Placher, *Domestication*, p. 38.

[40]Byrne, *Natural*, pp. 18-21

[41]*De servo arbitio* 18, quoted in Beiser, *Sovereignty*, pp. 150-151.

[42]*Institutes* 3, 23, 2, quoted in Beiser, *Sovereignty*, pp. 150-151.

[43]E.g. MacKenzie, *Order*, pp. 4-5.

[44]Beiser, *Sovereignty*, p. 41; Reardon, *Reformation*, pp. 190-191.

[45]Perkins, *Works*, 1612, 1:355, 358-359, 363a, 367a-b, 424-425 & 2:13-15; Beiser, *Sovereignty*, pp. 152-5.

[46]Beiser, *Sovereignty*, pp. 142-6.

[47]The evidence is unclear because of the popularity of false accusations. See Thomas, *Magic*, Chapter 15.

[48]Reventlow, *Authority*, p. 166.

[49]Reardon, *Reformation*, pp. 55-59.

[50]Erasmus-Luther, *Discourse on Free Will*, trans & ed. Winter, E G, New York: 1961, p. 103, quoted in Shapiro, *Probability*, p. 76.

[51]*Institutes*, 2.7.5, quoted in Reardon, *Reformation*, p. 183.

[52]Bebbington, *Evangelicalism*, pp. 43-44 & 56.

[53]Chadwick, *Bossuet*, p. 34; Scholder, *Birth*, pp. 14-15.

[54]Bettenson, *Documents*, p. 260, quoting Ignatius Loyola, *Spiritual Exercises*.

[55]Beiser *Sovereignty*, pp. 108-10.

[56]Grant, *Reason*, p. 311.

[57]Toulmin, *Cosmopolis*, pp. 77-78.

[58]Para 127.

NOTES TO CHAPTER 4

[1]I discussed this in Clatworthy, *Good God*.

[2]Beiser, *Sovereignty*, p. 156.

[3]Hooker, for example, had a four-stage account. Voak, *Hooker*, pp. 72-5.

[4]Stout, *Flight*, pp. 38-41.

[5]Shapiro, *Probability*, pp. 4-5, 9-10, 16-17; Popkin, *Scepticism*, p.

216.

6Mandelbaum, *Reason*, p. 19.

7Toulmin, *Cosmopolis*, pp. 54-55.

8The arguments are found in the *Discourse on Method* and the *Meditations*. For the ontological argument and the comparison with geometry see *Discourse 4* and *Meditation 5* (Descartes, *Discourse*, pp. 55, 57 and 144-149); for the cosmological argument, *Meditation 3* (Descartes, *Discourse*, pp. 119-131).

9*Meditation 4.*

10Shapiro, *Probability*, pp. 83-84.

11*Meditations 1 & 4.*

12Descartes, *Discourse*, pp 73-75.

13Descartes, *Discourse*, p. 21.

14Locke, *Essay*, 1.2. There is a discussion of these points in Dunn, *Empiricists*, Chapter 3.

15Locke, *Essay*, 4, 18, 4.

16Locke, *Essay*, 4,18,10.

17Locke, *Essay*, 4,19,14.

18Cragg, *Puritanism*, p. 117.

19Locke, *Essay*, 4, 10.

20Locke, *Essay*, 4,15,2.

21Locke, *Essay*, 4,16,3. Byrne, *Natural*, pp. 43 & 96-97, discusses the point.

22*City of God* 21.8.

23*Summa Theologiae* 1.105.7. Later still even the Socinians, whose rational approach to religion was developed before the popularization of mechanistic science, saw no reason why the interruption of the causal sequence should be against reason. Scholder, *Birth*, p. 42. See also Kaiser, *Creation*, p. 5.

24For a detailed discussion of this, see Armstrong, *Law*.

25Gaskin, *Hume*, p. 143.

26Shapiro, *Fact*, p. 170.

27Byrne, *Natural*, pp. 101-102.

28So argued Spinoza. Popkin, *Scepticism*, p. 242.

29Middleton, *A Free Enquiry into the Miraculous Powers*, London: 1749. Byrne, *Natural*, pp. 91-92.

[30]Hume, *Enquiry*, pp. 114-115.

[31]Gaskin, *Hume*, p. 161.

[32]Hume, *Enquiry*, pp. 116-119.

[33]Hume, *Enquiry*, pp. 119-120.

[34]Gaskin, *Hume*, pp. 136-143.

[35]Locke, *Essay*, 4, 10.

[36]Letter to Richard Bentley, 1692, quoted in Kaiser, *Creation*, p. 180.

[37]Kaiser, *Creation*, pp. 158-161.

[38]Gaskin, *Hume*, pp. 17-37. Hume makes his point rhetorically in *Enquiry*, p. 138.

[39]Merchant, *Nature* describes this process.

[40]Gaskin, *Hume*, pp. 94-106.

[41]*Essay Concerning Toleration*, Creed, *Religious Thought*, pp. 238-243.

[42]Jodock, *Modernity*, p. 18.

[43]Mandelbaum, *Reason*, pp. 11-12.

[44]At the time of writing Dawkins' *The God Delusion* is attracting much publicity. An example is 'Scientists divided over alliance with religion', *The Guardian*, 29 May 2007.

[45]Mandelbaum, *Reason*, pp. 10-11.

[46]Mandelbaum, *Reason*, pp. 16-18.

[47]*Journal of Philosophy* 84 (October 1987), p. 548, quoted in Helm, *Faith and Reason*, p. 265.

[48]So argues, for example, Rorty, *Mirror*.

[49]Trigg, *Reality*.

[50]Hanfling, *Positivism*, pp. 10, 111 & passim; Graham, *Mind*, pp. 44-51.

[51]The Sea of Faith movement continues this tradition today.

[52]'Belief' because a person who knows a fact should believe it to be true; 'true' because if the object of belief is false there is no real knowledge; 'justified' because the reason for believing must be a genuine reason for its truth. Michael Polanyi's *Personal Knowledge* has been influential in the change.

[53]Hospers, *Analysis*, pp. 50-67.

NOTES TO CHAPTER 5

[1]Lake, Peter, *Anglicans and Puritans? Presbyterian and English Conformist thought from Whitgift to Hooker*, London, 1988, p. 239.

[2]Voak, *Hooker*, pp. 3-12, 158-159 & 274.

[3]*Laws of Ecclesiastical Polity* 5.8.2.

[4]Reardon, *Reformation*, p. 262.

[5]Allchin, *Participation*, pp. 9-10, quoting *Laws of Ecclesiastical Polity* 1.9.2.

[6]*Laws of Ecclesiastical Polity* 2.1.4, quoted by Beiser, *Sovereignty*, pp. 70-3; Avis, *Anglicanism*, pp. 63-64.

[7]*Laws of Ecclesiastical Polity* 2.8.14 & 3.8.14. See Reardon, *Reformation*, pp. 226 & 263; Beiser, *Sovereignty*, p. 75. The point about it being a circular argument is that anyone can write a book claiming supreme authority; if we are to accept the claim we do so on other grounds.

[8]Avis, *Anglicanism*, pp. 41-2.

[9]D'Entrèves, A. P., *The Medieval Contribution to Political Thought: Aquinas, Marsilius, Hooker*, New York 1959, p. 120.

[10]*Laws of Ecclesiastical Polity* 5.8.2.

[11]*Laws of Ecclesiastical Polity* 2.7.5, quoted in Voak, *Hooker*, p. 73.

[12]Voak, *Hooker*, pp. 31-2, 115-117.

[13]Beiser, *Sovereignty*, pp. 116-7.

[14]Hales, *Works*, 1.81, quoted in Beiser, *Sovereignty*, p. 118.

[15]Beiser, *Sovereignty*, pp. 113-118.

[16]Beiser, *Sovereignty*, pp. 99 & 118-125.

[17]Chillingworth, *The Religion of Protestants*, 1.6.56; 2.410-411, quoted in Beiser, *Sovereignty*, p. 115.

[18]Beiser, *Sovereignty*, pp. 85-94, 125-6.

[19]Beiser, *Sovereignty*, pp. 111-112.

[20]Beiser, *Sovereignty*, p. 122, citing Chillingworth, *Religion of Protestants*, Answer to Preface, No. 26; I, 82. Cf. I, i, 8; I, 115.

[21]Beiser, *Sovereignty*, pp. 114-5, 120.

[22]Reventlow, *Authority*, p. 150; Beiser, *Sovereignty*, p. 123.

[23]Beiser, *Sovereignty*, p. 134.

[24]*Aphorisms*, 33 & 76, quoted in Cragg, *Puritanism*, p. 42.

[25]Beiser, *Sovereignty*, pp. 136 & 165-175; Shapiro, *Probability*, pp. 105-6.

[26]Beiser, *Sovereignty*, pp. 135-8.

[27]Beiser, *Sovereignty*, pp. 173-4.

[28]Beiser, *Sovereignty*, p. 138.

[29]Shapiro, *Probability*, pp. 108-110.

[30]*Analogy of Religion*, London, 1889, p. 219, quoted in Avis, *Anglicanism*, pp. 229-230 & 281.

[31]McAdoo, *Anglicanism*, p. 336.

[32]McAdoo, *Anglicanism*, pp. v, 1.

[33]Avis, *Anglicanism*, p. 279.

[34]Chadwick, *Bossuet*, pp. 76-77.

[35]Chadwick, *Bossuet*, pp. 60 & 79.

[36]Chadwick, *Bossuet*, p. 57.

[37]Herbert, E, *A Dialogue Between a Pupil and his Tutor*, London: 1768, pp. 10-11 and 14-15. Byrne, *Natural*, pp. 24-25.

[38]Reventlow, *Authority*, pp. 187-188; Byrne, *Natural*, pp. 23-33, quoting *De Religio Gentilium*, tr. W. Lewis as *The Antient Religion of the Gentiles*, London, 1705, p. 7.

[39]Byrne, *Natural*, pp. 26-7.

[40]Whichcote, B, *Aphorisms*, 771, quoted in McAdoo, *Anglicanism*, p. 312.

[41]Taylor, Jeremy, *Works*, Collected Edition by R Heber, 1828, Vol 9, p. 73, quoted in McAdoo, *Anglicanism*, p. 78.

NOTES TO CHAPTER 6

[1]Clark, *Biology*, p. 82. The argument was advanced by Philip Gosse, *Omphalos*, J van Voorst: London, 1857.

[2]Barbour, *Religion*, Chapter 4.

[3]Thus Cragg, noting that it excludes intuition and religious experience, writes that 'The change in the character of religious thought in the later seventeenth century resulted in the arid intellectualism of the succeeding age', *Puritanism*, pp. 226-7. Similarly Worrall remarks that by the beginning of the nineteenth century, 'religion, as it was understood by the majority of clergy and

laymen, had become formal and was lacking in spiritual vitality and depth' *Making*, p. 2. See also Vidler, *Revolution*, p. 31.

[4]Byrne, *Natural*, p. 157.

[5]*On Religion: Speeches to its Cultured Despisers*, 1799, trans Richard Crouter, CUP 1988, 101-2, quoted in Helm, *Faith and Reason*, pp. 206-7.

[6]Schleiermacher, Friedrich, *On Religion: speeches to its cultured despisers*, tr. John Oman, Harper and Row, 1965, p. 18; and *The Christian Faith*, ed. H.R. Mackintosh and J.S. Stewart, Edinburgh, 1948, p. 12. Byrne, *Natural*, pp. 164-5; Crowther, *Embattled*, pp. 43-44; Badham, *Authority*, p. 118.

[7]Ritschl, A, *The Christian Doctrine of Justification and Reconciliation*, trans. Mackintosh, H R and Macaulay, A B, Edinburgh: 1900, pp. 214-216, quoted by Welch, *Protestant Thought*, pp. 5-6. See also p. 9.

[8]*Lux Mundi*, London: 1890, quoted by Welch, *Protestant Thought*, pp. 34-35.

[9]*Outlines of a Philosophy of Religion Based on Psychology and History*, New York, 1902, pp. 27, 291 & 311, quoted by Welch, *Protestant Thought*, pp. 36-37.

[10]*Religions of Authority and the Religion of the Spirit*, New York: 1904, pp. 327-336, quoted by Welch, *Protestant Thought*, pp. 36-37.

[11]*The Idea of the Holy*, Oxford: 1968 edition, pp. 5-6, quoted by Welch, *Protestant Thought*, p. 121.

[12]Michael Van Horn has shown that it is true of all branches of Protestantism. Whatever foundations they may have claimed for their faith, since the Enlightenment they have consistently appealed to inner subjective experience as the basis for their faith. Intellectual belief in the authority of the Bible became, in practice, secondary; what mattered was being 'slain in the Spirit' or 'born again'. Preaching characteristically appealed to the emotions to trigger a conversion experience, and the centrality of the conversion experience was celebrated in their hymns and choruses. Badham, *Authority*, pp. 125-6.

[13]Bebbington, *Evangelicalism*, pp. 7-8, 79 & 91.

[14]Vidler, *Revolution*, p. 77.

[15]Bebbington, *Evangelicalism*, pp. 93-4.

[16]Chadwick, *Church 1*, p. 169.

[17]The Keswick conventions became a focus for this teaching. Unfortunately the conviction that one could not be tempted to sin convinced some that what they were tempted to do was not sinful, and some sexual scandals followed. Bebbington, *Evangelicalism*, pp. 151-2, 170.

[18]Bebbington, *Evangelicalism*, pp. 102-4.

[19]Bebbington, *Evangelicalism*, pp. 212-6.

[20]Bebbington, *Evangelicalism*, pp. 81-83.

[21]Bebbington, *Evangelicalism*, pp. 13-14 & 86-87.

[22]Chadwick, *Bossuet*, pp. 87-8.

[23]Avis, *Anglicanism*, p. 283; Chadwick, *Bossuet*, pp. 89-92, 127-128.

[24]McAdoo, *Tradition*, p. 5.

[25]Avis, *Anglicanism*, p. 281. See also Nockles, P, 'Survivals or new arrivals?', Platten, *Anglicanism*, p. 183.

[26]Vidler, *Revolution*, pp. 71, 148, 151, 183 & 185; Jodock, *Modernity*, pp. 9-10, 18, 94-96 and 196-198.

[27]*The Papal Encyclicals*, vol. III: 1903-1939, ed. Claudia Carlen, Raleigh, North Carolina: McGrath Publishing Company, 1981, p. 89, para 39, quoted in Jodock, *Modernity*, p. 1.

[28]Ibid., p. 73, para 3.

[29]Crowther, *Embattled*, pp. 13-14.

[30]Vidler, *Revolution*, p. 252.

[31]Bebbington, *Evangelicalism*, p. 128; Chadwick, *Church 1*, p. 4.

[32]Bebbington, *Evangelicalism*, p. 128.

[33]The papacy was determined to resist this development, but its own emphasis on spiritual phenomena and infallible revelation paved the way. See Jodock, *Modernity*, pp. 18 & Daly on p. 92. The general point is often noted. Vidler comments that the long papacy of Pius IX turned Catholicism into a 'close corporation' (Vidler, *Revolution*, p. 156). Similarly Worrall states that Pius IX separated the Roman Catholic Church from modern thought and turned it into an alternative society with an alternative vision of reality (Worrall, *Making*, p. 162).

[34]Lindbeck, *Doctrine*, pp. 16-19.

[35]Chadwick, *Church 2*, p. 132.

[36]For example, Murphy, *Beyond*, pp. 36-61; McGrath, *Doctrine*, pp. 20-21; Hunsinger in Vanhoozer, *Postmodern Theology*, p. 44. Murphy's account of the experiential-expressivist theology of Tracy and Kaufman no doubt represents some academic theologians who call themselves liberals; it is far too non-realist to represent the views of the vast majority of liberal Christians.

[37]McGrath, *Doctrine*, pp. 20-25 & 37.

[38]Murphy, *Beyond*, p. 51.

[39]Murphy, *Beyond*, p. 51.

[40]Reardon, *Romanticism*, p. 26.

[41]Reardon, *Reformation*, p. xii.

NOTES TO CHAPTER 7

[1]Harris, *Fundamentalism*, pp. 26-8.

[2]Reid, T, *Inquiry*, 1764 and *Essays on the Intellectual Powers of Reason*, 1785. Harris, *Fundamentalism*, pp. 95-105.

[3]Shapiro, *Fact*, pp. 195-196.

[4]Harris, *Fundamentalism*, pp. 96-115.

[5]Harris, *Fundamentalism*, p. 101.

[6]Bebbington, *Evangelicalism*, pp. 89-90.

[7]Hodge, Charles, *Systematic Theology*, Vol. 1, London: Thomas Nelson, 1871, pp. 9-18, 163, quoted in Harris, *Fundamentalism*, pp. 119 & 137 and Murphy, *Beyond*, p. 34.

[8]Harris, *Fundamentalism*, p. 137, quoting Hodge, C, *Systematic Theology*, Vol. 1, London: Thomas Nelson, 1871, pp. 152-154.

[9]Harris, *Fundamentalism*, p. 137, quoting Hodge, Charles, *Systematic Theology*, Vol. 1, London: Thomas Nelson, 1871, p. 170.

[10]Harris, *Fundamentalism*, p. 138.

[11]Ironically, Warfield was confident about this procedure because, unlike most conservatives, he was sympathetic to biblical criticism; he believed that the original autographs would indeed be found, and apparent errors would be explained away. Harris, *Fundamentalism*, pp. 139-141.

[12]Bebbington, *Evangelicalism*, pp. 85-89 & 194.

[13]Marsden, *Culture*, p. 213.

[14]Harris, *Fundamentalism*, pp. 28-34.

[15]Harris, *Fundamentalism*, pp. 2-4 & 31-48.

[16]E.g. Packer, James, *'Fundamentalism' and the Word of God*, 1958; Wenham, John, *Christ and the Bible*, 1972; see Harris, *Fundamentalism*, pp. 86-87.

[17]Harris, *Fundamentalism*, pp. 155 & 170. Harris cites Lindsey, H, *The Late Great Planet Earth*, London: Marshall Pickering, 1970, p. 119.

[18]Harris, *Fundamentalism*, pp. 63, 86, 147 & 155-156.

[19]Harris, *Fundamentalism*, pp. 66-67 & 73; Barr, *Fundamentalism*, pp. 120-3, 127-8.

[20]McGrath, A, *Christian Theology: An Introduction*; Harris, *Fundamentalism*, p. 8.

[21]Stott, J, et al, *The Anglican Communion and Scripture: Papers from the First International Consultation of the Evangelical Fellowship in the Anglican Communion*, Carlisle: EFAC and Regnum, p. 21, quoted in Harris, *Fundamentalism*, pp. 164-166.

[22]Harris, *Fundamentalism*, p. 119 & 164-6.

[23]Harris, *Fundamentalism*, pp.57 & 61-63; Barr, *Fundamentalism*, pp. 1, 11 & 37 and *Explorations in Theology 7: The Scope and Authority of the Bible*, London: SCM, 1980, p. 79.

[24]Harris, *Fundamentalism*, pp. 62-63; Barr, *Fundamentalism*, pp. 16-28, 166-179 & 268-9.

[25]Harris, *Fundamentalism*, pp. 64-5, quoting Barr, J, *Explorations in Theology 7: The Scope and Authority of the Bible*, London: SCM, 1980, p. 80.

[26]Harris, *Fundamentalism*, pp. 61; Barr, *Fundamentalism*, p. 1, & 183. This was brought home to me in the 1980s, when I was an Anglican university chaplain, in a discussion with two Christian Union members. After 20 minutes' discussion about Christianity, the younger of the two responded to a remark of mine with 'Oh, so you are a Christian too, are you? I didn't realize that'. He knew I was a chaplain, and could see my clerical collar. Behind his surprise lay that prevalent claim that chaplains and Anglican

clergy are not Christians, a claim which has its roots in polemics but which he, like many others, took at face value.

[27]Harris, *Fundamentalism*, pp. 61-62; Barr, *Fundamentalism*, pp. 23-8, 169-72.

[28]Harris, *Fundamentalism*, pp. 173-174. Harris cites the American Association of Christian Schools, which claims that 'all subject matter is related to God' and therefore the Bible is 'the central subject in the school's curriculum' and 'the point of reference whom which we can evaluate all areas and sources of knowledge'. For this reason pupils are expected to bring a bible to every class, though an exception is made for physical education.

[29]Harris, *Fundamentalism*, pp. 154-5.

[30]Harris, *Fundamentalism*, p. 176.

[31]Harris, *Fundamentalism*, pp. 180-181, 293-302.

[32]Harris, *Fundamentalism*, pp. 12, 57 & 121.

[33]'Are Evangelicals Fundamentalists?', *Christianity Today*, Sept 1978, p. 46.

[34]Harris, *Fundamentalism*, pp. 7-8 & 68-71.

[35]Vidler, *Revolution*, pp. 113-114.

[36]Barton, *People*, p. 2.

[37]Harris, *Fundamentalism*, p. 184.

[38]Harris, *Fundamentalism*, pp. 182-3.

NOTES TO CHAPTER 8

[1]Lyotard, *The Postmodern Condition: A Report on Knowledge*, Manchester University Press 1984, p. 30; Vanhoozer, *Postmodern Theology*, pp. 9-15; Reader, *Beyond*, p. 35.

[2]MacIntyre, *Justice*, p. 335.

[3]MacIntyre, *Justice*, pp, 166-7, 351-7.

[4]Milbank, *Social Theory*, pp. 346-7. See also p. 330.

[5]Kuhn, Thomas, *The Structure of Scientific Revolutions*, University of Chicago Press, 1970. See also Lindbeck, *Doctrine*, p. 10.

[6]Lakeland, *Postmodernity*, pp. 8-11.

[7]Bruce, Steve, 'The Problems of a Liberal Religion', in

Chapman, *Future*, p. 228.

[8]Hays, *Moral Vision*, p. 296.

[9]Vanhoozer, *Postmodern Theology*, pp. 16-17.

[10]McGrath, *Doctrine*, pp. 152 & 199; see also Gavin Hyman, 'Postmodern Theology' in Chapman, *Future*, p. 203.

[11]Hunsinger, 'Postliberal Theology', Vanhoozer, *Postmodern Theology*, pp. 47 & 53.

[12]Chapman, *Future*, p. 9.

[13]Hobson, Theo, 'Ecclesiological Fundamentalism', p. 52; Lindbeck, *Doctrine*, p. 24; Küng, Hans, *Theology for the Third Millennium*, New York: Doubleday, 1988, pp. 271-5.

[14]Harris, *Fundamentalism*, pp. 205-229.

[15]*Campus Crusade for Christ*, Leväsjoki, Finland: Myllykummun kirjapaino, 1986, pp. 1-2, quoted in Harris, *Fundamentalism*, p. 195.

[16]Harris, *Fundamentalism*, pp. 195-9.

[17]Macquarrie, *Thought*, p. 321.

[18]*Church Dogmatics*, Edinburgh: T & T Clark, 1961, 3.3, p. 403 & 4.3, p. 109, quoted by Hunsinger, *Barth*, p. 52.

[19]*Church Dogmatics*, Edinburgh: T & T Clark, 1956, 1.2, p. 774, quoted in Markham, *Engagement*, p. 8.

[20]*Church Dogmatics*, Edinburgh: T & T Clark, 1957, 2.1, pp. 314-5, quoted in Hunsinger, *Barth*, p. 35.

[21]Hunsinger, *Barth*, p. 68 & 72.

[22]*Church Dogmatics*, Edinburgh: T & T Clark, 1975, 1.1, p. 305, quoted in Hunsinger, *Barth*, p. 72.

[23]*Church Dogmatics*, Edinburgh: T & T Clark, 1956, 2.1, p. 150, quoted in Hunsinger, *Barth*, p. 40.

[24]*Church Dogmatics*, Edinburgh: T & T Clark, 1956, 1.2, pp. 724-725, quoted in Hunsinger, *Barth*, p. 51.

[25]Badham, *Challenge*, p. 32.

[26]Badham, *Challenge*, p. 35.

[27]Gorringe, *Discerning Spirit*, p. 12.

[28]de Gruchy, John W, *The Church Struggle in South Africa*, London: Eerdmans, Second Edition, 1986, p. 20.

[29]Barr, *Faith*, pp. 111-117.

[30]The argument is used by Roman Catholics too. See Lash, N,

The Beginning and the End of 'Religion', Cambridge: CUP, 1996, and a critique of it in Reader, *Beyond*, pp. 56-58.

[31]Milbank, *Social Theory*, p. 262.

[32]Milbank, *Social Theory*, p. 327.

[33]Milbank, *Social Theory*, p. 388.

[34]Milbank, *Social Theory*, p. 246.

[35]Milbank, *Social Theory*, p. 231.

[36]Milbank, *Social Theory*, p. 262.

[37]Milbank, *Social Theory*, p. 330; italics in original.

[38]Milbank, *Social Theory*, p. 384.

[39]Milbank, *Social Theory*, p. 328.

[40]Milbank, *Social Theory*, p. 263.

[41]Milbank, *Social Theory*, p. 267.

[42]Clark, *God, Religion & Reality*, p. 41.

[43]Reader, *Beyond*, pp. 64-74.

[44]I discuss this further in my *Good God*.

[45]MacIntyre, *Justice*, p. 353.

[46]Paul Murray, 'A Liberal helping of Postliberalism Please', in Chapman, *Future*, pp. 213-5. He cites the ordination of women as an example of a tradition accepting the values of outsiders.

[47]Vanhoozer, *Postmodern Theology*, p. 161; Lindbeck, *Doctrine*, p. 115.

NOTES TO CHAPTER 9

[1]A typical example is the correspondence on the subject in the letters columns of the Church of England Newspaper in August 2007.

[2]Brown, *Body*, especially pp. 53, 60, 66, 77 and 84.

[3]'I've been given a responsibility to try and care for the church as a whole, the health of the church. That health has a lot to do with the proper and free exchange between different cultural and political and theological contexts... and it's got a lot to do, therefore, with valuing and nurturing unity, not... as an alternative to truth, but actually as one of the ways we absorb truth' (*The Guardian*, 21 March 2006).

[4]*The Windsor Report* para 127.
[5]*The Windsor Report* para 51.
[6]*The Windsor Report* para 32.
[7]*The Windsor Report* para 68.
[8]*The Windsor Report* para 69.
[9]*The Windsor Report* para 93.

NOTES TO CHAPTER 10

[1]Trigg, *Reality*, p. 5.
[2]Herodotus, *Histories*, p. 255.
[3]Ian Barbour's classification describes four ways in which science and religion are said to relate: conflict, independence, dialogue and integration. Barbour, *Religion*, pp. 77-105. The view I am taking here is the integrationist one.
[4]Markham, *Truth*, p. 80.
[5]Trigg, *Reality*, especially pp. 5, 9, 61-62.
[6]E.g. *The Gospel of Truth* 28-30. Robinson, *Nag Hammadi*, p. 45; and the Seventh Hermetic Tractate 2.3, Rudolph, *Gnosis*, p. 114 (and see also the discussion on pp. 90-92).
[7]Markham, *Truth*; Hebblethwaite, *Ocean*; Plantinga, A, *Warrant and Proper Function*, Oxford: OUP, 1993.
[8]O'Hear, *Science*, Chapter 2.
[9]Boyd, *Science*, p. 299.
[10]Among the best known are Stephen Hawking's *A Brief History of Time* and Paul Davies' *The Mind of God*. Steven Dick, Ed, *Many Worlds*, London: Templeton Foundation, 2000, explores some of the issues.
[11]Cunliffe-Jones, *History*, pp. 590-591.
[12]*Laws of Ecclesiastical Polity* 5.8.2.
[13]This is well expressed in the Church of Uganda Position Paper on Scripture, Authority, and Human Sexuality, 2005. It is available on http://www.aco.org/listening/world/docs/doc6.cfm.
[14]Article 37.
[15]McAdoo, *Anglicanism*, p. 1.

[16]Peter Hodgson's list of characteristics of religious liberals is similar. Chapman, *Future*, pp. 114-111.

BIBLIOGRAPHY

Ackroyd, P R and Evans, C F, Ed, *The Cambridge History of the Bible: From the Beginnings to Jerome,* Cambridge: CUP, 1970.

Allchin, A. M., *Participation in God,* London: DLT, 1988.

Aquinas, Thomas Maurer, Armand, trans, *Thomas Aquinas: Faith, Reason and Theology,* Toronto: Pontifical Institute of Mediaeval Studies, 1987.

Armstrong, D M, *What Is A Law Of Nature?,* Cambridge: CUP, 1983.

Avis, Paul, *Anglicanism and the Christian Church,* Edinburgh: T & T Clark, 1989.

Ayers, Robert, *Language, Logic and Reason in the Church Fathers,* New York: Georg Olms Verlag, 1979.

Badham, Paul, *The Contemporary Challenge of Modernist Theology,* Cardiff: University of Wales Press, 1998.

Barbour, Ian, *Religion and Science: Historical and Contemporary Issues,* London: SCM, 1998.

Barr, James, *Holy Scripture: Canon, Authority, Criticism,* Oxford: OUP, 1983.

Barr, James, *The Bible in the Modern World,* London: SCM, 1973.

Barr, James, *Biblical Faith and Natural Theology,* Oxford: Clarendon, 1993.

Barr, James, *Fundamentalism,* London: SCM, 1977.

Barton, John, *Ethics and the Old Testament,* London: SCM, 1998.

Barton, John, *The People of the Book?: The Authority of the Bible in Christianity,* : SPCK, 1998.

Barton, John, *The Spirit and the Letter: Studies in the Biblical Canon,* London: SPCK, 1997.

Bebbington, D W, *Evangelicalism in Modern Britain: A History from the 1730s to the 1980s,* Grand Rapids, Michigan: Baker Book House, 1992 edition (first published 1989) .

Beiser, Frederick C, *The Sovereignty of Reason: The Defence of Rationality in the Early English Enlightenment,* Princeton: Princeton University Press, 1996.

Bettenson, H, *Documents of the Christian Church*, Oxford: OUP, 1963 edition (first published 1943).

Boyd, Richard et al, *The Philosophy of Science*, Massachusetts: MIT Press, 1992.

Byrne, Peter, *Natural Religion and the Nature of Religion: The Legacy of Deism*, London: Routledge, 1989.

Byrne, Peter, *God and Realism*, Aldershot: Ashgate, 2003.

Chadwick, Owen, *From Bossuet to Newman*, Cambridge: CUP, 1957.

Chadwick, Owen, *The Victorian Church: Part 1 1829-1859*, London: SCM, 1970.

Chadwick, Owen, *The Victorian Church: Part 2 1860-1901*, London: SCM, 1970.

Chapman, Mark Ed, *The Future of Liberal Theology*, Aldershot: Ashgate, 2002.

Chapman, Mark, *Why the Enlightenment Project Does Not Have to Fail*, Heythrop Journal 39 (1998), pp 379-93.

Church of England Doctrine Commission, *Believing in the Church*, London: SPCK, 1981.

Church of England Doctrine Commission, *Christian Believing*, London: SPCK, 1976.

Clark, Gordon H, *Religion, Reason and Revelation*, Hobbs, NM: The Trinity Foundation, 1995.

Clark, S R L, *God's World and the Great Awakening*, Oxford: Clarendon, 1991.

Clark, S R L, *Biology and Christian Ethics*, Cambridge: CUP, 2000.

Clark, Stephen RL, *God, Religion & Reality*, London: SPCK, 1998.

Clatworthy, Jonathan Ed, *By Whose Authority?: Papers of the Modern Churchpeople's Union Annual Conference July 2002*, Liverpool: MCU, 2003.

Clayton, Philip, *The Problem of God in Modern Thought*, Grand Rapids, Michigan and Cambridge: Eerdmans, 2000.

Copleston, F. C, *Aquinas*, London: Penguin, 1988 edition (first published 1955) .

Cragg, G R, *From Puritanism to the Age of Reason*, Cambridge: CUP, 1966.

Creed, J M and J S Boys Smith, *Religious Thought in the Eighteenth Century: Illustrated from Writers of the Period*, Cambridge: CUP, 1934.

Crowther, M A, *Church Embattled: Religious Controversy in Mid-Victorian England*, Newton Abbot: Archon, 1970.

Cunliffe-Jones, Hubert Ed, *A History of Christian Doctrine*, Edinburgh: T & T Clark, 1978.

Descartes, René, *Discourse on Method and The Meditations*, London: Penguin, 1968.

Dunn, John, et al, *The British Empiricists*, Oxford: OUP, 1992.

Esler, Philip F Ed, *The Early Christian World Volume 1*, London: Routledge, 2000.

Esler, Philip F Ed, *The Early Christian World Volume 2*, London: Routledge, 2000.

Evans, G R, *Problems of Authority in the Reformation Debates*, Cambridge: CUP, 1992.

Frei, Hans, *The Eclipse of Biblical Narrative: A Study in Eighteenth and Nineteenth Century Hermeneutics*, New Haven: Yale UP, 1974.

Gaskin, J C A, *Hume's Philosophy of Religion*, London: Macmillan, 1978.

Gillispie, Charles Coulston, *Genesis and Geology: The Impact of Scientific Discoveries Upon Religious Beliefs in the Decades Before Darwin*, New York: Harper & Row, 1959.

Gore, Charles, *Lux Mundi: A Series of Studies in the Religion of the Incarnation*, London: John Murray, 1890.

Gorringe, T J, *Discerning Spirit: A Theology of Revelation*, London: SCM, 1990.

Graham, George, *Philosophy of Mind: An Introduction*, Oxford: Blackwell, 1993.

Grant, Edward, *God and Reason in the Middle Ages*, New York: Cambridge UP, 2001.

Greenslade, S L, *Cambridge History of the Bible Vol 3*, Cambridge: CUP, 1963.

Gustafson, James M., *Protestant and Roman Catholic Ethics*, Chicago: University of Chicago Press, 1978.

Habermas, Jürgen, *Religion and Rationality: Essays on Reason, God and Modernity,* : MIT, 2002.

Hanfling, Oswald Ed, *Essential Readings in Logical Positivism,* Oxford: Blackwell, 1981.

Harries, Richard, *God Outside the Box: Why Spiritual People Object to Christianity,* London: SPCK, 2002.

Harris, Harriet, *Fundamentalism and Evangelicals,* Oxford: Clarendon, 1998.

Hastings, Adrian, *A History of English Christianity 1920-1985,* London: Collins, 1986.

Helm, Paul Ed, *Faith and Reason,* Oxford: OUP, 1999.

Helm, Paul, *Faith and Understanding,* Edinburgh: EUP, 1997.

Herodotus, *The Histories,* London: Penguin, 1966 edition (first published 1954).

Hick, John, *An Interpretation of Religion: Human Responses to the Transcendent,* Basingstoke: Macmillan, 1989.

Hookway, Christopher, *Scepticism,* London: Routledge, 1990.

Hospers, John, *An Introduction to Philosophical Analysis,* London: Routledge, fourth edition 1997.

House of Bishops of the General Synod of the Church of England, *The Nature of Christian Belief,* London: Church House Publishing, 1986.

Hunsinger, George, 'Postliberal theology', Vanhoozer, Ed, *Postmodern Theology,* Cambridge: CUP, 2003.

Jobling, J'annine and Markham, Ian, Eds, *Theological Liberalism: Creative and Critical,* London: SPCK, 2000.

Jodock, Darrell Ed, *Catholicism Contending with Modernity: Roman Catholic Modernism and Anti-Modernism in Historical Context,* Cambridge: CUP, 2000.

Kaiser, Christopher, *Creation and the History of Science,* London: Marshall Pickering, 1991.

Kent, John, 'Religion and Science' in Smart, Ninian, *Nineteenth Century Religious Thought in the West,* Cambridge: CUP, 1985.

Koch, Klaus, *The Prophets Volume One: The Assyrian Period,* London: SCM, 1982.

Lakeland, Paul, *Postmodernity: Christian identity in a Fragmented Age,* Minneapolis: Fortress, 1997.

Lampe, G W H Ed, *The Cambridge History of the Bible Volume 2: The West from the Fathers to the Reformation,* Cambridge: CUP, 1969.

Lash, Nicholas, *The Beginning and the End of 'Religion',* Cambridge: CUP, 1996.

Lee, Philip J, *Against the Protestant Gnostics,* Oxford: OUP, 1987.

Leff, Gordon, *Mediaeval Thought: From Saint Augustine to Ockham,* London: Penguin, 1958.

Leff, Gordon, *William of Ockham: The Metamorphosis of Scholastic Discourse,* Manchester: Manchester UP, 1974.

Levi, Anthony, *Renaissance and Reformation: The Intellectual Genesis,* New Haven & London: Yale UP, 2002.

Lindbeck, George, *The Nature of Doctrine: Religion and Theology in a Postliberal Age,* London: SPCK, 1984.

Lindblom, J., *Prophecy in Ancient Israel,* Oxford: Blackwell, 1962.

Locke, John, *An Essay Concerning Human Understanding,* London: Collins, Fount 1984.

Lyotard, J-F, *The PostModern Condition,* Manchester: Manchester UP, 1979.

MacIntyre, Alasdair, *Whose Justice? Which Rationality?,* London: Duckworth, 1988.

MacKenzie, Iain M, *God's Order and Natural Law: The Works of the Laudian Divines,* Aldershot: Ashgate, 2002.

Macquarrie, John, *Twentieth Century Religious Thought,* London: SCM, Second edition 1971.

Major, Henry, *English Modernism: Its Origin, Methods, Aims,* Cambridge, Massachusetts: Harvard UP, 1927.

Mandelbaum, Maurice, *History, Man and Reason: A Study in Nineteenth Century Thought,* Baltimore: John Hopkins Press, 1971.

Markham, Ian, *Plurality & Christian Ethics,* Cambridge: CUP, 1994.

Markham, Ian, *A Theology of Engagement,* Oxford: Blackwell, 2003.

Markham, Ian, *Truth & The Reality of God,* Edinburgh: T & T Clark, 1998.

Marsden, George M, *Fundamentalism and American Culture: The Shaping of 20th Century Evangelicalism 1870-1923,* Oxford: OUP,

1980.

McAdoo, H R, *The Spirit of Anglicanism: A Survey of Anglican Theological Method in the Seventeenth Century*, London: A & C Black, 1965.

McAdoo, H R, *Anglicans and Tradition: and the Ordination of Women*, Norwich: Canterbury Press, 1997.

McGrath, Alister, *The Genesis of Doctrine*, Oxford: Blackwell, 1990.

McGrath, A, *Intellectual Origins of the Reformation*, Oxford: Blackwell, 1992.

McGrath, Alister, *Reformation Thought: An Introduction*, Oxford: Blackwell, 1993 edition.

Milbank, John, *Theology and Social Theory: Beyond Secular Reason*, Oxford: Blackwells, 1990.

Murphy, Nancey, *Beyond Liberalism and Fundamentalism*, Valley Forge: Trinity Press International, 1996.

O'Hear, Anthony, *An Introduction to the Philosophy of Science*, Oxford: OUP, 1991.

Osborn, Eric, *The Emergence of Christian Philosophy*, Cambridge: CUP, 1993.

Pagels, Elaine, *The Gnostic Gospels*, London: Weidenfeld & Nicolson, 1979.

Peacocke, A R, *Creation and the World of Science*, Oxford: Clarendon, 1979.

Penelhum, Terence, *God and Skepticism: A Study in Skepticism and Fideism*, Reidel: Dordrecht, 1983.

Pippin, Robert B, *Modernism as a Philosophical Problem*, Oxford: Blackwell, 1991.

Placher, William C, *The Domestication of Transcendence: How Modern Thinking about God Went Wrong*, Louisville: Westminster/John Knox Press, 1996.

Platten, Stephen Ed, *Anglicanism and the Western Christian Tradition: Continuity, Change and the Search for Communion*, Norwich: Canterbury Press, 2003.

Popkin, Richard, *A History of Scepticism from Savonarola to Bayle*, Oxford: OUP, 2003.

Popper, Karl, *The Logic of Scientific Discovery*, London: Hutchinson, 1968 edition.

Rabinowitz, Isaac, *A Witness Forever: Ancient Israel's Perception of Literature and the Resultant Hebrew Bible*, Bethesda, MD: Cornell UP, 1993.

Reader, John, *Beyond All Reason: The Limits of Postmodern Theology*, Cardiff: Aureus, 1998.

Reardon, Bernard M G, *Religious Thought in the Reformation*, London: Longman, 1995 edition.

Reventlow, Henning Graf, *The Authority of the Bible and the Rise of the Modern World*, London: SCM, 1984.

Richardson, R D, *The Gospel of Modernism*, London: Skeffington, 1933.

Rodd, Cyril, *Glimpses of a Strange Land: Studies in Old Testament Ethics*, Edinburgh: T & T Clark, 2001.

Rorty, Richard, *Philosophy and the Mirror of Nature*, Oxford: Blackwells, 1980.

Rowell, Geoffrey Ed, *The English Religious Tradition and the Genius of Anglicanism*, Wantage: Ikon, 1992.

Rudolph, Kurt, *Gnosis*, Edinburgh: T & T Clark, 1983.

Saggs, H W F, *The Encounter with the Divine in Mesopotamia and Israel*, London: Athlone, 1978.

Saxbee, John, *Liberal Evangelism: A Flexible Response to the Decade*, London: SPCK, 1994.

Scholder, Klaus, *The Birth of Modern Critical Theology: Origins and Problems of Biblical Criticism in the Seventeenth Century*, : SCM/Trinity Press International, 1990.

Shanks, Andrew, *God and Modernity: A New and Better Way to Do Theology*, London: Routledge, 2000.

Shapiro, Barbara J, *A Culture of Fact: England 1550-1720*, London: Cornell UP, 2000.

Shapiro, Barbara J, *Probability and Certainty in Seventeenth Century England*, Princeton University Press, 1983.

Stout, Jeffrey, *The Flight from Authority: Religion, Morality and the Quest for Autonomy*, Notre Dame: University of Notre Dame Press, 1981.

Sykes, Stephen, *The Integrity of Anglicanism*, London: Mowbrays, 1978.

Thiselton, A C, 'Premodern Bible, Postmodern World?', Gifford, Paul, Ed, *2000 Years and Beyond: Faith, Identity and the 'Common Era'*, London: Routledge, 2003.

Thomas, Keith, *Religion and the Decline of Magic: Studies in Popular Beliefs in Sixteenth- and Seventeenth-Century England*, London: Penguin, 1971.

Toulmin, Stephen, *Cosmopolis: The Hidden Agenda of Modernity*, University of Chicago Press, 1990.

Trigg, , *Reality at Risk*, Brighton: Harvester, 1980.

Vanhoozer, Kevin J Ed, *The Cambridge Companion to Postmodern Theology*, Cambridge: CUP, 2003.

Voak, Nigel, *Richard Hooker and Reformed Theology: A Study ofReason, Will, and Grace*, Oxford: OUP, 2003.

Welch, , *Protestant Thought in the Nineteenth Century: Volume 2, 1870-1914*, New Haven & London: Yale UP, 1985.

Young, Frances, *Biblical Exegesis and the Formation of Christian Culture*, Peabody, Massachusetts: Hendrickson, 1997.

INDEX

BOOKS

O books
O is a symbol of the world, of oneness and unity. In
different cultures it also means the "eye", symbolizing
knowledge and insight, and in Old English it means "place
of love or home". O books explores the many paths of
understanding which different traditions have developed
down the ages, particularly those today that express
respect for the planet and all of life.

For more information on the full list of over 300 titles
please visit our website
www.O-books.net

SOME RECENT O BOOKS

Gays and the Future of Anglicanism
Andrew Linzey and Richard Kirker

This book breathes toleration. It invites thought. It abhors the polemical. It is very Anglican - in the best sense - in that it tries to bring understanding, be inclusive and avoid expulsion. Yet it has authority, without being bossy and authoritarian. Readers will find much to chew on to help them think about what is the nature of church for which they strive. "Gays and the Future of Anglicanism" is about much more than homosexuality and is highly recommended. RENEW

190504738X 384pp £17.99 $29.95

Good As New
John Henson

A short review cannot begin to persuade readers of the value of this book. If you feel you can really face what Jesus and the writers of the New Testament really meant rather than have your ears dulled by the versions we normally hear, then buy this book-and read it. But only if you are brave enough. RENEW

1905047118 448pp £11.99 $19.95

Life in Paradox
The Story of a Gay Catholic Priest
Paul Edward Murray

This memoir is the compelling story of an honest, sensitive priest, and the tragic tale of a hierarchy that has lost its way in its desire to control the Church rather than nurture it. No book sets out more clearly and

urgently the tragedy and the prospects of the current crisis of Catholicism. **Bruce Chilton,** Bernard Iddings Bell Professor of Religion, Bard College

9781846941122 240pp £11.99 $24.95

Thoughtful Guide to Faith
Tony Windross

These delightful essays raise the questions of faith and values that all modern people raise and Windross offers a refreshing, challenging alternative to the religion of control. This book will escape the walls of the church and be debated everywhere. **John Shelby Spong,** former Bishop of Newark

1903816688 224pp £9.99 $14.95

Let the Bible Be Itself
Learning to read it right
Ray Vincent

An honest book about what the Bible is and is not! Vincent exposes why millions of people misuse the Bible and cause havoc with it. All this is laid bare and a different, positive view of the Bible is offered to replace it. A necessary and excellent book! **Adrian Thatcher,** Professorial Research Fellow in Applied Theology at the University of Exeter, UK

978-1-84694-148-1 160pp £11.99 $24.95